DATE DUE

DEMCO 38-296

AMERICA's
CITIES

OPPOSING VIEWPOINTS®

Other Books of Related Interest in the Opposing
Viewpoints Series:

AMERICA's CITIES

OPPOSING VIEWPOINTS®

David L. Bender & Bruno Leone, *Series Editors*

Charles P. Cozic, *Book Editor*

OPPOSING VIEWPOINTS SERIES®

Greenhaven Press, Inc. PO Box 289009 San Diego, CA 92198-9009

Library of Congress Cataloging-in-Publication Data

America's cities : opposing viewpoints / Charles P. Cozic,
book editor.
    p.   cm. — (Opposing viewpoints series)
  Includes bibliographical references and index.
  Summary: An anthology of articles debating issues related
to America's cities, including the decline of the cities,
measures to improve urban housing, the reduction of
homelessness and urban crime, and how cities can be
improved. Includes critical thinking activities.
  ISBN 0-89908-195-9 (lib. : alk. paper). —
  ISBN 0-89908-170-3 (pbk. : alk. paper)
  1. Cities and towns—United States. 2. Urban policy—
United States. [1. Cities and towns. 2. Urban policy.
3. Critical thinking.] I. Cozic, Charles P., 1957- . II. Series:
Opposing viewpoints series (Unnumbered)
HT123.A668 1993
307.76'0973—dc20   92-40708
                                CIP
                                AC

"Congress shall make no law . . . abridging the freedom of speech, or of the press."

First Amendment to the U.S. Constitution

The basic foundation of our democracy is the first amendment guarantee of freedom of expression. The Opposing Viewpoints Series is dedicated to the concept of this basic freedom and the idea that it is more important to practice it than to enshrine it.

Contents

Why Consider Opposing Viewpoints?

"The only way in which a human being can make some approach to knowing the whole of a subject is by hearing what can be said about it by persons of every variety of opinion and studying all modes in which it can be looked at by every character of mind. No wise man ever acquired his wisdom in any mode but this."

John Stuart Mill

In our media-intensive culture it is not difficult to find differing opinions. Thousands of newspapers and magazines and dozens of radio and television talk shows resound with differing points of view. The difficulty lies in deciding which opinion to agree with and which "experts" seem the most credible. The more inundated we become with differing opinions and claims, the more essential it is to hone critical reading and thinking skills to evaluate these ideas. Opposing Viewpoints books address this problem directly by presenting stimulating debates that can be used to enhance and teach these skills. The varied opinions contained in each book examine many different aspects of a single issue. While examining these conveniently edited opposing views, readers can develop critical thinking skills such as the ability to compare and contrast authors' credibility, facts, argumentation styles, use of persuasive techniques, and other stylistic tools. In short, the Opposing Viewpoints Series is an ideal way to attain the higher-level thinking and reading skills so essential in a culture of diverse and contradictory opinions.

In addition to providing a tool for critical thinking, Opposing Viewpoints books challenge readers to question their own strongly held opinions and assumptions. Most people form their opinions on the basis of upbringing, peer pressure, and personal, cultural, or professional bias. By reading carefully balanced opposing views, readers must directly confront new ideas as well as the opinions of those with whom they disagree. This is not to simplistically argue that everyone who reads opposing views will—or should—change his or her opinion. Instead, the series enhances readers' depth of understanding of their own views by encouraging confrontation with opposing ideas. Careful examination of others' views can lead to the readers' understanding of the logical inconsistencies in their own opinions, perspective on why they hold an opinion, and the consideration of the possibility that their opinion requires further evaluation.

Evaluating Other Opinions

To ensure that this type of examination occurs, Opposing Viewpoints books present all types of opinions. Prominent spokespeople on different sides of each issue as well as well-known professionals from many disciplines challenge the reader. An additional goal of the series is to provide a forum for other, less known, or even unpopular viewpoints. The opinion of an ordinary person who has had to make the decision to cut off life support from a terminally ill relative, for example, may be just as valuable and provide just as much insight as a medical ethicist's professional opinion. The editors have two additional purposes in including these less known views. One, the editors encourage readers to respect others' opinions—even when not enhanced by professional credibility. It is only by reading or listening to and objectively evaluating others' ideas that one can determine whether they are worthy of consideration. Two, the inclusion of such viewpoints encourages the important critical thinking skill of objectively evaluating an author's credentials and bias. This evaluation will illuminate an author's reasons for taking a particular stance on an issue and will aid in readers' evaluation of the author's ideas.

As series editors of the Opposing Viewpoints Series, it is our hope that these books will give readers a deeper understanding of the issues debated and an appreciation of the complexity of even seemingly simple issues when good and honest people disagree. This awareness is particularly important in a democratic society such as ours in which people enter into public debate to determine the common good. Those with whom one disagrees should not be regarded as enemies but rather as people whose views deserve careful examination and may shed light on one's own.

Thomas Jefferson once said that "difference of opinion leads to inquiry, and inquiry to truth." Jefferson, a broadly educated man, argued that "if a nation expects to be ignorant and free . . . it expects what never was and never will be." As individuals and as a nation, it is imperative that we consider the opinions of others and examine them with skill and discernment. The Opposing Viewpoints Series is intended to help readers achieve this goal.

David L. Bender & Bruno Leone,
Series Editors

Introduction

"We will neglect our cities to our peril, for in neglecting them we neglect the nation."
John F. Kennedy, statement to Congress, January 30, 1962.

For decades, America's cities flourished as centers of trade and manufacturing. Americans took pride in their cities and depended on those vital to the economy, such as Detroit and Pittsburgh, where the automobile and steel industries reigned. As these cities and industries prospered, waves of Americans and immigrants flocked to them for jobs and a better standard of living.

But along with success in the cities came problems such as crime and poverty. Today, such problems have become pervasive, and cities are in perhaps their worst shape ever, in many cases suffering from extreme economic stagnation, depopulation, and social and physical decay. In 1991, for example, a fiscal crisis threatened to bankrupt Philadelphia, the nation's fourth largest city. Also, Detroit's population has dropped dramatically from two million in 1950 to approximately one million in 1990, nearly one-quarter of which depends on welfare. And rampant poverty and crime have laid waste to many inner-city areas.

Clearly, crime and poverty are two of the most imposing crises threatening cities. From 1980 to 1990, poverty in cities increased at four times the rate for the nation, according to Census Bureau figures. Similarly, the violent crime rate in large cities is four times higher than in suburban areas. In the inner cities, acute poverty and crime have residents and families living in turmoil in the midst of unemployment, gangs and guns, and drug-related crime and abuse.

Consider, for example, the effects of crack cocaine on inner-city residents. Ishmael Reed, a writer in Oakland, California, described his neighborhood in 1988: "What was once a tranquil North Oakland zone is occupied by a deadly army. . . . Members of the black working class are the victims of the drive-by shootings, the burglaries, rapes, and assaults committed by the crack dealers and their clients." In East Oakland, grandmothers are raising grandchildren because their crack-addicted mothers cannot. In some cases, parents have even attempted to sell a child for crack. One woman, who could not locate her drug-addicted granddaughter, had to take in her two great-grandsons, including a five-month-old, eleven-pound baby near death, to prevent their adoption or foster home placement.

The problems associated with crime and poverty burden not only the people in inner cities but society as a whole. For example, increases in drug-related and gang-related crime overload courts and jails, resulting in public funds' being spent to hire more police or to build more prisons. Also, addicts gathering in so-called shooting galleries risk spreading AIDS through shared needles and sex and giving birth to babies addicted to heroin or crack. Drug addiction and unemployment increase chances of becoming homeless. Those afflicted with these problems of crime, poverty, and addiction require medical care, housing, and other social services, the costs of which fall on the shoulders of the public through higher fees and taxes.

Many Americans believe that the nation must act immediately to reverse the decline of cities and address their alarming rates of unemployment, crime, and infant mortality. In a May 1992 *New York Times*/CBS poll, 61 percent stated that the nation was spending "too little money" on the problems of cities, compared to 35 percent who expressed this view in 1988. This increase mirrors growing public concern that America must rescue its cities. Many mayors and urban activists argue that healthy cities remain vital to the nation and have called for an offensive to rebuild cities and restore them to their former strength and stature. As New York City mayor David N. Dinkins stated in 1990:

> Cities . . . serve as our commercial and intellectual marketplaces, where economics and philosophy, entertainment and art, science and technology, ideas and emotions, flourish and enrich the American experience. Like a mighty engine, urban America pulls all of America into the future: 77 million Americans, almost one-third of our population, live within the limits of our cities. As our cities go, so goes America and our unique civilization.

The struggle of inner-city residents and urban America to endure is just one of the issues explored in *America's Cities: Opposing Viewpoints*. The anthology examines the physical and economic decline of cities and what can be done to save them in the following chapters: Why Are America's Cities in Decline? How Can Urban Homelessness Be Reduced? How Can Urban Crime Be Reduced? What Measures Would Improve Urban Housing? How Can Urban Conditions Be Improved? Tragically, too many cities, because of budgetary constraints, are forced to reduce the very services that might save them. They must lay off teachers, reduce police forces, and shut down hospitals, even while crime and poverty threaten to destroy residents' very lives. Although the authors disagree on what exactly can save the cities, they agree that this is a task the nation cannot ignore.

Why Are America's Cities in Decline?

Chapter Preface

Today, most American cities are spending more money on schools, police, and the poor than they receive in taxes and other income. Indeed, according to the National League of Cities 1992 annual report, expenditures exceeded revenues in 54 percent of cities.

This cash shortage can be traced to factors such as drastic reductions in federal aid, which cities once counted on to fund mass transit and other services. Cities have also suffered from the demise of many industries that once provided numerous manufacturing jobs, increasing unemployment. Furthermore, much of the middle class has moved out of cities to suburbs, which has lowered cities' tax base.

Such events have left cities struggling to survive. Similarly, neighborhood businesses no longer thrive as they once did, often disappearing as more working families moved. In the economically depressed inner cities, what often remains are the eyesores of abandoned homes and boarded-up storefronts. Crime and drug abuse can easily thrive in these impoverished neighborhoods, making them ever more unattractive to new residents and businesses.

Clearly, cities owe much of their decline to economic hardship. Crime, drug abuse, vandalism, and racial conflict among residents also contribute to the decline. The authors in this chapter consider these factors in analyzing the decline of America's cities.

"American cities are succumbing to a process of planned de-urbanization."

Government Is to Blame for Urban Decline

Daniel Lazare

Some urban experts believe that cities and their residents are victims of government's anti-urban policies. In the following viewpoint, Daniel Lazare agrees and argues that many government policies harm America's cities while benefitting surrounding suburbs. Lazare contends that government subsidies for suburban home mortgages far outweigh those for public housing in cities and that subsidies for highway systems have encouraged people to purchase automobiles and ignore mass transit. Lazare believes that these anti-urban policies are responsible for "white flight," the move of much of the white population from cities to suburbs. Lazare is a free-lance writer in New York City.

As you read, consider the following questions:

1. How do cities use energy more efficiently than suburbs, according to Lazare?
2. In Lazare's opinion, how do wealthy suburbanites exclude unwanted businesses and residents?
3. According to the author, why does the overabundance of local government units harm regional planning?

The 1980s, according to people like [former New York mayor] Ed Koch, were supposed to be the years cities came into their own. Instead, this was the decade they fell off a cliff. Despite pockets of gentrification, cities across America found themselves playing host to more poor people than ever before, laying off employees, slashing services, emitting Oliver-Twistian appeals for help from unsympathetic state governments and the feds.

Better than 25 per cent of 525 American cities reported budget gaps in 1991 of 5 per cent or more. (New York's deficit was 10 per cent.) Bridgeport, Connecticut, the biggest city in the most affluent state, filed for bankruptcy, while Chelsea, Massachusetts, a small municipality on the northern edge of Boston, ran out of cash and had to be taken over by the state. A study by the National League of Cities found that the gap in personal income between major cities and their surrounding suburbs leapt from 11 per cent in 1980 to an astounding 41 per cent in 1987. (No more recent figures were available.)

This occurred not in spite of the longest boom in postwar history, but because of it. Savings and Loans doled out hundreds of billions to sunbelt developers, causing shopping malls and suburban tract housing to spring up like mushrooms after a thaw, yet cities found themselves shut out as never before. For the urban poor, the consequences of this capital flight have been catastrophic, as jobs and economic opportunity head out for the countryside. In the 'burbs, an entire generation has come of age thinking of cities as badlands filled with crack, guns, and AIDS. Rather than attending to such problems, government investment policies allow the middle class to slam shut the gates and leave the urban poor behind.

Planned De-Urbanization

None of this is inevitable. Rather than dying of natural causes, as the Republicans would have it, American cities are succumbing to a process of planned de-urbanization that began early in the century, took off after World War II, and accelerated at a madcap pace under Reagan and Bush. Despite abundant evidence that millions of Americans want to live in cities (rents wouldn't be so high if they didn't), the system makes it all but impossible. Through a carrot-and-stick approach, society has rendered cities unlivable by redirecting the flow of tax breaks and infrastructure subsidies to auto-based suburbs. As a consequence, millions of city dwellers have been lured to the countryside, where they end up living in culturally sanitized suburban "developments," undergo hours of political re-education in front of the tube, and spend their "free" time wandering through pseudo-public expanses known as malls.

There's nothing covert about this process. Rather, in countless laws passed by Congress and policy decisions by administrative agencies, it's been open and above board. Since the turn of the century, anti-urbanism has been at least as fundamental to American culture as racism. Cities are crowded and jumbled, matrices of political ferment and new ideas. Since the Middle Ages, they've been a nonstop threat to the political order. Suburbs are the opposite. Specifically designed as havens from urban tumult, they're places where people go to spend and own—not rebel. From the point of view of the ruling class at the birth of the auto age, they opened up a new opportunity for mass consumption and political control. America, once a country of clanging trolley cars and husky, brawling cities, was promptly redefined by the vine-covered cottage and two-car garage.

Henry Ford, the small-town fascist who did more than anyone else to get the new system going, is famous for two aphorisms: "History is bunk" and "We shall solve the city problem by leaving the city." As he foresaw, the new ex-urbanites would be without collective memory. A culture of mass consumption, fixated on the present, would ensnare them in a system of private ownership, and thereby push them to the right. Meanwhile, in the abandoned urban cores, underconsumption would reign, along with underinvestment, alienation, and free-form rage. How does America destroy cities? Let us count the ways.

Housing and Transportation

1. *Subsidized Private Housing:* Each year, the federal government doles out an estimated $70 billion or more in annual tax subsidies to bolster an ostensibly private suburban home market. And that doesn't count federal mortgage guarantees, S&L bailouts, infrastructure investments, and additional billions in tax breaks and benefits kicked in by state and local governments—all to buttress home ownership. By comparison, the federal government allocated just $1.8 billion in 1990 for public housing and $150 million for various programs for the homeless.

Whether all this public subsidization has boosted the home-ownership rate is debatable (Canada's rate is nearly identical to ours, though its tax code is not as favorable), but there's little doubt about its impact on urban areas. Runaway subsidization has tilted the market toward bigger homes and larger lots. Heavy borrowing, encouraged by the feds since the 1930s, has led to high-volume, high-speed construction and hence the ticky-tacky look that is the hallmark of suburban development.

At the same time, no country treats its urban tenants more meanly. Lacking comparable tax deductions, renters wind up paying what is in effect a penalty for the crime of not owning

19

property. (Home ownership in New York City is half that of Westchester County and a third of Nassau's.) If their building is knocked down to make way for a highway, they get zero compensation. If their landlord sells out to developers, their only thanks is to be thrown out onto the "free market" to search for another place to live. In much-abused neighborhoods in Brooklyn and the Bronx, the scene of so much Robert Moses-wrought devastation, tenants got the message early in the post-war period that if stability was what they were after, they would be wise to buy a piece of the rock out in Jersey or Long Island. Suburban developers gained, as did mortgage lenders. But cities lost.

© Pierotti/Rothco. Reprinted with permission.

2. *Cars, Cars, Cars:* As Henry Ford predicted, the automobile has revolutionized land use as thoroughly as railroads and trolleys did, although in completely different ways. Whereas trains and trolleys facilitated urban concentration, cars encouraged the opposite: wider streets; low-density suburbs; highways that slice

through crowded neighborhoods like "a meat ax," as Moses once put it. Urbanologists like Lewis Mumford correctly identified the private auto as Urban Enemy Number One.

But they were wrong in blaming the problem on a headlong infatuation with technology and progress. Technology has nothing to do with it. A political system dedicated to the illusion of individualism and "free" choice, on the other hand, does. Cars flatter motorists into believing they're self-sufficient, when in fact they'd be immobilized were it not for huge public expenditures for roads and bridges, traffic cops and ambulance squads. Cars don't take drivers where they want to go, but where society has invested in the necessary infrastructure.

The investment has been enormous. Relative to population, the U.S. has built the most elaborate highway system in the world, yet charges the lowest rates among advanced capitalist nations for the privilege of using it. While gas prices in this country hover around $1 a gallon, stiff highway taxes have pushed them above $3 across Western Europe and over $5 in parts of Scandinavia. (Europeans also pay annual fees—based on the size of one's motor—totaling several hundred dollars, while progressive little Denmark imposes a purchase tax that effectively triples the price of a new car.) The difference between the environmental and social cost of all this driving and the price paid by the motorist is the public subsidy, estimates of which start at $4 a gallon and go well into the double digits. That's $500 billion and up for the country as a whole per year. It's why the U.S. has up to twice as many cars per capita as other advanced industrial economies, as well as the worst traffic jams this side of Bangkok, the worst urban smog this side of Mexico City, and some of the developed world's worst mass transit.

By footing much of the bill, the government has succeeded in driving jobs and population out of the central cities and into the great highway-bound wastes beyond.

Energy Consumption

3. *Petro-Profligacy:* A few years ago, a couple of Australian environmental scientists named Peter Newman and Jeffrey Kenworthy traveled the globe checking out energy consumption in 32 cities. What they found is not terribly surprising: the most densely populated cities use energy most sparingly, while the most thinly populated use it like water. At one extreme are the hive-like Asian metropolises of Tokyo, Singapore, and Hong Kong; at the other are the sprawling sunbelt "conurbations" of Phoenix and Houston. Somewhere in between are Manhattan, Copenhagen, Vienna, and Amsterdam, with gasoline consumption levels 50 per cent or more higher than the Asians but less than a sixth the gasoline appetite of sunbelt Americans.

21

But which came first: high energy consumption or sprawl? For decades, it's been an article of faith in American politics that Americans naturally like things big—big cars, big lawns, big drafty houses—and engage in Saudi-style energy consumption in order to have them. But it ain't necessarily so. America also once meant big, densely populated cities. But since this would have reduced energy demand to a fraction of the current level and reduced profits for the oil companies, they were phased out. To bolster oil production the federal government set about cultivating a domestic market, which has meant systematically encouraging high energy consumption and discouraging efficiency. Ever since the Model T, waste has been sanctified.

Until the recession put a damper on real estate, the fad among Wall Streeters was for 6000-square-foot hideaways in places like upper Westchester County and the Hamptons (partially financed by the federal government via the tax code, of course) that are so expensive to heat and air-condition they practically require their own Kuwaiti oil well. Middle-class exurbs in Central Jersey and elsewhere are so auto-dependent that, according to one study, an average household generates 12 to 14 car trips per day. Try as they might, cities are incapable of waste on such a colossal scale, which is why there's no place for them in the current high-consumption economic order.

Government Segregation

4. *Racism:* Not the whole reason for American deurbanization, but certainly a big part of it. On one hand, the forces of urban decline were evident as early as World War I, before blacks were a major presence in big cities. Whatever the reasons city-dwellers left for the suburbs, hatred of blacks was well down the list. On the other hand, the racist backlash engendered by the black migration wave of the '30s, '40s, and '50s vastly accelerated the process already underway. Initially, blacks making their way to New York, Newark, or Detroit met with racist cops, foremen, and mobs, but more recently they've met with something even more insidious: the emptiness of the postmodern ghetto. As jobs have fled to the suburbs, inner-city blacks and Latinos who lack a ticket of admission in the form of a private car and suburban home are excluded as never before. Instead of last hired and first fired, they're simply shut out.

The important thing about white flight is that, like urban decline in general, it would never have gone so far without active government assistance. The process began in the 1930s when New Deal housing agencies adopted mortgage guidelines so racist that that famed urban planner Charles Abrams once compared them to the Nuremberg laws of Nazi Germany. Neighborhoods deemed most worthy of federal investment were those in which homes were owned by "American business and professional men," i.e., native-born white Christians. Neighborhoods with blacks or any other "undesirable element" were the least worthy. In Brooklyn, the presence of a single black family in 1939 was enough to render an entire block ineligible for federal mortgage assistance. When the Federal Housing Authority expressed concern about the proximity of an "inharmonious" racial group in a Detroit suburb in 1941, an enterprising local developer responded by building a concrete wall between a black neighborhood and the surrounding white area. The FHA took a second look and granted the mortgage guarantees—but only to whites.

Years of Government Neglect

A dozen years of Government actions such as spending 25 percent of tax dollars on defense while reinvesting a paltry 1 percent in our cities and towns have forced people to accept only grief and despair.

If Washington had maintained the level of aid it gave New York City 10 years ago, we would have received some $3.9 billion more in 1992 for operating expenses and capital construction.

David N. Dinkins, *The New York Times*, May 5, 1992.

Thus, Franklin Roosevelt, the father of modern liberalism, did more to foster housing segregation up North than any number of politicians before him. The upshot is a home-grown version of the South African Group Areas Act, in which the federal government engages in token efforts to combat racial discrimination while simultaneously investing billions in support of *deepening* suburban segregation. Where blacks and whites once at least passed one another on city streets, a kid growing up in Ocean or Hunterdon County, New Jersey, where the black population is less than 3 per cent, may not see a nonwhite face for weeks.

Institutionalized Chaos

5. *Political Fragmentation:* According to the Census, the U.S. now has some 83,000 government units, everything from cities and townships to library boards and fire districts, each with a high degree of fiscal autonomy and power to levy taxes. This is one unit of government for every 3000 Americans, and if it sounds like the sort of Jeffersonian democracy the rest of the world might envy, think again: it's actually a form of institutionalized chaos. As suburban development overwhelms the coun-

tryside, regional planning is nil, duplication of services rampant, and tax raiding epidemic. . . .

State governments pile obligations like Medicaid on financially strapped cities, knowing they're too weak to fight back. Some people gain under such a system, mainly well-off white people who live close to cities with museums and theaters they can enjoy without having to pay for the cops that protect them, and who can afford to be choosy about what people and businesses they let into their leafy suburban enclaves. Developers make out like bandits as well since if any town government gives them trouble, they can always threaten to take their projects to the next community down the line.

Cities, which get saddled with huge welfare populations and a diminished tax base, lose big. But suburbanites saddled with rising traffic, eyesore development, and rising taxes due to multiplying layers of government lose as well. So does anyone who values clean air and an uncluttered landscape. . . .

Due to their greater economic efficiency, the result of people and businesses concentrated in a compact space, cities should not only be self-supporting but, in a reasonable world, would be the economic powerhouses that carry the rest of the country on their back. Rather than places where unemployment benefits are disbursed, they should be places where jobs are created. Rather than catchment zones for the chronically unemployed—in New York City one resident in seven and one child in four is on welfare—they should be places where people go to *find* work.

Demanding a fair shake for urban centers suggests that cities and suburbs should somehow be on equal footing. They shouldn't. The compact, energy-efficient urban mode of life should take precedence. Suburbanization boils down to the privatization of space, with private cars crowding out public transit and private backyards replacing the hustle and bustle of crowded city streets. The appropriation of public space facilitates a higher degree of regimentation—not to mention consumption. The more people try to escape into the privacy of their car and home, the more ensnared in a web of commercialism they become.

There still is some public space left in the city, however; places where people can walk, be by themselves and think, or simply hang out with friends; places where different classes and races still jostle one another in the streets—and sit side by side in the subways. Democracy is impossible without urbanism. Rising regimentation in the rest of the country is the chief reason why people still flock to cities, despite innumerable barriers placed in their path. They're seeking freedom and relief. If this isn't a reason for defending cities, what is?

"The wounds of the central cities are self-inflicted."

Cities Are to Blame for Their Own Decline

Stephen Moore and Dean Stansel

Large cities in the Northeast and Midwest have suffered from an exodus of people and companies, and some have nearly declared bankruptcy. In the following viewpoint, Stephen Moore and Dean Stansel argue that these cities' fiscal woes are the result of their own harmful policies. Moore and Stansel contend that the cities are spending far too much money and allowing their budgets to soar out of control. Declining cities, the authors maintain, levy higher taxes and pay their employees greater salaries than the growing cities in the South and the West. Moore and Stansel believe that the troubled cities can prosper only when they reduce taxes and operating costs. Moore is the director of fiscal policy studies and Stansel is a research assistant at the Cato Institute, a Washington, D.C., think tank.

As you read, consider the following questions:

1. Why do Moore and Stansel object to increases in federal aid to cities?
2. According to the authors, why do declining cities argue for the need to increase personal and business taxes?
3. Why do the authors believe declining cities should reduce their number of personnel?

Stephen Moore and Dean Stansel, "The Myth of America's Under-Funded Cities," *Cato Policy Analysis*, December 1992. Reprinted with permission.

For more than a quarter-century now Americans have been voting with their feet against the economic policies and social conditions of the inner cities. Since 1965, 15 of the largest 25 U.S. cities have lost a combined four million people, even while the total U.S. population rose by 60 million. This is no longer just "white flight": minorities are now leaving the cities in record numbers.

In recent years the exodus of businesses, jobs, and middle-income families from the old central cities has begun to resemble a stampede. For example, since the late 1970s more than 50 Fortune 500 company headquarters have fled New York City. A stunning 370,000 jobs have left New York since 1989 alone and another 130,000 are expected to disappear by the end of 1992. Cleveland, Detroit, Philadelphia, St. Louis, and other major U.S. cities are also suffering from severe out-migration of capital and people. These once-mighty industrial centers are becoming hollow cores of poverty and crime.

The Myth of Urban Neglect

What is the cause of this urban sclerosis? Ever since the Los Angeles riots and looting, the urban lobbyists—including the mayors, the public employee unions, urban scholars, and many members of Congress—have been arguing that the inner cities are victims of a neglectful federal government under Ronald Reagan and George Bush. "There was, quite literally, a massive federal disinvestment in the cities in the 1980s," says congressional delegate Eleanor Holmes Norton of Washington, D.C. To revive the cities, the U.S. Conference of Mayors is asking for $35 billion in new federal funds—a "Marshall plan for the cities."

Unfortunately, the federal government has already tried the equivalent of some 25 Marshall Plans to revive the cities. Since 1965 the federal government has spent an estimated $2.5 trillion on the war on poverty and urban aid. (This includes all welfare spending, Medicaid, housing, education, job training, infrastructure, and direct aid to states and cities.) Economist Walter Williams has calculated that this is enough money to purchase all of the assets of the Fortune 500 companies *plus* all of the farmland in the United States. But it has not spurred an urban revival. In 1992 federal aid to states and cities will rise to $150 billion. After adjusting for inflation, this is the largest amount of federal intergovernmental aid ever. This is hardly a "massive disinvestment."

The budgets of Cleveland, Detroit, Philadelphia, New York, St. Louis, and other large central cities have not been shrinking, they have been rapidly expanding for decades. In constant 1990 dollars local governments spent $435 per resident in 1950; $571 per resident in 1965; and $1,004 in 1990. The largest cities saw an even faster budget rise. In real dollars, New York City's budget nearly tripled from $13 billion in 1965 to $37 billion in 1990. Philadelphia, another near-bankrupt city, has allowed its budget to rise by 125 percent—from $1.6 billion to $3.5 billion— since 1965, a period in which it lost 20 percent of its population. If doubling and even tripling the budgets of New York, Philadelphia, and other cities has not prevented the urban bleeding, there is no reason to suspect that giving cities more money to spend will help solve the urban crisis.

Many Cities Are Booming

Not all cities are in a state of decline. Among the 75 largest U.S. urban areas there are dozens of cities—many on the West Coast, in the Sunbelt region, and in the Southeast—that have been booming financially and economically for at least the past twenty years. Las Vegas, Nevada; Phoenix, Arizona; Arlington and Austin, Texas; Sacramento and San Diego, California; Raleigh and Charlotte, North Carolina; and Jacksonville, Florida, all have rapidly rising incomes, populations, and employment; and low poverty and crime rates.

The key policy question addressed in this study is this: What do growth cities—Phoenix, Raleigh, and San Diego, for example—do differently from shrinking cities, such as Buffalo, Cleveland, and Detroit? The answer is at least partially contained in the fiscal policies of these cities. Using Census Bureau City Finance data from 1965, 1980, and 1990 for the 80 of the largest cities, we find significant and consistent patterns of higher spending and taxes in the low growth cities as compared to the high growth cities. [Our data] shows the following:

Spending is almost twice as high in shrinking cities as in growth cities. Expenditures in the high growth cities average $673 per person and 5.7 percent of personal income versus $1,152 and 11.8 percent in the shrinking cities.

Taxes are roughly twice as high in the shrinking cities as in growth cities. A family of four pays $2,352 in taxes in shrinking cities, while it pays $1,216 in taxes in the high growth cities.

Shrinking cities are much more likely to impose an income tax on residents than high growth cities. None of the 15 highest growth cities have an income tax, whereas ten of the 15 lowest growth cities do. With very few exceptions, every city in America with a city income tax is getting poorer.

Shrinking cities have twice as large a bureaucracy as growth cities. The high growth cities have 99 city employees per 10,000 residents; the shrinking cities 235.

Cities with high spending and taxes in 1980 lost population in the 1980s; cities with low spending and taxes gained population. High spending and taxes are a cause, not just a consequence, of urban decline. The fastest growing cities in the 1980s had very low spending—$577 per resident—at the start of the period. The cities with the most severe population losses had 1980 spending of $995 per resident. Taxes were $257 per person in the growth cities and $497 in the shrinking cities in 1980.

The primary reason expenditures are high and rising in large central cities is that these governments generally have higher unit costs in educating children, collecting garbage, building roads, policing neighborhoods, and providing other basic services. For example, in 1988 the shrinking cities spent roughly $4,950 per pupil on education, whereas the high growth cities spent $3,605. This $1,350 cost differential cannot be explained by superior schools in places such as Detroit and Newark.

Municipal Unions Raise Costs

The influence of municipal employee unions largely explains the high unit costs of declining central cities. Compensation for unionized local employees tends to be roughly 30 percent above wages for comparably skilled private sector workers. In New York City, the average school janitor is paid $57,000 a year. In Philadelphia, the average municipal employee receives more than $50,000 a year in salary and benefits. These high salaries are typical of large cities. According to the Census Bureau, cities with populations over 500,000 pay their mostly nonunionized workers more than 50 percent more than do cities with populations under 75,000. In short, thriving cities are places where costs are lower, bureaucracies are smaller, and services are better.

Absurd Union Rules

Philadelphia's arcane unionized work rules offer city employees 14 paid holidays (most workers get 8), require that the art museum be fully staffed on Mondays and holidays when it is closed, and once prevented for months the firing of a worker who repeatedly skipped work to play pinball and video games. The unions claimed that pinball is a gambling addiction, and thus a handicap. Philadelphia is also near bankruptcy.

Stephen Moore, *National Review*, October 5, 1992.

Some city officials are beginning to recognize this economic reality. The Democratic mayor of Philadelphia, Edward Rendell, is challenging the entrenched municipal unions and other spending constituencies with a budget plan that calls for $1.1 billion in cost savings over five years. He has spurned more federal aid as the poison that has produced Philadelphia's near-insolvency in 1991. Meanwhile, Chicago Mayor Richard J. Daley and Indianapolis Mayor Stephen Goldsmith have contracted out dozens of services to private providers and have slowed the growth of massive and bloated budgets to a crawl.

There is no inevitability to the decline of America's major cities. They can and should be saved. For generations they have served as the nation's centers not only of industrial might, but of culture, diversity, and intellect. Through an aggressive agenda of budget control, tax reduction, privatization, and deregulation, America's declining cities can rise again in prominence and prosperity. . . .

Cities' Self-Imposed Policies

In the conventional analysis of the urban crisis, cities are portrayed primarily as victims of national trends and conditions beyond their control. These factors include the recession, Reagan budget cuts, suburbanization, the decline in manufacturing, the rise of the automobile, an aging infrastructure, racism, AIDS, homelessness, urban gangs, guns, and drugs. Each of these conditions can place considerable strain on municipal budgets, yet city officials are impotent in combating them.

There is some truth to this. The recent recession is painful evidence that no city is immune from the impact of national economic conditions and policies. From the 1950s through the 1980s most of the cities of California enjoyed spectacular rates of growth. California was widely considered recession-proof. The recession has had a devastating impact on California localities—many of which are at the top of the list of growth cities. One-third of all the job losses from 1990 to 1992 have occurred in California. Another example is the impact that wide fluctuations in international oil prices in the 1970s and 1980s had on the economies and budgets of Texas cities.

Unquestionably there are regional factors at play in determining the relative rates of growth of cities. Most of the declining cities in our survey are the once-mighty industrial centers in the Northeast and Midwest—the rustbelt. Most of the growth cities are in the Sunbelt, the West Coast and the Southeast. A related factor that tends to correlate with the rate of economic growth of a city is its age—with older cities tending to do worse. This is often attributed to the aging infrastructure of older cities.

Still, the fact that for long periods of time some cities have been flourishing as others are deteriorating, suggests that the self-imposed policies of cities play an important role in determining their economic fates. The regional differences in economic growth rates of cities and states are largely a result of the fact that *the policies* of Southeastern cities and states are different from those of the Northeast. People and businesses are not moving from New York City and Philadelphia to Raleigh or Dallas entirely because of the weather. Moreover, there are substantial differences among cities within states that clearly cannot be explained by regional or state factors. Why is Oakland a declining city, but Santa Ana growing? Why is Arlington doing so much better than Fort Worth, or Colorado Springs than Denver? Our answer to this question is that their spending and taxing policies are very much different. Growth cities have pro-growth fiscal policies; declining cities have anti-growth fiscal policies. . . .

High Taxes and Spending

The urban lobby and urban scholars invariably argue that low growth cities spend more than high growth cities because of more spending requirements. Poor cities must pay for anti-poverty spending, subsidized child care, homeless assistance, drug abatement and rehabilitation, crime control, job training, and so on. And because these cities have less wealth and fewer workers and businesses to support the cost of these kinds of programs, declining cities have to charge higher tax burdens on their residents and businesses to raise the same amount of revenue as wealthy and prospering cities. In sum, higher spending and taxes in low growth cities are allegedly not a *cause*, but a *consequence* of urban decline.

To investigate this issue, we need to determine whether spending and tax levels at the *beginning* of each period of analysis are related to rates of economic growth and well-being in *later* periods. If cities with high spending and taxes in 1970, for example, have large increases in poverty from 1970 to 1990, the high spending and taxes clearly cannot be a consequence of the subsequent poverty. In other words, high spending and taxes *in 1990* may be a consequence of a large increase in poverty from 1970 to 1990. But it would be impossible for high spending and taxes *in 1970* to be a consequence of large increases in poverty from 1970 to 1990. Indeed, this would be strong evidence that the high spending and taxes contributed to the poverty.

[Our data] shows that indeed the levels of city spending and taxes in 1965 are negatively correlated with subsequent rates of urban economic progress. This is true for four measures of economic growth we examined: population change from 1965-1990, employment change from 1960-1990, poverty from 1970-1990, and per capita income from 1969-1987. High-employment growth cities had per capita tax revenues of $361 in 1965, whereas low-employment growth cities had per-capita tax revenues of $605. Per capita income growth is the only economic measure for which the relationship appears to be weak. For the other growth measures, spending and taxes were typically 50 to 100 percent higher in slow growth cities.

High Spending Yields Little Growth

	Expenditures per Capita (less health, education, welfare)		Tax Revenue Per Capita	City Employees	
	1990	1965-90 Increase		Number Per 10,000 residents	Monthly Payroll Per Capita
Highest Growth Cities Over 100% Growth	$695	$232	$314	107	$27
High Growth Cities 50% to 100% Growth	$890	$515	$371	146	$33
Average Growth Cities 10% to 49% Growth	$860	$453	$414	134	$31
Low Growth Cities –15% to 9% Growth	$1,142	$652	$670	243	$61
Lowest Growth Cities Over 15% Shrinkage	$1,169	$662	$577	217	$51

Source: Stephen Moore, Cato Institute, 1992.

The negative relationship also holds true with even greater force for the period of the 1980s. Cities with high spending and taxes in 1980 lost population in the 1980s; low tax and spend cities in 1980 gained substantial population in the 1980s. Cities with high taxes and spending can be expected to experience urban decline. . . .

Low Growth Versus High Growth

Cities quite clearly do have direct control over their own economic fortunes. Cities in decline are victims of bad public policies that are mostly self-generated and in some cases are generated by policymakers at the state level. Comparing the fiscal policies of low growth cities versus high growth cities, we make the following nine conclusions:

1) Low growth cities have expenditures that are up to twice the level of high growth cities.

2) Low growth cities have tax burdens that are up to twice the level of high growth cities.

3) Low growth cities have much higher payroll costs. On average, low growth cities have twice the number of municipal em-

31

ployees per 10,000 residents as do high growth cities.

4) Low growth cities are much more likely to impose a local income tax than high growth cities.

5) Low growth cities tend to rely more heavily on income and property taxes for revenues, whereas high growth cities rely more heavily on sales taxes.

6) Low growth cities spend as much as 50 percent more per student on education expenses than high growth cities.

7) State-local tax burdens are substantially higher in low growth cities than in high growth cities.

8) State-local income tax levels are much higher in low growth cities than in high growth cities.

9) High spending and taxes in low growth cities are a cause of their decline. High taxes and expenditures at the beginning of a period are consistently associated with subsequent slow economic growth rates in cities. It may be that big government is both a cause and a consequence of urban distress. High spending and taxes lead to city decline, which may promote further city spending and taxes, which may lead to a further exodus of people and businesses, and so on. . . .

Self-Inflicted Wounds

Urban advocates are right when they say that America's inner cities have been victims of destructive government policies. They have—but not those of Reagan or Bush. The wounds of the central cities are self-inflicted. A 1988 private audit of near-bankrupt Scranton, Pennsylvania, professed that "the city government appears to exist for the benefit of its employees instead of the people." Regrettably, this could describe the operating principles and skewed priorities of too many ailing cities. Unless and until America's central cities start putting people first, through cutting service costs and anti-growth tax rates, no amount of federal aid can reverse the decline of urban America.

"If the market is allowed to take job growth to the extreme fringe of our metropolitan areas, our center cities may well require full-time military occupation."

The Loss of Jobs to Suburbs Harms Large Cities

Christopher B. Leinberger

Many high-paying jobs in cities are moving to, or being created in, suburbs. In the following viewpoint, Christopher B. Leinberger argues that this trend harms cities because poorer inner-city residents have no access to these distant jobs. Leinberger contends that unless this trend is slowed, economic conditions in cities will worsen and hopelessness among the poor will increase. Leinberger proposes to slow the trend by encouraging city-based corporations to provide job training and to make business districts safe for workers. He also advocates controlling cities' growth to ensure that jobs are kept in, and closer to, large cities. Leinberger is managing partner of Robert Charles Lesser & Co., a real estate advisory and metropolitan public policy firm in Los Angeles.

As you read, consider the following questions:

1. How will the existence of high-paying jobs in the suburbs increase urban flight, according to Leinberger?
2. Why does Leinberger believe it is important for cities and suburbs to share tax revenues?
3. According to the author, why is it important to provide affordable housing in the suburbs?

From Christopher B. Leinberger, "Where Jobs Go: Business Flees to the Urban Fringe." The article is reprinted from *The Nation*, July 6, 1992, © 1992 The Nation Company, Inc.

As a direct result of the postindustrial economy that America has been creating over the past couple of decades, the locations of the best-paying new jobs are changing radically. These jobs are now overwhelmingly concentrated in obscure crossroads like King of Prussia (Philadelphia metropolitan area), Newport Beach (Los Angeles area), Tyson's Corner (Washington, D.C., area) and Schaumburg (Chicago area). These new suburbs are fourteen, forty, sixteen and twenty-five miles, respectively, from the central business district.

Types of Metropolitan Jobs

There are three distinct types of employment in our metropolitan areas, two generally well paying and a third almost always at the bottom of the wage scale. About one-third of metropolitan jobs are with companies that "export" goods and services outside the metro area. These are the highest-paying jobs, injecting fresh cash into the local economy. In Los Angeles, for example, those jobs are in aerospace, defense, software development, entertainment, international trade, oil refining and a number of other industries. In Seattle, the export industries are aerospace, software development and international trade; in Philadelphia they include pharmaceuticals, higher education, oil refining and computer hardware development.

Export jobs in turn create demand for the second type of employment, regional-serving jobs, which include finance, real estate, utilities, the local news media and professional services of various kinds. These represent about a quarter of all jobs in most metropolitan areas and on average pay slightly less well than export jobs. It is important to note that export and regional-serving jobs tend to locate in a few concentrations, variously referred to as urban villages, edge cities or urban cores. Most large metropolitan areas have ten to thirty urban cores, the downtown being just one of them.

The third category is local-serving jobs, representing about half of all employment and paying the least well. These jobs are located near where people live and include such occupations as schoolteacher, store clerk, police and local professionals such as neighborhood doctors and "storefront" lawyers. Virtually every job in South Central Los Angeles is—or was—local serving. Following the Watts riots in 1965, most of the export jobs, generally in manufacturing, abandoned the area, leaving only low-wage, local-serving employment.

The export and regional-serving jobs in every metropolitan area in the country have followed the same pattern over the past twenty years. In any metro area in late twentieth-century America, if one knows the layout of the freeway system; where the existing white, upper middle class lives and where the new

34

white middle-income housing is; and where minority populations are concentrated, one can determine where 80 to 100 percent of the new upwardly mobile export and regional-serving
jobs are located. With few exceptions, these high-paying jobs
have concentrated in the predominantly white upper-middle-
and middle-income sections of the metropolitan region, generally on the opposite side of the metro area from the highest concentration of minority housing. Low-income residents and the
new high-paying, upwardly mobile export and regional-serving
jobs are now located farther apart than ever. . . .

Less Access to Good Jobs

If, as many indicators suggest, jobs in the 1990s, particularly
the high-paying ones, become available in the extreme fringe of
the metropolitan area in the same proportion as they did in the
near-in suburban locations over the past two decades, many inner-city residents will be too far away to commute daily to the
new exurban ones. In the 1970s and 1980s the new jobs in relatively close-in suburban locations were at least within commuting distance for many city dwellers. The new relocation trend to
the extreme fringe will certainly continue, and could accelerate,
the post-World War II exodus of the middle class from the center cities, leaving poorer residents behind.

A Hemorrhaging of Urban Jobs

As corporations spread out into the outer rings of the metropolis,
many of the largest cities face a continuing hemorrhaging of jobs,
tax dollars, and people. Those forces only exacerbate the growing
social pathology of the inner cities, raising the specter of the
once-great cities as abandoned, burned-out congregations of the
poor, the sick, and the homeless.

Business Week, September 25, 1989.

These trends affecting the location of export and regional-serving jobs are firmly imbedded in the economy and real estate
market. Short of massive federal and state intervention in the
marketplace (an unlikely event that would undoubtedly produce
as many problems as it would solve), the trends must be viewed
as something that can be influenced but not reversed. However,
here are four ideas, tried and proved in this country and Europe,
that might ameliorate some of the intended and unintended consequences of the decentralization of our metropolitan areas.
    The first is to try to slow down the trend through a kind of
holding action by center-city economic development agencies

and public/private partnerships, working with those institutions and corporations that have a commitment to the center city. Targeting the existing concentration of export and regional-serving sections of the center city, particularly downtown, these groups must launch programs that increase job training opportunities and enhance security. A well-trained work force and freedom from fear of crime are prerequisites to maintaining the existing job base.

An example of this effort is provided by the more than twenty public/private partnerships in New York City. The Grand Central Partnership, for instance, supplements municipal services in the fifty-three-block section of Manhattan surrounding Grand Central Terminal with its own fifty-person security force, a forty-person sanitation force that sweeps the sidewalks and streets twelve hours a day, and a $2-million-a-year program for the homeless at a former Catholic boys' school. Hundreds of these "business improvement districts" are now operating in cities throughout the country.

Sharing Tax Revenues

The second strategy is to encourage a regional approach to government, particularly toward tax-sharing. This strategy requires a recognition that the center city cannot—and should not have to—bear the cost of serving the bulk of the metropolitan area's needy. The growing fiscal and social problems of our center cities have been ignored too long by the suburban jurisdictions. Violent and property crime, homelessness and drug trafficking know no political boundary. These problems have not been magically confined within the center city limits and have resulted in a new trend of declining property values and quality of life for close-in suburbs throughout the country. An example of the kind of tax-sharing needed can be found in the Minneapolis-St. Paul metro area, where 60 percent of new commercial property tax revenues go to the local municipality and 40 percent go to the other metro area jurisidictions.

In addition, a regional approach could allow for the establishment of an urban growth boundary around the metropolitan area, beyond which jobs and suburban housing could not go, as Portland, Oregon, and nearly every European metropolitan area have done. This would force jobs back closer to, and possibly back into, the center cities as well as protect the rural land around our metropolitan areas from sprawling development. While growth boundaries are not without flaws—they can artificially inflate land prices and thus rents and home prices, for example—they do seem to slow lopsided growth toward predominantly white neighborhoods while maintaining the integrity of downtown.

Los Angeles has already created a de facto regional government in the form of the South Coast Air Quality Management District. This body also increasingly regulates traffic congestion, job growth and land use. Even in 1987, regional government in the Los Angeles area was considered a fantasy. Today, most metropolitan-area leaders do not question that it is a reality. The next step would be to add social issues to the regional agenda.

Decentralization of Jobs and People in Nine Large Cities in the North and East, 1950-1980 (percentage)

	1950		1980	
	Central City	Suburban Ring	Central City	Suburban Ring
Population	64.0	36.0	42.0	58.0
Employment				
Manufacturing	69.0	31.0	43.0	57.0
Retail trade	74.0	26.0	38.0	62.0
Wholesale trade	90.0	10.0	51.0	49.0
Selected services	83.0	17.0	56.0	44.0
Total	74.0	26.0	45.0	55.0

Source: U.S. Census Bureau.

A third approach is to encourage affordable and public housing in the near-in and fringe suburbs, enabling low-income residents to live closer to the new jobs. Orange County, California, has in the past required that 20 percent of all new residential projects be set aside for affordable housing. Columbia, Maryland, recently issued a taxpayer-supported bond to build low-income housing for minorities. While these measures are unlikely to be widely adopted, the business community could be a powerful ally. Many companies had a hard time filling lower-level jobs in the near-in suburbs during the 1980s, and this situation will be exacerbated in the 1990s. One promising approach is for corporations to team up with nonprofit affordable-housing organizations, such as the Bridge Housing Corporation in San Francisco and Habitat for Humanity, based in Americus, Georgia. An interim measure is the organizing of car pools and setting up of van pools to bring city residents to distant corporate jobs.

Fourth, we must improve the efficiency of central city public services. The cost of maintaining existing infrastructure and providing services in the center city is higher than the cost of building new infrastructure and providing services in the fringe suburbs, even if the extra cost of delivering social services to the needy is subtracted. The trade-off many companies face is either moving to a suburb with lower costs and fewer social problems or staying in the high-cost center city with overwhelming social problems. It is not hard to see that moving out makes more sense economically.

The Downward Spiral of Cities

If present trends continue, the center city's future—and the future of many of the close-in suburbs—is likely to be similar to the present-day fate of Camden and Newark, New Jersey; of Chester, Pennsylvania; or of South Central Los Angeles. The "Camdenization" of our major cities, resulting in their being populated primarily by an underclass in an environment of hopelessness, has obviously begun. It is probable that the 1990s offer the last chance to reverse this trend, because if most of the 24 million new jobs that the Labor Department estimates will be created between 1990 and 2005 are located at the fringe of our metro areas, the downward spiral of the center cities may become irreversible.

As a nation we are used to moving away from our problems, striking out to new frontiers. If the market is allowed to take job growth to the extreme fringe of our metropolitan areas, our center cities may well require full-time military occupation. The fires in Los Angeles are a warning that an escapist strategy no longer works. The costs are too steep and the stakes are too high.

"The [lost] office jobs . . . have been mostly in the big, aging companies—the ones most likely to head for suburbia and to bomb when they do. "

The Loss of Jobs to Suburbs Does Not Harm Large Cities

William H. Whyte

William H. Whyte is a researcher of city and suburban life who has written several books on these topics, including *The Organization Man*. In the following viewpoint, Whyte argues that the relocation of corporations and jobs to suburbs does not harm large cities because these companies are less competitive and profitable than corporations that remain in cities. Whyte cites his New York City regional study, which shows that the average stock market performance of relocated companies was far poorer than those that remained in cities. Whyte asserts that new, smaller companies will thrive and grow larger in cities, replacing those that have relocated.

As you read, consider the following questions:

1. Why did many firms choose to leave New York City, according to Whyte?
2. According to the author, how did problems within the relocated companies cause their poor performance?
3. Why does Whyte believe that central city locations are vital to new, small companies?

The out-migration started slowly. The first to move was General Foods, to White Plains in 1954. Ten years later IBM moved out, to Armonk. Then Olin, to Stamford. In 1970 the momentum picked up. A few corporations headed for the Sunbelt. Most headed for the suburbs, to Connecticut's Fairfield County in particular. By 1976 over thirty major corporations had moved out of New York City, and more were leaving—including one of the biggest, Union Carbide. Office vacancy rates were climbing. With the city on the edge of bankruptcy, it looked as if a full-fledged rout was in the making.

High time, many people said. Even New Yorkers joined in the reprehension. Couldn't blame Union Carbide, the *New York Times* editorialized; the city had let it down. Dr. George Sternlieb, director of Rutgers' Center for Urban Policy Research, who had been prophesying such events, fairly chortled at their arrival. "It takes a man who's been shot in the head a while to realize he's dead," Sternlieb observed. "New York may not realize it, but if you look at the numbers it's clear that New York is dead."

New York Avoids Disaster

But the rout did not come off. The bad news about New York had been so bad that a classic bottom was being formed. Any corporation that had not yet decided to leave probably would not leave. The ones who had left had long before signaled their intentions. In our research on public spaces we had found an early warning indicator. It was the corporation's own building. Often it would give an advance tip that the corporation was not long for the city.

Union Carbide's headquarters on Park Avenue was one such. This sleek black building was one of Skidmore, Owings, and Merrill's best, and it was superbly located. In operation, however, it bristled with distrust of the city. Large strips of empty space bordered its sides and fronts, and with nary a bench or a ledge for anyone to sit on. Guarding entry was a corps of guards. It should have come as no surprise when the company announced in 1976 that it was forswearing the city and would move to Danbury, Connecticut.

Union Carbide's timing was not very good. The mass exodus was just about over. Preposterous as it may have seemed then, the bad news was peaking just as the city's competitive position took some decided turns for the better. Overseas business had become a great stimulant; there was an influx of foreign firms, especially in finance. International divisions of corporations were expanding and it was in New York that they were doing it. A number of firms that had earlier contemplated leaving the city had second thoughts. Philip Morris announced it would stay. So did Pfizer. New York's troubles were by no means over, but there was to be a respite, and time for mulling over some lessons. . . .

After the 1976 departures the outward movement slowed to a trickle, averaging about two firms a year. Then in 1986 the pace picked up: four moved out and several others announced they were going to: Exxon, J.C. Penney, Mobil, AT&T. As in the mid-seventies, the news thoroughly alarmed the city. This time, many said, the city really had had it.

A Return to the Inner City

For more than three decades, business has staged a mass exodus from the mean streets of America's inner cities—driven by fear of crime, high operating costs and lack of skilled labor.

But with many suburban and downtown retail markets nearly saturated—and with wages and real estate costs becoming increasingly attractive in depressed urban areas—some experts believe that basic economics favor a return to the inner city. Hopes are especially high in the Los Angeles area, where the Long Beach rapid rail transit line and the Century Freeway could help fuel new business development in South Los Angeles.

Jube Shiver Jr., *Los Angeles Times*, November 27, 1991.

There was a widespread disposition to see the move-outs' side, and to see their departure as a damning indictment of the city: its high taxes, crime, and stress and strain. The moves had been preceded by exhaustive study of all factors, the firms emphasized, and certainly this must have included the experience of the previous move-outs. It was generally assumed that they had done very well in their suburban campuses, and in financial as well as environmental terms.

Tracking Companies' Performance

But had they? When I did my 1976 study, not enough time had elapsed to draw valid conclusions. But now ten years had gone by and there was hard data. To follow up, I tracked the performance of the 38 companies that had moved out and 36 that had not, and by that most hard-boiled of measures, the valuation of the marketplace.

The first discovery was that seventeen of the thirty-eight move-out firms had lost their identify. They had been bought out, raided, or merged, and in no case as the dominant partner. That left twenty-two companies. For each I traced the stock valuation for the eleven-year period December 31, 1976, to December 31, 1987. The average increase was 107 percent—

somewhat better than the 93 percent increase of the Dow-Jones Industrial Average.

What about the companies that had stayed in New York? The results were downright startling. For the thirty-six major corporations that stayed the average increase was 277 percent—over two and one half times the increase of the move-outs.

Assigning cause and effect is difficult. There are just too many variables. It could be that the sojourn in suburbia did dull reflexes, as some prophesied it would. But it could also be argued that the companies were the better for having moved and would have fared worse had they not moved.

I think the die was cast well before the companies moved out. The impulse seems to have been internal, the consequence of cyclical changes within the companies, and independent of the city and its problems. In a word, they were not doing very well. Some had grown old and fat and slow. Several had identity problems. (American Can got out of the can business entirely, changed its name to Primerica, and went into finance.) To paraphrase Dr. Johnson, if a company is tired of New York, it is tired.

Understandably, companies that were unhappy became unhappy with the city. Frequently they telegraphed their intentions by citing somebody else's complaints; the recalcitrant yokel was a favorite. When the companies finally did announce, it was with a vengeance. The leave-takings were acts of renunciation, a turning of the back to the past. The sheer mechanics of the migration, the planning studies, and the design work promised to be a shot in the arm. And so it was—for the top management group, at any rate, if not for the underlings who were unable to pick up roots and join the move. Sorry about that.

Similar Results Found

Another study revealed a wide disparity between the performance of move-outs and that of stayers. In a 1980 assessment for the Regional Plan Association, Regina Belz Armstrong analyzed three kinds of firms: those that stayed in New York City; those that moved to the suburbs; those that moved out of the region entirely. The factors she checked were productivity, profitability, and growth.

Of the twenty-three companies that had moved to the suburbs in the period 1972-75, the majority had profitability lower than average for companies in their industry in the region, and the growth rate was only a half that of the others. The twenty firms that had moved out of the region had performances moderately below average for their group.

As in my study, firms that remained in New York City did very well, some spectacularly well. The average value of output and profit per dollar of labor input increased much faster than both the regional and national average, and faster yet than the average of the move-out firms.

Costs? Both studies are illuminating on this score. At the top of the list of reasons advanced for moving out has been the cost of New York. They are indeed high, and for a range of things: for a house, anywhere; for commutation; for schooling. High too are costs of office space, it being more expensive to be at the crossroads than up a back road.

But costs are relative. What is the payoff? What is the profit earned from the lower costs? The expenditures for housekeeping are far less important to a balance sheet than profitability and performance. On this score, both studies speak loudly. The lower costs enjoyed by the move-out companies did not correlate with excellent performance. The higher costs of the New York companies did.

New Jobs: San Francisco and New York Benefit

In a study of San Francisco's experience between 1972 and 1984, David L. Birch found that small firms were creating the new jobs. Larger firms with 100 employees or more, were shedding jobs. Company age was a factor too: firms less than four years old produced a net gain of 30,597 jobs over the period, but those twelve years old or more had a net loss of 13,382 jobs.

New York has been enjoying similar gains. In 1986 it has a net gain of 64,000 office jobs and about the same was expected for 1987. Some of the gain has come from the expansion of local firms, most markedly in financial services. This expansion has been so buoyant as to be unsettling and has absorbed most of the space vacated by the move-outs. Firms moving into New York, including several from the Sunbelt, have brought jobs. What in time may prove the most fruitful source are the jobs created through the start-up of entirely new companies.

William H. Whyte, *City*, 1988.

There will probably be more move-outs. More companies will be growing older and fatter, and as a normal consequence they will leave. This will be painful for the cities they leave, especially when the moves come in bunches, as they seem to do from time to time.

They too are losing back-office work to their suburban office parks, and sometimes they lose headquarters as well. When firms move South and Southwest, furthermore, they will not necessarily move to a downtown. J. C. Penney did not. To the discomfiture of Dallas it moved all the way from New York, not to Dallas, but to the town of Plano. Some Dallas leaders were incredulous. Plano?

City Businesses Prevail

On balance, the center city is competing rather well. The office jobs that it has been losing have been mostly in the big, aging companies—the ones most likely to head for suburbia and to bomb when they do. The new-job increases have been mostly in newer, smaller firms. They are local companies, most of them, but as [author] Jane Jacobs has observed, local economies are where it all starts. The small companies need access to a wide range of specialized services and people. They cannot have this in-house. They are not big enough. They cannot have this out in some isolated location. They need to be in the center—or as close to it as rents and space will permit.

Turnover is brisk. Many will fold, but here and there some of the companies will become big companies. Eventually, some of them may defect to the suburbs, but in their dynamic years they will thrive in the city. So, at least, our comparison study would indicate. As a group, the companies that competed in the city proved to be tougher and more profitable than the companies that did not—and by an impressive margin. The crossroads, it would appear, is a very good place to be.

"Urban America is not only divided by a line with blacks on one side and whites on another, . . . it is a mixture of other races, languages and religions."

Racism Divides America's Cities

Bill Bradley

Bill Bradley is a U.S. senator from New Jersey. In the following viewpoint, Bradley argues that misapprehensions and tensions among racial groups divide America's cities. Bradley asserts, for example, that white stereotypes of minorities as lawless or violent instill an unfounded fear that prompts whites to avoid minorities. Similarly, Bradley contends, minority groups view white criticisms of individual acts as criticisms of all members of a particular group. Bradley believes that all inhabitants of cities must be more tolerant of each other and interact peacefully regardless of race.

As you read, consider the following questions:

1. Why will economic progress increasingly depend on minority workers, according to Bradley?
2. In Bradley's opinion, how can pessimism toward the possibility of justice lead to chaos and irresponsibility?
3. According to Bradley, how will continued racial strife and violence affect the upper, middle, and lower classes?

Bill Bradley, "A Plea for Racial Dialogue: A Plan for Saving Our Cities," *In These Times*, May 13-19, 1992. Reprinted with permission.

The future of American cities is inextricably bound to the issue of race and ethnicity. By the year 2000, only 57 percent of the people entering the workforce in America will be native-born whites. That means that the economic future of the children of white Americans will increasingly depend on the talents of non-white Americans.

If we allow them to fail because of our penny-pinching or timidity about straight talk, America will become a second-rate power. If they succeed, America and all Americans will be enriched. As a nation, we will find common ground together and move ahead, or each of us will be diminished.

Urban America is not only divided by a line with blacks on one side and whites on another. Increasingly, it is a mixture of other races, languages and religions, as new immigrants arrive in search of economic promise and freedom from state control. More than 4.5 million Latinos and nearly 5 million Asians and Pacific Islanders have arrived in America since 1970.

Even though our American future depends on finding common ground, many white Americans resist relinquishing the sense of entitlement skin color has given them throughout our national history. They lack an understanding of the emerging dynamics of "one world," even in the U.S., because to them non-whites always have been "the other."

Racial Differences

On top of that, people of different races often don't listen to each other on the subject of race. It's as if we're all experts, locked into our narrow views and preferring to be wrong rather than risk changing those views. Black Americans ask of Asian-Americans, "What's the problem? You're doing well economically." Black Americans believe that Latinos often fail to find common ground with their historic struggle, and some Latino Americans agree, questioning whether the black civil-rights model is the only path to progress. White Americans continue to harbor absurd stereotypes about all people of color. Black Americans take white criticism of individual acts as an attempt to stigmatize all black Americans. We seem to be more interested in defending our racial territory than recognizing we could be enriched by another race's perspective.

In politics for the last 25 years, silence or distortion has shaped the issue of race and urban America. Both political parties have contributed to the problem. Republicans have played the race card in a divisive way to get votes—remember Willie Horton—and Democrats have suffocated discussion of self-destructive behavior among the minority population in a cloak of silence and denial. The result is that yet another generation has been lost. We cannot afford to wait longer. It is time for candor, time for truth and time for action.

America's cities are poorer, sicker, less educated and more violent than at any time in my lifetime. The physical problems are obvious: old housing stock, deteriorated schools, aging infrastructure, a diminished manufacturing base, a health-care system short of doctors that fails to immunize against measles, much less educate about AIDS. The jobs have disappeared. The neighborhoods have been gutted. A genuine depression has hit cities, with unemployment in some areas at the levels of the '30s.

Yet, just as Americans found solidarity then in the midst of trauma and just as imaginative leadership moved us through the darkest days of the Depression, so today the physical conditions of our cities can be altered. What it takes is collective will, greater accountability and sufficient resources.

The Importance of Meaning

What is less obvious in urban America is the crisis of meaning. Without meaning, there can be no hope; without hope there can be no struggle; without struggle there can be no personal betterment. Absence of meaning derived from overt and subtle attacks from racist quarters over many years—and furthered by an increasing pessimism about the possibility of justice—offers a context for chaos and irresponsibility.

Development of meaning starts from the very beginning of life. Yet more than 40 percent of all births in the 20 largest cities of America are to women living alone. Among black women, out-of-wedlock births are over 65 percent. While many single women do heroic jobs in raising kids, there are millions of others who get caught in a life undertow that drowns both them and their children. Many of these children live in a world without love and without a father or any other male supportive figure besides the drug dealer, the pimp or the gang leader. They are thrown out on the street early without any frame of reference except survival.

To say to kids who have no connection to religion, no family outside a gang, no sense of place outside the territory, no imagination beyond the cadence of rap or the violence of TV, that government is on their side rings hollow. Their contact with government has not empowered but diminished them. To them, government at best is incompetent—look at the schools, the streets, the welfare department—and at worst corrupt—the cops and building inspectors on the take, the white-collar criminal who gets nothing but a suspended sentence, the local politicians with gross personal behavior. And replacing a corrupt white mayor with a corrupt black mayor won't make the difference.

The physical conditions of American cities and the absence of meaning in more and more lives come together at the barrel of a gun. If you were to select the one thing that has changed in cities since the '60s, it would be fear. Fear covers the streets like a sheet of ice. Every day the newspaper tells of another murder. Both the number of murders and violent crimes has doubled in the 20 largest cities since 1968. Ninety percent of all violence is committed by males, and they are its predominant victims. Indeed, murder is the highest cause of death for young black males.

For African-Americans in cities, the violence isn't new. You don't have to see *Boyz 'N the Hood* to confirm it; just visit public housing projects where mothers send their kids to school dodging bullets, talk with young girls whose rapes go uninvestigated, listen to elderly residents express their constant fear of violation, and remember the story of a former drug dealer who once told me he quit only after he found his partner shot, with his brains oozing onto the pavement.

Lingering Racism

The Willie Horton ads in the 1988 presidential election, the emotional reactions to a gang rape in New York's Central Park in April, 1989, and an elaborate hoax to frame a black man for the brutal murder of a pregnant white woman in Boston in January, 1990, indicate that racial animosity lurks very near the surfaces of our urban veneers.

Len M. Nichols, *USA Today*, November 1990.

But what is new is the fear of random violence among whites. Most politicians want to avoid the need to confront the reality that causes the fear. They don't want to put themselves at risk by speaking candidly about violence to both blacks and whites and saying the same things to both groups. Essentially, they're indifferent to the black self-destruction. And violence only hardens their indifference—not only to the perpetrator but to all African-Americans.

Physically, more white Americans leave the city—from 1970 to 1990, more than 4 million white Americans moved out of our big cities. Psychologically, white Americans put walls up to the increasingly desperate plight of those, both black and white, who can't leave—those Americans who are stuck trying to raise kids in a war zone, holding jobs in a Third World economy, establishing a sense of community in a desert where there is no water of hope and where everyone is out for themselves.

Now, it's not that there isn't racism. It's alive and well. It's not that police brutality doesn't exist. It does. It's not that police departments give residents a feeling of security. Few do.

But, when politicians don't talk about the reality that everyone knows exists, they cannot lead us out of our current crisis. Institutions are no better than the people who run them. Because very few people of different races make real contact or have real conversations with each other, the white vigilante groups and the black TV spokespersons educate the uneducated about race.

The result is that the divide among races in our cities deepens with white Americans more and more unwilling to spend the money to ameliorate the physical conditions or to see why the absence of meaning in the lives of many urban children threatens the future of their own children.

The Future of Cities

So, the future of urban America will take one of three paths: abandonment, encirclement or conversion.

Abandonment means recognizing that, with the billions of investment in the national highway system (which led to suburbia, corporate parks and the malling of America) and with communications technology advancing so fast that the economic advantages of urban proximity are being replaced by the computer screen, the city has outlived its usefulness.

"Massive investment in urban America would be throwing money away," the argument goes, "and to try to prevent the decline will be futile."

Encirclement means that people in cities will live in enclaves. The racial and ethnic walls will go higher. The class lines will be manned by ever-increasing security forces, and communal life will disappear. What will replace it are deeper divisions with politics amounting to splitting up a shrinking economic pie into ever smaller ethnic, racial and religious slices.

It will be a kind of *Clockwork Orange* society in which the rich will pay for their security; the middle class will continue to flee as they confront violence; and the poor—the poor will be preyed upon at will or will join the army of violent predators. What will be lost for everyone will be freedom, civility and the chance to build a common future.

Conversion means winning over all segments of urban life to a new politics of change, empowerment and common effort. Conversion is as different from the politics of dependency as it is from the politics of greed. Its optimism relates to the belief that every person can realize his or her potential in an atmosphere of nurturing liberty. Its morality is grounded in the conviction that each of us has an obligation to another human being simply because that person is another human being.

There will not be "a charismatic leader" here but many "leaders of awareness" who champion integrity and humility over self-promotion and command performances. Answers won't come from an elite who has determined in advance what the new society will look like. Instead, the future will be shaped by the voices from inside the turmoil of urban America, as well as by those who claim to see a bigger picture.

Conversion requires listening to the disaffected as well as the powerful. Empowerment requires seizing the moment. The core of conversion begins with a recognition that all of us advance together or each of us is diminished; that American diversity is not our weakness but our strength; that we will never be able to lead the world by example until we've come to terms with each other and overcome the blight of racial division on our history.

The first concrete step is to bring an end to violence, intervene early in a child's life, reduce child abuse, establish some rules, remain unintimidated and involve the community in its own salvation. As a young man in dreadlocks said at one of my town meetings, "What we need is for people to care enough about themselves so that they won't hurt anybody else."

A Better World

Steven Vincent Benet once said about American diversity; "All of these you are; and each is partly you; and none of them is false; and none is wholly true." Another way of saying: Out of many, one. He was describing America. . . .

For those who came generations ago, there is a need to reaffirm principles—liberty, equality, democracy—principles that have always eluded complete fulfillment. The American city is where all these ideas and cultures have always clashed—sometimes violently. But all, even those brought here in chattel slavery and subsequently freed, are not African or Italian or Polish or Irish or Japanese. They're Americans.

What we lose when racial or ethnic self-consciousness dominates are tolerance, curiosity, civility—precisely the qualities we need to allow us to live side by side in mutual respect. The fundamental challenge is to understand the suffering of others as well as to share in their joy. To sacrifice that sensitivity on the altar of racial chauvinism is to lose our future. And we will lose it unless urgency informs our actions, passing the buck stops, scapegoating fails and excuses disappear.

The American city needs physical rejuvenation, economic opportunity and moral direction, but above all what it needs is the same thing every small town needs: the willingness to treat another person of any race with the respect you show for a brother or sister with the belief that together you'll build a better world than you would have ever done alone, a better world in which all Americans stand on common ground.

> *"Idle, ignorant, and often criminal, the proletariat can ruin a great city—and nation."*

Moral Failure Causes Urban Decay

Russell Kirk

Analyses of urban decay often blame individuals who commit crime, abuse drugs, or are unwilling to work. In the following viewpoint, Russell Kirk agrees that these individuals, or "proletarians," lack moral values and have no sense of personal responsibility or family unity and contribute nothing to their communities. Kirk is a writer and a college lecturer and is the president of Educational Reviewer, an educational foundation in New York City.

As you read, consider the following questions:

1. Why doesn't Kirk blame all poor people for urban decay?
2. In the author's opinion, why does welfare dependency persist throughout some family generations?
3. How can religious groups fortify communities, according to Kirk?

From Russell Kirk, "Prospects for the Proletariat," *St. Croix Review*, December 1991. Reprinted with permission.

From time to time, I am asked what I believe to be the greatest difficulty the American Republic confronts nowadays. I reply that our most puzzling and distressing social misfortune is the growth of a proletariat. Let us define our terms. The words proletariat and proletarian come down to us from Roman times. In the Roman signification of the term, a proletarian is a man who gives nothing to the commonwealth but his progeny. Such a being pays no taxes, subsists at public expense, fulfills no civic duties, performs no work worth mentioning, and knows not the meaning of piety. As a mass, the collective proletarians, the proletariat, are formidable; they demand entitlements—principally, in antique times, bread and circuses; in our day, much larger entitlements, which are granted to them lest they turn collectively violent. To the state, I repeat, the proletarian contributes only his offspring—who in their turn, ordinarily, become proletarians. Idle, ignorant, and often criminal, the proletariat can ruin a great city—and nation. . . .

Who the Proletarians Are

Now in America today, whom do we specify when we talk of a proletariat, a rootless and discontented class that is a burden upon the commonwealth? It is necessary first to specify groups that we do *not* have in mind.

The proletariat is not identical with "the poor." Although most proletarians are poor, a man may be rich and yet a proletarian if he is nothing better than a vexation to the commonwealth and has the mind of a proletarian. Also, there are many people of very modest income who nevertheless are people of commendable character and good citizens. Incidentally, I am given to quoting an aside by Robert Frost when he was conversing with liberal friends: "Don't talk about the poor all the time!" The poor we have always with us, as Jesus of Nazareth instructs us.

The proletarian is not identical with "the workingman"—indeed, it is characteristic of the proletarian that he does *not* work voluntarily. I was reared almost literally in the Pere Marquette railway yards outside Detroit, my father a locomotive engineman and fireman; we were not proletarians, nor were my schoolmates and their parents.

The proletarian is not identical with the "welfare recipient," even though the vast majority of proletarians are on the welfare rolls. For of course among the recipients of local, state, and federal relief and entitlements are many elderly, infirm, or otherwise distressed people who are not so unfortunate as to share the proletarian mentality and morality. . . .

The proletariat, in short, is a mass of people who have lost—if ever they possessed—community, hope of betterment, moral convictions, habits of work, sense of personal responsibility, intellectual curiosity, membership in a healthy family, property, active participation in public concerns, religious associations, and awareness of ends or objectives in human existence. Most proletarians live, as dogs do, from day to day, unreflective. The *lazzaroni* of Naples, I suppose, for centuries have existed in such a proletarian condition; but the *lazzaroni* of American cities and countryside, proliferating in recent years, are more aggressive than their Neapolitan counterparts.

The cores of many American cities now are dominated by the proletariat; or if not the core in some cities, then a grim and dangerous urban ring encircling the core. Some thirty years ago, dining with the economist Colin Clark at an Oxford inn, I remarked that I did not know what would become of America's cities. Professor Clark replied, "*I* know: They will cease to exist." He went on to suggest that suburbs beyond a city's political boundaries would survive, surrounding a devastated and demolished and depopulated accumulation of ruins, the former urban area looking much as if it had been showered with gel bombs, after the fashion employed against Dresden at the end of World War II. With dismaying speed just that has been coming to pass.

The Decay of Detroit

Permit me to turn to striking instances. I have known the city of Detroit ever since I was a small boy—that is, for more than half a century, during which the "arsenal of democracy" has been quite thoroughly proletarianized. When I was a college student and wandered the streets of Detroit every weekend, the city had a population of two million; now it has one million. The art institute, the public library, the Detroit historical museum, and Wayne State University survive, for the present, along with some tall stone churches, in the midst of an overwhelming decadence. On the campus of the University, telephone kiosks have been erected at short intervals. In these structures, the telephone is installed at ground level, so that persons wounded or violated conceivably may crawl to the kiosk and pull the phone off its hook; even if no words are spoken, a police patrol is supposed to investigate. Such is the intellectual life of Detroit.

Tempting although it might be to offer to you vignettes of existence in proletarian Detroit, I have not world enough and time. Some persons already may have read the book by Ze'ev Chafets, *Devil's Night and Other True Tales of Detroit*; or have seen my own article on Detroit's Devil's Night, published in *Newsday*; or have seen the television program that infuriated the foul mouthed demagogue who is mayor of Detroit; or have been somewhat startled by a piece in the *New Yorker* revealing the miserable and depraved proletarian condition in which that mayor deliberately keeps the rising generation virtual prisoners in a ghetto. In any event, I do not suppose that any person today is quite uninformed concerning the degradation of what once was a booming and hopeful city with some culture of its own.

What worked the ruin of Detroit, proletarianizing the place? The complex causes of this decay have been at work in most other American cities, too; but they were especially acute in Detroit. I venture to list some of the principal afflictions.

Impact of the Automobile

First, the automobile, though it brought a great deal of money into the city and much increased its population, nevertheless did mischief to what had been a rather pleasant and peaceful big town on a principal inland waterway. Ford and the other automobile manufacturers recruited labor wherever they could find it, especially from Central and Eastern Europe and from the Southern states, the masses of semi-skilled or unskilled men who came to the automobile factories were uprooted, cut off often from some traditional rural culture. With American thought, politics, and manners most of them never obtained much acquaintance. They became deculturalized, rather than acculturated, and demagogues found them easy prey. So as late as 1932, by the way, the most conservative "minority" or ethnic group in the city were the blacks of the Paradise Valley ward, stout Republicans who stood by Herbert Hoover. They were also very nearly the poorest bloc in Detroit.

Second, the triumphant automobile made it possible for the more affluent Detroiters to build houses in the suburbs, particularly in the Grosse Pointes, abandoning their mansions near the heart of the city. With the coming of the New Deal, this outflow of ability and wealth from the old city was much accelerated by the Home Owners Loan Corporation and later programs of low-interest loans, federally backed, available to people who were good credit risks; thus increasingly the old city was drained of merchants, manufacturers, professional people, bankers and skilled craftsmen—leaving a vacuum to be filled successively by ethnic and economic groups of decreasing means and talent for leadership. The shifting of Henry Ford from a little house on Bagley Avenue, near the city's heart, to a great rustic estate near Dearborn, is sufficient illustration of this. The same flitting occurred in most other American cities, of course—New York and San Francisco being the chief, if partial, exceptions.

Impact of the War

Third, military production in "the arsenal of democracy" during the Second World War attracted to Detroit great numbers of industrial workers, chiefly Appalachian whites ("hillbillies" to natives of Michigan) and Southern blacks. To the number of the latter were soon added more Southern blacks left technologically unemployed by the perfection of the mechanical cotton picker and other alterations of the economic patterns of Dixie. People whose ancestors had been settled for several generations in place and in customs south of the Mason-Dixon Line found themselves in Detroit, bewildered, often resentful, and shaken in their beliefs and habits.

Fourth, with the ending of war production these people were short of work and money—and often in social or moral confusion. Divorce, and desertion of wives and children, became common in Detroit and other cities; out of this arose the successive programs for Aid to Dependent Children, federally financed, and well intentioned. But out of this humanitarian scheme came the one-parent family, the welfare household on a huge scale, the street-corner gangs of bored and idle youths who looked up to the brother keeper, the numbers racketeer and presently the drug pusher, those ingenious, successful men. And presently the first generation of such dependent children fathered a second dependent generation; the second generation fathered a third—these true proletarians giving nothing to the commonwealth but their progeny—which progeny in turn would emulate their fathers and mothers.

No Chance to Lead a Good Life

Let's not kid ourselves: So many people who go into these gangs, deal drugs and commit acts of violence were never the most important person in the world to anyone. They were never connected to a better future. They were never given enough love or discipline, enough order or emotion to build a healthy life. We must do that within the communities.

Bill Clinton, *Los Angeles Times*, May 26, 1992.

Much of the old city grew shabby, and some of it dangerous, in consequence of the changes I suggested just now; yet still, in the forties, I walked mean streets unarmed, at all hours. By the fifties, I adopted the precaution of wearing a sheath knife when I walked those mean streets, Michigan Avenue included, nocturnally; later, I carried a pistol. By the sixties, it was well not to walk those streets except under necessity. . . .

Among causes of the forming of the classless society in Detroit—that is, a society consisting of a single class, the proletariat—has been the crumbling of the public school system.

Compulsory integration turned out to be worse schooling for both blacks and whites, not better; the abandonment of neighborhood schools alienated both parents and pupils; the tax basis for the school system dwindled. Schools became unpleasant and dangerous places where teachers' energies were spent mostly in maintaining some semblance of physical order. Public opinion polls showed that both white and black parents strongly objected to massive busing—but their mere opinion did them no good, decisions being in the hands of omniscient judges, those infallible educators.

The causes of Detroit's sickness indeed are complex: it is almost as if some evil genius had plotted intricately the undoing of a great metropolis. Woe unto the city! But let me name [another] major cause of Detroit's undoing, the latest of the terrible afflictions: the frightful curse of the narcotics traffic and of widespread narcotics addiction. Possibly the city of Washington is worse off in this malady than is Detroit—but I doubt that. (True, Washington has deprived Detroit of its former proud distinction as "Murder Capital of the United States.") Presumably it is unnecessary for me to describe to you the fatal consequences, personal and social, of the curse of narcotics. It is the proletarian who seeks hallucinatory drugs, because he retains no objective in life; and narcotics addiction will convert people of good prospects into empty proletarians.

Christian Churches Offer Hope

You may be asking yourselves at this point in my long tale of woe, what it is that still keeps Detroit half-alive, and functioning after a fashion. What resists proletarian despair? The Christian churches do. It is said that within the boundaries of Detroit stand some two thousand, five hundred churches, from cathedrals to scruffy store-front Bethels. Some of the black temples and tabernacles may be remarkably eccentric varieties of religious experience; but even the wildest of them offers some sort of hope and consolation beyond the decayed City of This Earth; even the smallest of these churches or quasi-churches is a surviving anchor of community. Fervent Christian profession still breathes into wrecked Detroit some life of the spirit.

The influence of the black preacher is undiminished. In 1973, at the climax of a bitter political contest over abortion, I gave the chief address to Michigan's principal pro-life organization, meeting in a big hall on the riverfront. Behind me on the platform, as moral and physical reinforcement, sat three or four ebony monoliths, huge black Baptist preachers. A white Protestant clergyman was there too, and one man—William Ryan, then Speaker of the Michigan House of Representatives. (No Catholic priests ventured to take a visible stand on the platform.) The presence of the ebony ministers signified that we pro-life partisans had won the day in Detroit. For when the statewide initiative for abortion-on-demand appeared on the ballot in November, the pro-choice people were defeated nearly two to one. Every black ward in Detroit voted against abortion by large majorities; in one ward, the ratio of ballots was sixteen to one against abortion. The proletarian, Marxist model has cast off the "fetters" of religion. But clearly there remains in Detroit one strong influence that impedes total proletarianization.

I have offered you the spectacle of Detroit because probably Detroit illustrates better than any other city the concurrent and converging causes of the reduction of a city's population to a miserable proletarian state. Some people tell me that Newark is worse stricken than Detroit; Washington might be worse off, were it not for the restraining power and the resources of the federal government. Possibly I have succeeded in persuading you that . . . the cities of America have become what Thomas Jefferson called them about the end of the eighteenth century, the social equivalents of sores upon the human body.

A Concern of Conservatives

The tendency of the American people toward a proletarian condition—often a drift more subtle than the processes I have mentioned—ought to be the urgent concern of all genuine conservatives. The devising of any remedies or palliatives will require high power of imagination. . . .

No effort at all is required to become a proletarian: one needs merely to submit to the dehumanizing and deculturizing currents of the hour, and worship the idols of the crowd. Much effort is required to conserve the legacy of order, freedom, and justice, of learning and art and imagination, that ought to be ours. Some malign spirits, in the name of equality, would have us all proletarians together: the doctrine of equal misery. The conservatives' impulse, *au contraire*, is to rescue as many men and women as possible from the submerged lot in life, without object and without cheer, which is the proletarian condition.

Evaluating Sources of Information

When historians study and interpret past events, they use two kinds of sources: primary and secondary. Primary sources are eyewitness accounts. For example, a researcher's study analyzing the movement of Americans from cities to suburbs would be a primary source. A magazine article summarizing the study's results would be a secondary source. Primary and secondary sources may be decades or even hundreds of years old, and often historians find that the sources offer conflicting and contradictory information. To fully evaluate documents and assess their accuracy, historians analyze the credibility of the documents' authors and, in the case of secondary sources, analyze the credibility of the information the authors used.

Historians are not the only people who encounter conflicting information, however. Anyone who reads a daily newspaper, watches television, or just talks to different people will encounter many different views. Writers and speakers use sources of information to support their own statements. Thus, critical thinkers, just like historians, must question the writer's or speaker's sources of information as well as the writer or speaker.

While there are many criteria that can be applied to assess the accuracy of a primary or secondary source, for this activity you will be asked to apply three. For each source listed on the following page, ask yourself the following questions: First, did the person actually see or participate in the event he or she is reporting? This will help you determine the credibility of the information—an eyewitness to an event is an extremely valuable source. Second, does the person have a vested interest in the report? Assessing the person's social status, professional affiliations, nationality, and religious or political beliefs will be helpful in considering this question. By evaluating this you will be able to determine how objective the person's report may be. Third, how qualified is the author to be making the statements he or she is making? Consider what the person's profession is and how he or she might know about the event. Someone who has spent years being involved with or studying the issue may be able to offer more information than someone who simply is offering an uneducated opinion; for example, a politician or layperson.

Keeping the above criteria in mind, imagine you are writing a paper on how important America's cities are to society. You decide to cite an equal number of primary and secondary sources. Listed below are several sources that may be useful for your research. *Place a P next to those descriptions you believe are primary sources. Place an S next to those descriptions you believe are secondary sources.* Next, based on the above criteria, *rank the primary sources, assigning the number (1) to what appears to be the most valuable, (2) to the source likely to be the second-most valuable, and so on, until all the primary sources are ranked. Then rank the secondary sources, again using the above criteria.*

P or S		*Rank in Importance*

_____ 1. A report by the U.S. Conference of Mayors _____ criticizing the lack of federal aid to cities.

_____ 2. A *New York Times* article about the flight of _____ companies and jobs from northeastern cities to their suburbs.

_____ 3. A suburbanite who describes the advantages _____ suburbs have over cities.

_____ 4. A *Washington Post* book review of Joel _____ Garreau's *Edge City: Life on the New Frontier*.

_____ 5. William Whyte's book *City*, which describes _____ the economic and social advantages of cities.

_____ 6. A University of Pennsylvania study describ- _____ ing the economic interdependence of Philadelphia and its suburbs.

_____ 7. A *U.S. News & World Report* article summa- _____ rizing the negative attitudes that corporations have toward cities.

_____ 8. A *Los Angeles Times* article describing how _____ that city appeals to a wide spectrum of immigrant groups.

_____ 9. A television interview with a university _____ president who boasts of the many college opportunities found in cities.

_____ 10. Articles in *National Review* describing Ronald _____ Reagan's policy to slash the amount of direct aid to cities.

Periodical Bibliography

The following articles have been selected to supplement the diverse views presented in this chapter.

Paul R. Bardack	"New Hope for Urban America," *USA Today*, July 1992.
Janice Castro	"Come on Down! Fast!" *Time*, May 27, 1991.
James Cook	"Exodus," *Forbes*, September 16, 1991.
Osborn Elliott	"March on Washington," *Newsweek*, April 8, 1991.
Raymond L. Flynn	"Dear Legislator: Don't Sweep Our Cities Under the Rug," *Governing*, January 1992. Available from Congressional Quarterly Inc., 2300 N St. NW, Suite 760, Washington, DC 20037.
Richard Lacayo	"This Land Is Your Land . . . This Land Is My Land," *Time*, May 18, 1992.
David Moburg	"Facing America's Urban Nightmare," *In These Times*, January 29-February 4, 1992.
Tom Morganthau	"Are Cities Obsolete?" *Newsweek*, September 9, 1991.
Will Nixon	"A Municipal Meltdown in Bridgeport, Connecticut," *In These Times*, January 22-28, 1992.
David Rusk	"America's Urban Apartheid," *The New York Times*, May 21, 1992.
Alvin P. Sanoff and Joel Garreau	"The Cities of the Future," *U.S. News & World Report*, September 23, 1991.
Elliott D. Sclar	"Back to the City," *Technology Review*, August/September 1992.
R. Emmett Tyrrell Jr.	"Unheavenly Cities," *The American Spectator*, July 1992.
Robert Wood	"Cities in Trouble," *Domestic Affairs*, Summer 1991. Available from 1545 New York Ave. NE, Washington, DC 20002.
The World & I	"Solving America's Urban Crisis," special issue, June 1991.

How Can Urban Homelessness Be Reduced?

Chapter Preface

Homelessness is a serious problem in America's largest cities. New York and Philadelphia, for example, estimated their homeless populations at fifty-five thousand, and thirty-five thousand, respectively in 1991. Perhaps even more tragically, many of the homeless seem to be families with children. In Norfolk, Virginia, 81 percent of the homeless are thought to be families with children, according to the U.S. Conference of Mayors.

Housing homeless people is expensive. In New York City, housing a family of four or more in a hotel can cost from $2,000 to $5,000 monthly, according to author Jonathan Kozol, with families living there an average of two years. While federal and state governments provide funding to reduce such costs, the *Economist* weekly magazine states that "The cities themselves have to bear most of the burden of caring for the homeless on their streets—and many cities are going bust."

Cities and relief organizations face a difficult task in reducing homelessness, not only because of high costs and a lack of funding, but because the root causes of the problem are so complex: unemployment, housing shortages, mental illness, and chemical dependency, among others. The authors in the following chapter examine these causes in proposing remedies to the homeless problem.

"I did not want to give up my membership in the human race, which is what you do if you sleep in one of these [shelters]."

Improving Homeless Shelters Would Help the Homeless

Joe Homeless

Joe Homeless is a pseudonym used by the author of *My Life on the Street*, a book describing the author's more than twelve years of homeless life in New York City. In the following viewpoint, excerpted from the book, the author describes his awful experiences in homeless shelters, including unsanitary living conditions and abuse and violence against the homeless. He argues that these deplorable conditions convinced him to never again seek shelter in such places. The author formerly owned a small mechanical contracting business and remains homeless.

As you read, consider the following questions:

1. What are some of the dangers homeless people face in shelters, according to the author?
2. In the author's opinion, why does a homeless person lose his or her dignity in a homeless shelter?
3. If you were homeless, would you seek food or sleep in a homeless shelter? Why or why not?

I still had nowhere to go. I headed down to the Bowery. Once there, I decided to try the Men's Shelter on East Third Street in Manhattan. . . .

I finally made it to the front of the City Shelter, and walked through a doorway with a lot of bums on each side. I found myself in a big room that was very clean and neat. In front of me were a bunch of glass partitions with signs over them labeled: Welfare, Clothing, etc. I did not know which window I should go to; so I tried the first one, and asked the middle-aged Hispanic man sitting behind it, "How do I get some food and a place to sleep?"

He asked, "You have any identification?"

I answered, "Yes," and showed it to him.

He scanned it for a minute, and gave me two cards. Then he spoke rapidly, with a strong accent. "One card is a meal ticket. Take it to the cafeteria in the basement and get breakfast, lunch, or dinner. It can be used ten times. We also give out clothes a few times a week. The other card is for shelter. You have to take it down the block to the private hotel that is rented by the City in the evening to get a bed. Make sure you get there early to get a bed, because these cards are given to everybody who gets a meal ticket and they are not dated or numbered. We are never sure of how many men will come for shelter on any one night."

"What kind of room will I get?" I asked hesitantly.

Flashing me an annoyed look he answered, "You do not get a room, you get a bed in a dormitory if you are early. If you are late, you are out of luck." Then he added, "Now go sit outside and wait 'til we open the cafeteria for lunch."

I said, "How will I know when it is time to come inside for lunch? I have no watch."

He gave a slight sigh, "When it's lunch time you'll know it, don't worry."

I nodded slowly, gratefully, "Okay, thank you." Then I went outside and sat down on the sidewalk, just like all the other bums. . . .

Abuse Inflicted on the Homeless

I . . . started talking to the man I was sitting next to. He had a patch covering one of his eyes. I asked him, "What's the hotel like?"

"Well," he told me, "the bums call the guard who works there 'Stromboli.'" (That was the evil puppeteer who kidnapped Pinnochio in the fairy tale.) "He continually curses them out. On cold days he likes to throw bums into the shower with all their clothes on, then push them into the street." He pointed to a man with one arm sitting on a car and said, "His name is Marty. Stromboli did that."

I said, "Did what?"

He said, "He made that guy lose his arm."

I asked, "How?"

He answered, "I just told you what Stromboli likes to do. One day he put Marty in the shower with all his clothes on, then threw him in the street, soaking wet. That day it was close to zero. At night, Marty tried to sleep in a doorway and the next thing he knew, a doctor was telling him he had to cut off his arm. I even heard Stromboli joke to one of his friends that he did Marty a favor because afterwards Marty got cleaned up and lived in a hotel for about a year, until Welfare closed his case and Marty had to come back down here."

I shook my head, "How come Stromboli did not get fired?"

The bum flashed me a crooked smile. "You've got a lot to learn.". . .

As Dangerous as the Streets

It seems distressingly perverse that the very places where homeless people seek asylum, the shelters, are often, albeit by no means universally, the sites of greater risk than are the streets. . . .

Theft in shelters is rife: retention of personal belongings is accomplished by guile or domination, as even the best-staffed facilities can provide little real security. Shelter clients may fear their fellows—some recently released from jail, prison, or mental hospital—who can be violent or exploitative; 34 percent of homeless people surveyed in Manhattan shelters and streets said they were afraid of being attacked in a shelter—a proportion similar to that of those who voiced fears of being attacked on the street.

Pamela J. Fischer, *Homelessness: A Prevention-Oriented Approach*, 1992.

Despair filled me. Not long ago I had been a person who had been able to give to others. Now I was one of those others. I shook off my dark thoughts. If I were to survive I had to move forward, forget about the past.

At least I had the other ticket, good for a hotel at which to sleep. I went down the block to look at it. It was a small gray building covered with graffiti, right near a gas station. The smell of gas fumes permeated the air. I shuddered. Some of the burned-out buildings at which I had stayed in the Bronx looked better.

Then I walked back to the shelter and looked again at the group of men waiting with me. The guy with the patch over his eye stood with some others, talking and staring at me hard. The men, who were bunched in a group, seemed to be part of a clique. Their heads were bent together as if they were conspirators planning something.

As they were talking, a bum with black, caked-together hair passed them carrying a full box of donuts he was just opening up. A muscular bum in the group strode over to him and demanded, "Give me a donut."

The man with the donuts said, "No."

The muscular guy grabbed the other bum's hand, bent it back, and pushed him to the ground. A guard stood outside the doorway of the shelter watching, but did nothing to stop the intimidation.

After observing that, I started to fear for my life, sleeping in a large dormitory with all these guys. They were hungry, broke, and desperate. If I slept soundly, anything could happen.

I decided to try a private shelter that some of the churches I'd been to had recommended. It wasn't that far away, so I walked there. The shelter was housed in a huge, red brick building that looked neat and had no graffiti.

Unfortunately, the homeless clustered about its entrance. One of them, a slight blond man, was sitting down on the sidewalk with his back resting on the building. I asked him, "Is this the way to the shelter?"

He answered, "Yes, if you want any more information, go inside and ask."

A paunchy, balding man was sitting at a table blocking the entrance to the shelter. "How do I get food and a place to sleep?" I asked.

"We're going to open the doors in a little while. Come in then and you can have food and possibly get a bed for the night."

I nodded, "All right."

The frustration of it all was beginning to get to me. . . .

Inside the Shelter

I looked at the beds and thought, at least I'll get off my feet for a little while. Then they informed us, we were all going to have to take a shower. I sighed and murmured, "Good, I could use one." Then I looked at the shower. It looked like the same kind of set-up they use at the zoo to bathe animals. There were brown colored tile stalls, just like the zoo has, and you were bathed in a group just like animals. "If I had any pride left," I thought, "this would really take it away."

The person doing the bathing was a tiny guy with a hump on his back. He reminded me of the little hunchback man, Fritz, who used to go running around pulling all the electrical switches in the old Frankenstein movies. It was his job to bring the Frankenstein monster to life. This shriveled guy looked just like him. And he had the same kind of mentality.

66

Sitting around waiting to go in the shower, I looked at some of the men strip down before they went into the shower. The ones with artificial limbs took them off and put them on a bench close to the shower stall entrance where they could watch them. Even artificial limbs can be hocked. I could see a large assortment of bugs coming out of some of the limbs. The bouncers saw them also. They began to search the limbs, plus everybody's clothes and possessions, for drugs and weapons. . . .

A Dangerous Environment

Next, I started talking to a short, stocky man next to me. "I'm here all the time," he observed, running his hand over his balding head.

"How safe is this place?" I asked.

He answered with another question, "Well, how sound do you sleep?"

I said, "I don't know."

He replied, "Well, if you sleep sound, it ain't that safe."

I said, "Well, don't they have guards at night?"

He said, "One guy sits in a chair, then he falls asleep. You got to protect yourself."

Shelter Population Grows More Violent

The proportion of men barred temporarily or permanently from the largest mission in Baltimore for causing problems, including violent behavior, arson, and stealing, increased from 5 percent in 1981, to 14 percent in 1986. As the shelter-using population has become younger and more violent, physical danger has escalated to the point where the most vulnerable homeless people—such as the elderly—have been "crowded out" of the shelters.

However, the threat not only emanates from shelter clients but may occasionally issue from staff as well, although this appears to be the exception. Both intimidation and physical abuse, including the murder of clients, have been attributed to the staff of some of the immense public shelters in New York City.

Pamela J. Fischer, *Homelessness: A Prevention-Oriented Approach*, 1992.

As we were talking, a fight broke out between two bums who had just come out of the shower. They were standing in line to get paper night gowns. As we watched, one of the guys brandished a single-edge razor blade which he had hidden in the bottom of a crush-proof box of cigarettes. I gasped as he cut off the ear of the man he was fighting with. The guy who got cut shook his head like a wet dog, trying to get the blood out of the ear he no longer had.

As he shook, his blood splattered all over the place. Reaching his left hand up, he realized he no longer had his ear attached to his head. "Fuck you," he yelled and knelt down frantically searching for it on the floor. Grasping the ear, he tried to put it back on his head.

The man who did the cutting began to run away. He was caught by the bouncers and began to fight them. They hit him over and over in the head with their night sticks. Finally, he fell to the floor unconscious.

The bouncers went over to the man who was cut. One handed him a towel to stop the blood. Then they helped him over to a bench. I heard them ask him for his ear, so they could put it on ice and give it to the doctor in the ambulance when it came. The bum slowly handed it to them. Then he pressed the towel to the side of his head. I continued looking at him as his face turned white and he passed out. A few minutes later, an ambulance and the cops came. Both men were taken away.

Salvaging Self-Respect

After they left, I decided to take a closer look at the beds. The sheets were dirty and had lice on them. Depressed I looked at some of the other bums. I could see myself mirrored in them. That's when the realization of where I was really sank in. I wanted to run away, to leave, because I did not want to be like the bums I saw there. I did not want to give up my membership in the human race, which is what you do if you sleep in one of these places. You become little more than an animal.

I could say it was for my safety's sake that I decided to go back on the street, but it was really more my ego and my self-respect. Until I could get my life back together, it would be the street and brutal, brutal cold weather. Would I be able to survive? I didn't know.

I would have to call on all the strength I had left to get through this winter without staying in a shelter. I felt that if I succeeded, I wouldn't be a bum or a derelict.

"A number of cities have adopted or are considering laws to curtail panhandling and put limits on where the homeless can sleep or congregate."

Eliminating Vagrancy Would Help The Homeless

Donald Kimelman

Many Americans object to homeless people who ask passersby for money or who sleep in public places. In the following viewpoint, Donald Kimelman argues that these homeless people are nuisances who must be removed from the streets because they harm commerce by driving away shoppers, tourists, and others from cities' downtown areas. Kimelman asserts that laws must be adopted to prohibit panhandling and loitering in these areas and to encourage the homeless to seek shelter and help for their problems. Kimelman is deputy editor of the editorial page for the *Philadelphia Inquirer* daily newspaper.

As you read, consider the following questions:

1. If a homeless person asked you for money, would you give it to him or her? Why or why not?
2. According to Kimelman, why do some people oppose laws prohibiting the homeless from sleeping in public?
3. In the author's opinion, how can cities reduce the size of their homeless shelter population?

From Donald Kimelman, "What Are the Rights of the Homeless in Downtown Philadelphia?" Reprinted from the Winter 1991/1992 issue of *The Responsive Community*, 2020 Pennsylvania Ave. NW, Suite 282, Washington, DC 20006.

We tried to find a way to ease into this subject, but there's no delicate way to put it: All of Philadelphia's compassionate efforts to shelter the homeless who live on the streets of Center City have failed to do the job. In many respects the situation is getting worse. So for the sake of everyone—including those sleeping in the city streets—it is time to take a harder line.

So began an editorial in my newspaper, the *Philadelphia Inquirer*, that took up the entire column on a July Sunday in 1989. Arguing that "everyone should be able to use [the city's] public spaces, but that no one should be permitted to abuse them," the editorial called for City Hall to forbid people from "camping out" on sidewalks or in the city's parks and squares. In place of civic passivity, we argued, the city ought to offer assistance to those willing to improve their circumstances (most of the street people were drug addicts or alcoholics) and tell the rest to either abide by accepted rules of behavior or move on. We also strongly advised the public to stop giving to panhandlers, as it just perpetuates the problem.

Vagrants' Rights Must Be Curtailed

While *The Responsive Community* and the intellectual movement that spawned it were not in existence at the time, the editorial was essentially making a "communitarian" argument, saying that broader community interests required that the rights of vagrants be curtailed. "The concern," we argued, "is that the continued presence of hundreds of homeless people in Center City—sprawled on steam grates or against the sides of buildings, befouling public squares and parks—will repel ordinary citizens whose presence downtown is often optional." And if shoppers, tourists, residents, and even office workers retreat from Philadelphia's commercial core, we concluded, "the city is going to be in deep trouble."

Needless to say, our hard-line stance did not win universal praise. On radio talk shows and in letters to the editor and op-ed responses, we were accused of being cowardly, mean-spirited, self-deceptive, and, of course, of "blaming the victim." One letter writer charged, "You have in effect given the public license to turn its back on the homeless."

But there was plenty of support out there as well, and we kept pounding away in the editorial column. In the end, the mayor took us up on our suggestion that he bring business leaders and homeless advocates together and try to work out some mutually acceptable approaches.

Two years passed, and the homeless, like the poor, are still with us. Our editorials did more to change public attitudes than the reality on the streets, though a once-worsening situation seems to have gotten a little better. The mayor's task force, on which I sat as a sort of *ex officio* member, created bonds between business leaders and homeless advocates that remain important today. But it produced disappointingly few tangible results.

One of the drawbacks of the communitarian approach, I was to learn, is that the community itself can't be counted on to act in its own long-term interests. It wants the homeless off its streets and doorsteps, but balks at providing the meaningful help that should be a part of any strategy.

A Plan to Discourage Panhandling

As an outgrowth of the task force's work, a group of downtown shop owners, with the blessings of leading homeless advocates, developed a plan to provide tokens, rather than cash, to panhandlers. The tokens, to be sold in downtown stores, would be redeemable at a nearby "dining center" ("Please," I was implored, "don't call it a soup kitchen"), where outreach workers would be on hand for counseling. Once the new center was opened, the shop owners would launch a heavy public relations campaign to discourage people from giving money to panhandlers.

It's a great idea. By organizing such a service, the merchants can stake out the moral high ground as they work to discourage panhandling. And if they succeed, they will destroy much of the incentive for street people to congregate downtown. But the project has stalled. It turns out that no landlord in the downtown area—and there are some pretty seedy blocks—has been willing to provide space for a facility that would attract that kind of clientele.

Similarly, the city's best-known angel of mercy, Sister Mary Scullion, formed an alliance with the local Board of Realtors to develop supervised rooming houses (known in the trade as SROs) for single men who can take care of themselves but who can't quite handle the independence, or cost, of an apartment. There's federal money for such projects, though the funds are hard to come by. . . .

Perhaps the editorial campaign's narrow focus was unrealistic. A good case can be made that we'll never get the homeless off our streets until we make major inroads against inner-city poverty. The vast majority of the people sleeping on Philadelphia's streets every night (as opposed to those sleeping in shelters) are young black men who are addicted to drugs or alcohol or both. These are the folks who are tough to rehabilitate, because in many cases they've never been "habilitated" in the first place. While the city, with state help, has developed a number of "clean and sober" shelters that are really turning some of these young men's lives around, there seems an endless supply of refugees from ghetto streets who are ready to fill the vacancies in doorways and on steam grates in Center City.

But that sort of fatalism leads only to despair. Even if this nation finally develops the will and the consensus to act, inner-city poverty will still be with us for a long, long time. Does that mean that the homeless are destined to become a permanent part of the landscape, damaging both the psyche and the economy of cities like Philadelphia that are struggling to remain viable? It can't be allowed to happen.

Plans to Oust the Homeless

Atlanta, the host-designate for the 1996 Olympics, considers itself the Mecca of the New South. But how magnetic can a city be, business people ask, with an estimated 10,000 homeless people scattered around town? Mayor Maynard Jackson proposed a "public nuisance" law [in June 1991] to give police broad powers to arrest beggars and to sweep the homeless from vacant buildings and parking lots. Jackson believes panhandlers alienate visitors, and police say that drug dealers take over buildings occupied by the homeless. Homeless advocates plan to fight back, but they know public sympathy is fading. "To see poor, raggedy homeless people," says Constance Curry, Atlanta's former director of human services, "irritates people now."

James N. Baker, *Newsweek*, June 24, 1991.

A number of cities have adopted or are considering laws to curtail panhandling and put limits on where the homeless can sleep or congregate. In Atlanta, as image conscious a city as you will find, Mayor Maynard H. Jackson is pushing such a proposal—and taking flak for trying to "sanitize" downtown in advance of the Olympics. Such measures, if they're upheld by the courts, could have some impact, but they smack of desperation and temporizing.

In Philadelphia, in response to our editorials, Mayor Wilson Goode formed a legal review committee to see what, if anything, could be done to impose legal limits on the behavior of the homeless. Not surprisingly, the committee split down the middle between the civil libertarians, who argued that any laws forbidding people from sleeping on the streets unconstitutionally discriminated against a particular social group, and communitarians, who argued that such a law could be constitutional if it provided options for the homeless.

Efforts to End Loitering

Two associates with a Center City law firm, who had been placed on the committee at the behest of a civic-minded business group called the Central Philadelphia Development Corporation, have actually drafted an ordinance that would make it illegal to "sleep, lie, or sit" on city sidewalks or on public property not intended for such use. For moral as well as legal reasons, police (who would often be accompanied on these missions by professional outreach workers) would not be permitted to charge anyone under the ordinance until they had first inquired whether the person was homeless and, if so, made an offer of assistance.

Recognizing the very different needs of drug addicts, the mentally ill, and the just plain destitute, the proposed law simply requires the city to offer "appropriate shelter" to those who need it. Anyone not interested in shelter may avoid arrest by getting up and moving. Those who refuse to budge, however, will be booked and released, getting them off the streets for a few hours and perhaps increasing their willingness to accept assistance the next time.

Such a law would draw no distinction between people who are aggressive and threatening and those—a majority, I believe—who are passive and sad. Aggressive behavior can be, and is, dealt with through existing laws. But none of these folks should be sprawled on downtown streets.

In an editorial in support of the ordinance, we wrote, "Such a law would thus present society with a choice: You can get people off the streets, but only if you're willing to provide for those who have no place to go." As daunting as that sounds, the editorial pointed out that city police do in fact go out on very cold nights and bring everyone in to shelters. To shift from the makeshift arrangements of mid-January to a more desirable, year-round mix of shelters, "transitional" housing, SROs, and the like would be more costly (we put the price tag at at least $4 million a year), but certainly not beyond this society's means.

One point we made frequently in our editorials is that while the homeless often seemed ubiquitous, there were only 500 to 600 people on downtown streets on any given night. (While people do live on the streets elsewhere in the city, by far the largest concentration is downtown.) Considering that 53,000 people live in Center City Philadelphia, and 285,000 people work there, that's not an unmanageable number.

Unlimited Shelter Is a Fool's Game

An ordinance like the one described above should not be confused with the creation of an indefinite entitlement to shelter to all who request it. That's how it works in New York City, to virtually everyone's dismay. You end up with the worst of both worlds: an expensive, unsafe shelter system, as well as a large street population that no one can touch. Philadelphia started

73

down that road early in the homeless crisis and realized that it's a fool's game. People flooded into shelters and stayed there, most of them continuing the kinds of self-destructive behaviors that had brought them so low to begin with.

Homeless Population in American Cities, 1991

City	Total	Mentally ill	Drug abusers
Alexandria, Va.	220	44	NA
Boston	3,613	2,602	1,301
Charleston, S.C.	600	160	80
Chicago	6,764	1,691	1,352
Cleveland	10,000	2,852	1,400
Kansas City, Mo.	13,000	1,950	1,260
Los Angeles	31,000	10,300	NA
Louisville	11,442	2,276	5,254
Nashville	942	424	289
New Orleans	10,500	3,205	1,663
New York City	55,000	18,150	4,538
Philadelphia	35,000	11,500	2,645
Phoenix	6,300	1,670	410
St. Paul, Minn.	1,023	165	110
Salt Lake City	2,000	500	250
San Diego	7,000	2,310	1,155
San Francisco	3,000+	2,000	1,000+
Santa Monica, Calif.	4,000	1,325	NA
Seattle	1,350+	700	650
Trenton, N.J.	600	150	75
Washington, D.C.	7,500	2,218	900

Note: Some of the figures are an average of a range provided by the cities.

Source: U.S. Conference of Mayors, 1991.

Over the past few years, Philadelphia has halved the size of its shelter system by imposing rules of behavior on the residents. No drugs or alcohol is one. Another requires residents to enroll in some kind of substance-abuse treatment or educational or job-training program. In short, with the exception of the mentally ill, no one can stay for any length of time in a shelter without working in some way toward self-sufficiency. While there are plenty of complaints about how the system works, the basic philosophy is sound. And for the most part, the hundreds of people bounced from shelters have melted back into the neighborhoods, rather than congregating on downtown streets.

Still, many of the street people in Center City are officially classified as "noncompliants." They've been in and out of the shelter system and various treatment programs, and, because they continue to smoke crack or drink heavily, they are no longer welcome. So the question arises: What does society owe them? The answer: Not much.

The prevailing thinking regarding addiction is that the addict has to hit bottom before he is willing to change. To give money to a panhandling addict is to postpone that moment at his—and society's—expense. But how would unrepentant addicts be handled under the law described above? What would be "appropriate shelter" for them? The best we could come up with was that addicts who did not play by the rules of the city's regimented, therapeutic "clean and sober" shelters or some comparable treatment program would be offered the absolute minimum: "big rooms with mattresses on the floor. They'd be heated, they'd have plumbing—and that's about it."

The alternative for the addicts and boozers would be to retreat, like the hobos of old, to godforsaken parts of the city where the neighbors didn't complain and the police looked the other way. Cruel as that sounds, it might inspire some of them to make the commitment to fight their addictions and change their lives. (In our writing, we always drew a distinction between substance abusers and people with serious mental illnesses. The mentally ill, who make up about one-fifth of the street population, require a different range of services and clearly wouldn't benefit from a disapproving refusal of assistance. But they, too, shouldn't be allowed to live on the streets.)

Suffice it to say that our editorializing in favor of such a law in the spring of 1990 did not launch a popular movement. It didn't even launch a debate. Philadelphia had become mired in fiscal chaos, and the attention of its political leaders was, and is, focused on avoiding insolvency. In such a climate, the homeless issue only comes up in terms of what existing programs can be cut. New commitments are out of the question.

Businesses Take the Initiative

Still, we're not despairing. The initiative has shifted from City Hall to the downtown business community, which, thanks to the legacy of the mayor's task force, has good relations with homeless advocates. Working together, they've already begun to talk about a renewed push to get people off the streets. . . . Mayor Edward Rendell recognizes that the success of the city's $500 million convention center, which is due to open in 1993, could hinge on whether downtown streets seem inviting or menacing.

Sister Scullion says that the advocates have come around on the need to vigorously discourage giving money to panhandlers and to better maintain public order through the enforcement of existing laws regarding public drunkenness and the like. "For the most part," she says, "we're just helping people to destroy themselves." Meanwhile, the business community recognizes that a "continuum of services" outreach efforts, shelters, halfway houses, treatment programs, SROs—is required, not just to get people off the streets but to keep them off. There's talk of creating a not-for-profit development corporation, which would be run by real estate hotshots rather than nonentrepreneurial do-gooders, that would take better advantage of the federal money that has recently become available for specialized housing for the homeless.

At this point, Scullion's attitude toward the grand trade-off implied in a law prohibiting sleeping in the streets is that the required services aren't in place, so why get civil libertarians all lathered up about a prospect that isn't imminent? Confrontation would only undercut the harmony that now exists on once-touchy matters such as the need to discourage panhandling.

She's probably right. The advocates and the business types both need to do more to win each other's trust and to make genuine inroads against the problem. Scullion is convinced that if the services are there, and income from panhandling plummets, 80 percent of the street people will either come inside voluntarily or disappear. Her assessment may be too optimistic, but it makes sense to give persuasion its best shot before turning to legal remedies. If after a few years of progress the city can argue that it is doing right by those who want help, there may be a political consensus to pass a just law that forbids people from sleeping in the streets.

"To be homeless . . . is to be alone, alienated from the lives of others, and thereby alienated from the dynamics of community life."

Strengthening the Community Would Help the Homeless

Gerald Campbell

Many people attribute homelessness to problems such as unemployment and substance abuse. In the following viewpoint, Gerald Campbell argues that America must look beyond these factors and address the more fundamental cause of homelessness: the alienation of many people from other community members and community life. Campbell maintains that individualism and a breakdown in interpersonal relationships are responsible for the decline of community and the dissatisfaction and loneliness many homeless people suffer. Campbell believes that many others who are not homeless are similarly alienated and that society must prevent further homelessness by rebuilding the community bonds that once united people. Campbell is president of Impact Group, a Washington, D.C.-area organization dedicated to improving community relations.

As you read, consider the following questions:

1. According to Campbell, why has the public become increasingly dissatisfied with the homeless?
2. Why does Campbell dismiss substance abuse as a principal cause of homelessness?

Gerald Campbell, "The Critical Moral Dimension." This article appeared in the December 1991 issue of and is reprinted with permission from *The World & I*, a publication of The Washington Times Corporation, © 1991.

There are few in America who have not had occasion to witness within their own communities some aspect of the plight of the homeless. Men and women going to and from work, children on their way to school, consumers at shopping centers, individuals going to health clubs, movies, or attending places of worship—all have been increasingly unable to disavow the presence of the tens of thousands of homeless persons standing in food lines, scattered about public parks, sleeping on public benches, or panhandling on public sidewalks.

To be sure, there have always existed those who—for whatever reason—have lived outside the system. In recent years, however, the number of homeless persons has grown into a major spectacle striking deep into the national consciousness. A survey of 30 cities by the U.S. Conference of Mayors reports that over 90 percent of them had to contend with a 22 percent average yearly increase in the demand for emergency shelter [for] six consecutive years. During the same period, 66 percent of these cities were able to satisfy only 80 percent of the demand for emergency shelter, and 97 percent of them anticipated that this need would continue to grow. Only Washington, D.C.—which has increased its support of prevention services and the rehabilitation of public housing—expected that the number of homeless persons seeking emergency shelter would decline, although this remains to be seen.

Generosity Toward the Homeless

In general, Americans have been generous in their support for public and private efforts to alleviate the problems of the homeless. Across the nation, spokesmen have emerged. Their personal inspiration and leadership have mobilized the collective action of tens of thousands of concerned citizens—and a vast array of charitable organizations—into a nationwide struggle to secure social justice for the homeless. Government support at the federal, state, and local levels has also been forthcoming, although some might argue that it has been insufficient.

Despite this considerable effort, the numbers of homeless persons continue to grow at an alarming and increasingly uncomfortable rate. Unemployment among them remains high, and even when they are employed, their wages are generally inadequate to meet the high cost of food and shelter. Alcohol and drug rehabilitation facilities remain in short supply, and those who receive treatment suffer from a recidivism rate as high as 90 percent during the first year. New mental-health facilities are in great demand, and the quality of existing services is generally inadequate. Sadly enough, no solution to the problem of the homeless seems to be on the horizon, leaving growing numbers unable to escape the street.

Critics contend that much more could have been done these past 10 years—particularly by the federal government—to alleviate this problem. No one who has taken the time to become acquainted with a homeless person can be unsympathetic to this argument. Yet this criticism reflects only part of the story. For it cannot be denied that considerable resources—both human and material—have been employed to lessen the burden of the homeless and to reintroduce them into mainstream society.

Impatience with the Homeless

Faced with this seemingly intractable dilemma, it is not surprising that even well-intentioned individuals have some impatience with the homeless. Of the 30 cities surveyed by the U.S. Conference of Mayors, 57 percent reported a "negative change in public attitudes toward homeless persons." The perception is growing that while individuals and social institutions have done their part to assist the homeless, the homeless have done little to help themselves. As one city reported in the mayors' survey, "there is an increasing tendency to blame the homeless for being homeless." Thus, the compassion and sympathy that were so prevalent during the 1988 presidential election—and that were symbolized in the phrase "a thousand points of light"—are slowly but steadily eroding and are being replaced with resentment and anger. Frustrated, otherwise responsible citizens are now turning to other concerns, hoping all the while that the problem of the homeless will just go away.

Fractured Relationships

The problems of the homeless are almost always a tangle of personal pathologies combined with fractured relationships. In one of the best empirical studies of the homeless it was discovered that about eight of ten had experienced some form of institutionalization for either drugs, mental problems, or crime. It is almost never alcoholism alone, or mental illness alone, that produces homelessness. Likewise, it is not poverty alone. . . . The proximate cause of homelessness, and what accounts most for the explosion in their numbers, then, is fractured relationships.

Dan McMurry, *Crisis*, February 1989.

Public officials at the state and local levels, reflecting this change in mood, have begun to dismiss the gravity of the homeless problem. Many are stating openly that the homeless have become a public nuisance and a social irritant, a powerful disincentive to commercial investment, and an excessive financial burden that the community can no longer abide. Going further, many officials—finding no workable solution to the problem of homelessness—are now eager to ignore the challenge it presents and to shift the entire burden of responsibility back to the homeless themselves.

Nonetheless, homelessness will not just disappear. For this reason, a reactive policy that bars the homeless from the most conspicuous public places—a policy that some cities have been implementing—will not work. At best, such policies can bring only a brief interval of relief from this most compelling social disorder, and they can only postpone the necessity to take more effective action.

Homelessness poses a challenge to America that must be addressed openly and more honestly than it has been to date.

Homelessness and Community

To most people, homelessness is a condition brought about by the lack of proper shelter and food, and occasioned by a variety of social dislocations including unemployment, drug abuse, alcoholism, and, in about 28 percent of the cases, mental illness. These conditions give rise to the pressing need for a variety of social programs: those providing treatment for alcohol and substance abuse, making available affordable housing and better employment opportunities, providing proper nourishment and health care, and offering a more humane way of assisting the mentally handicapped.

Yet, prevalent as these conditions are among the homeless, they do not offer a complete explanation of homelessness. Take the case of substance abuse, for instance. It cannot be denied that use of alcohol and drugs is widespread and excessive among homeless people. This is a fact they themselves will readily admit. But it does not necessarily follow that such abuse can be judged a principal cause of homelessness. A more basic question must be asked: Does an individual begin his self-destructive journey? Is it that the ruinous aspects of alcohol and drugs come to light only after continued use—or is there a deeper cause?

The answer is clearly yes, and the truth of this argument is borne out by the homeless themselves.

Has society wrongly interpreted and judged the symptoms of homelessness to be the causes of homelessness?

It has become evident that homelessness is a much deeper problem than most people realize. Indeed, every indication is that something more fundamental is at work.

Each homeless person with whom I conversed related to me his own particular journey toward homelessness. Some spoke of their inability to cope with the stresses that follow upon economic and social uncertainties, while others referred to a lack of self esteem or a difficulty in relating to others. No two persons told the same story. It was as if there existed an endless variety of situations and circumstances, each having the potential to radically alter the course of a life.

The Impact of Loneliness

And yet, despite this diversity, most spoke of a fundamental void that in some way disposed them to accept their worsening condition. They all referred to a growing sense of dissatisfaction—and then aloneness—that slowly but relentlessly enveloped their lives, eventually severing their connection with the future and undermining whatever meaning and purpose they once had. Each person said that this aloneness affected his ability to think and to act purposefully. As one person told me, being so terribly alone left him with an inner emptiness and paralysis that even his closest friends could not bridge or help overcome.

The following vignettes are illustrative:

> Mike related how hard he had worked to meet his house and car payments and to provide a nice home for his wife and two children. But he felt unappreciated, at work and at home, and sensed that no one cared about him. Life began to lose meaning, until, finally, he could no longer continue. One day he left home and sought refuge on the street.

> Joe was manager of a shoe store in New York City. During a holdup, he was shot in the knee and lower leg. While he was in therapy, his girlfriend convinced him to move to Washington and stay with her mother. As he recovered, he began to help around the house. The mother began to demand more work and soon insisted that he give her his disability checks. He said he would give her half, but she refused, phoned the police, and had him evicted that very evening. Alone and feeling betrayed, he had become a street person whose basic possessions were a cane and a Bible, which he said gave him inner strength and peace.

> John was panhandling. He asked me for a quarter. I introduced myself, and we began to talk. He related stories about him and children, his Catholic religion, and his attendance at Mass every day. When we finished talking. I gave him two dollars. He looked at me and said: "I can always get food and shelter. I will use the money to buy some soup, and I appreciate it. But more than ever, I appreciate the time you took to talk to me. You know," he said, with tears in his eyes, "my life has been so lonely."

These stories—along with countless others—make it clear that homeless individuals see their situation somewhat differently than does the general public or the policymaker. In fact, if we allow that the homeless are the more perfect witnesses of their own predicament—which I am willing to do—it follows that the basic causes of homelessness remain a mystery to most Americans and to American policymakers.

Betrayed by Society

Whatever particular griefs men may have experienced on their way to homelessness, there is one final and crippling sorrow all of them share: a sense of betrayal at society's refusal to recognize their needs. Most of us—men and women—grow up expecting that when things go terribly wrong someone, from somewhere, will step forward to help us. That this does not happen, and that all watch from the shore as each of us, in isolation, struggles to swim and then begins to sink, is perhaps the most terrible discovery that anyone in any society can make. When troubled men make that discovery, as all homeless men do sooner or later, then hope vanishes completely.

Peter Marin, *The Nation*, July 8, 1991.

To be homeless, as these individuals are, is to be alone, alienated from the lives of others, and thereby alienated from the dynamics of community life.

This is the substantial core of what it means to be homeless. Yet, it is a truth that has relevance for us all. For in a most powerful and graphic way—too graphic for many—the homeless person is revealing to us something about ourselves.

To understand this more fully, it is helpful to reflect on the role that the notion of community has played in the life of the individual over the past 30 years, and what its current diminished relevance signifies for America's future.

The decline of community in America has loosened the bonding that has traditionally united individuals. To an alarming extent, the individual now pursues a life as independent from others as is practically possible. Relations among individuals increasingly are depersonalized and defined in terms of utilitarian and hedonistic needs.

To a degree that can only be termed troublesome, the United States has, over the past three decades, been evolving into a society where there is little common purpose, where there are only small pockets of community, and where the forces of alienation and dehumanization have in many instances reached an advanced stage.

The consequences of these changes affect us all. Personal relationships—whether within a family, among friends, at work, or with strangers—have become increasingly antagonistic over the past three decades. Social atomism is on the rise. Children take legal action against their parents. The elderly are often left alone. Child abuse has become a national scandal. These trends have been reinforced by a litigious mentality that has transformed the legal system and enshrined it as a means of enhancing personal gain.

In short, what we are witnessing throughout society is a phenomenon not unlike that found among homeless street people—an increased isolation and alienation of the individual from the life of the community.

Alienation Affects Many People

Thus, the notion that homelessness today is a phenomenon pertaining exclusively to street people is incorrect. The casual drug user, the addict, the alcoholic, the conspicuous consumer, the person who betrays his family obligations, or the individual who violates the public trust—all these individuals, to one degree or another, are alienated from community.

The main difference between the two groups is that the people of the street—whose material deprivation is perhaps more deplorable than that of any other group in America—symbolize this alienation in the most graphic way.

For this reason, homelessness—as it exists today—cannot be adequately addressed simply by changing this or that condition. A person who is given food or shelter, but nothing more, remains alienated. He is just not any worse. A person who enters a drug treatment program but who remains outside of community faces overwhelming odds of having a relapse. As the homeless say, their problem goes far beyond the need for food and shelter, drug and alcohol treatment, or affordable housing. It strikes to the very depths of the human spirit. . . .

What is needed in America today is a renaissance of community and a rebuilding of bonds that have traditionally united people in the dynamics of community life.

This is a goal that only individuals—working together in small groups but inspired by a common vision—can accomplish. For to the degree and the extent that individuals are engaged in helping each other, they unleash a social and political dynamic. Once set in motion, it slowly but relentlessly rebuilds those relationships of justice, law, and friendship that are essential to the good life of the individual.

Apart from such a renewed individual commitment to community, all other efforts to deal effectively with the growing problem of homelessness will fall short. If we continue to address only the symptoms, and not the root of the problem, even the status quo will be difficult to maintain.

> *"Housing regulations are to blame for a lot of homelessness."*

Removing Housing Regulations Would Help the Homeless

William Tucker

William Tucker is a housing expert and the author of *The Excluded Americans: Homelessness and Housing Policies*. In the following viewpoint, Tucker argues that local housing regulations, such as rent control laws and laws prohibiting construction, have made rental housing difficult to find and have forced many people into homelessness. Tucker blames both cities and suburbs for enacting exclusionary laws designed to drive poor tenants out of their jurisdictions. Tucker is a former media fellow at the Hoover Institution, a think tank located in Palo Alto, California.

As you read, consider the following questions:

1. In Tucker's opinion, how are conservatives and liberals both mistaken about local and national housing availability?
2. Why does Tucker believe that some cities are anxious to close down and ban downtown single-room occupancy hotels?
3. Why does the author discount stereotypes of "slumlords" and conclude that these landlords are necessary?

From William Tucker, "How Housing Regulations Cause Homelessness." Reprinted from: *The Public Interest*, No. 102 (Winter 1991), pp. 78-88, © 1991 by National Affairs, Inc.

The problem of homelessness in the 1980s has puzzled liberals and conservatives alike. Both have tended to fit the problem into their preconceived views, without looking at what is new and different about the phenomenon. . . .

There were indeed homeless people long before 1980, and their numbers have always been difficult to count. But it is hard to ignore the almost unanimous reports from shelter providers (many of them old-line conservative church groups) that the problem has been getting steadily worse since 1980. The anecdotal evidence is also abundant. Anyone who has walked the streets of New York or Washington over the last decade knows that there are more beggars sitting on the sidewalks and sleeping on park benches than there were ten years ago.

Although many of the homeless are obviously alcoholics, drug addicts, and people who are clinically insane, large numbers appear only to be down on their luck. The most widely accepted statistical breakdown was first proposed in a 1988 Urban Institute paper: "Feeding the Homeless: Does the Prepared Meals Provision Help?" According to authors Martha Burt and Barbara Cohen, one-third of the homeless can be categorized as released mental patients, one-third as alcoholics and drug abusers, and one-third as people who are homeless for purely economic reasons.

Thus the component of homeless people who are not affected by personal pathologies is large. It should also be noted that being a chronic alcoholic or drug addict does not condemn a person to living in the streets. Even "winos" or "stumblebums" were able to find minimal housing in the past.

And so paradoxes remain. How can we have such a large homeless population at a time when rental vacancy rates are near postwar highs? How can there be plenty of housing but not enough "affordable housing"? In short, how can there be scarcity in the housing market when so much housing is still available?

Variations Among Housing Markets

These paradoxes can be resolved when we recognize that the housing market is not a national market but is instead the sum of many regional and local markets. Rental vacancy rates probably serve as the best measure of the availability of affordable housing, since most poor people rent. These rates vary widely from city to city. During the 1980s, rental vacancy rates in Dallas and Houston were rarely below 12 percent—a figure that is about twice what is considered a normal vacancy rate. At the same time, housing has been absurdly scarce in other cities. New York has not had vacancy rates over 3 percent since 1972. San Francisco had normal vacancy rates during the 1970s, but they plunged to 2 percent during the 1980s, where they remain today.

Since the poor tend to be limited in their mobility, vacancy rates signifantly affect their ability to find housing. Although southern and southwestern cities claim to receive a regular seasonal migration of homeless people during the winter months, there is little evidence that people are moving from city to city to find housing. Other factors, like work opportunities, proximity to family members, and sheer inertia, seem to dominate people's choice of locale.

Affordable housing in America

Renault, *Sacramento Bee*. Reprinted with permission.

What should be far more mobile is the capital that builds housing and has created such a superabundance in specific cities. If it is difficult to find tenants for new apartments in Dallas and Phoenix, why don't builders shift to Boston or San Francisco, where housing is desperately needed?

Once we start asking this question, the impediments in the housing market suddenly become visible. It is obviously not equally easy to build housing in all cities. In particular, the local regulatory climate has a tremendous impact on the housing supply. Dallas and Houston are free-wheeling, market-oriented cities with little or no zoning regulation and negligible anti-growth sentiment. They have been able to keep abreast of housing demand even as their populations grew rapidly. Boston and San Francisco, on the other hand, have highly regulated housing markets. Both are surrounded by tight rings of exclusionary suburbs, where zoning and growth-control sentiment make new construction extremely difficult. In addition, both have adopted rent control as a way of "solving" local housing shortages. As a result, both have extremely high housing prices and extremely tight rental markets. The median home price in each approaches $200,000, while in Dallas and Phoenix the median price is below the national median of $88,000.

Thus it makes little sense to talk about a national housing market's effect on homelessness. Local markets vary widely, and municipal regulation seems to be the deciding factor.

This is what has misled both liberals and conservatives. Conservatives look at the national superabundance of housing and conclude that local problems do not exist. Liberals look at local shortages and conclude that there is a national housing problem. In fact, housing shortages are a local problem created by local regulation, which is the work of local municipal governments. . . .

Eliminating Unwanted Housing

No-growth ordinances and rent control have not, of course, been embraced everywhere; but city administrations have often produced comparable results through intense housing-code enforcement, designed to drive "undesirable" housing (and the people who live in it) out of their jurisdictions.

In *New Homeless and Old: Community and the Skid Row Hotel*, Charles Hoch and Robert Slayton have traced the disappearance of the single-room occupancy (SRO) and "cubicle" hotels that once provided cheap housing to thousands of marginal tenants in downtown Chicago. Over 8,000 of these hotel rooms—still available to Chicago's low-income transients in 1963—have disappeared, leaving barely 2,000 today. These lost accommodations were all supplied by the private market. Although remarkably inexpensive (often costing only $2 a night), these rooms offered residents exactly what they wanted—security and privacy. Most of the hotels had elaborate security systems, with desk clerks screening visitors and protecting residents from unwanted ones. In addition, the cheap hotels were usually convenient to stores and public transportation, allowing low-income residents with few family connections to lead frugal but relatively dignified lives.

What happened to these old SRO hotels? Almost without exception, they became the target of urban-renewal efforts and municipal campaigns to "clean up downtown." Intense building-code enforcement and outright condemnation drove most of them out of business. Strict zoning ordinances have since made it virtually impossible to build replacements. Hoch and Slayton conclude:

> We do not believe that the demise of Skid Row and the SRO hotels was the inevitable result of market forces, or that Skid Row residents embodied peculiar social and psychological characteristics that produced deviant and pathological social behavior. . . . [Instead,] this loss was the result of decades of antagonism from civic and business leaders, legitimated from the 1950s on by social scientists, and incorporated into dramatic change-oriented programs like urban renewal.

Nor have these policies abated today. Despite the hue and cry over the loss of SRO hotels, their replacement is still generally forbidden by zoning ordinances. In Los Angeles, there is a movement afoot to close down SRO hotels—even those subsidized by the city government—because they are not built to withstand earthquakes. Peter Smith, president of the New York City Partnership for the Homeless, comments: "It's essentially illegal for private developers to build SRO hotels in New York anymore."

Restricting Development

What is causing homelessness, then, is the familiar phenomenon of government regulation. This regulation tends to escape the attention of the public and the enthusiasts of deregulation, because it is done at the local rather than the state or national level.

The truth is that cities and towns do not always welcome new development. At bottom, even the most enthusiastic advocates of progress would often prefer to see their own neighborhoods remain just as they are. People will usually settle for higher-priced housing, because it raises the value of their own homes; but few want tenements, rentals, or other forms of "low-income" housing.

Through regulation, most cities and towns hold a tight rein on their housing markets. Suburbs are particularly exclusionary, zoning out everything but high-priced single-family homes (which require large lot sizes), and prohibiting the rental of rooms or apartments. Cities themselves, although sometimes offering rhetorical welcomes, often play the same exclusionary games.

An example can be seen in Takoma Park, Maryland, a nine-teenth-century "streetcar suburb" of Washington, D.C., which until recently had a long history of tolerant housing policies. Takoma Park is a hodgepodge of two-, three-, and four-family homes within easy commuting distance of Washington. During World War II, homeowners rented attics and spare bedrooms to wartime officials who could not find housing in Washington. This tradition continued after the war, when many returning GI's sought housing while attending nearby Columbia Union College. Many homeowners permanently converted their homes to two- and three-family units.

Government Must End Bad Policies

Policy makers love to write laws to address problems they've created instead of getting rid of the mischievous policy. Rent controls give landlords incentive to convert units into condominiums. Then politicians legislate anti-condominium conversion laws. These actions reduce the incentives for builders to enter the market. Then the politicians call for housing subsidies. Politicians never change because they never look back at their last policy. Years ago, Congress took the federal bulldozer to low-income housing in downtown areas. They replaced it with high-income high rises and office skyscrapers. Now they wonder about lack of "affordable" housing in cities.

Walter E. Williams, *The Union Leader*, February 22, 1990.

During the 1970s, however, a group of homeowners living in a recently constructed, more suburban part of the city asked Montgomery County to enforce a sixty-year-old zoning ordinance that prohibited rentals in single-family zones. (Zoning is controlled by county governments in Maryland.) After a long dispute, the city council adopted a compromise in 1978, which permitted anyone who was renting before 1954 to continue to do so for another ten years. In 1988 the reprieve expired, however, and evictions began. More than six hundred tenants were forced to leave their homes.

The Importance of Skid Rows

It is important to realize that housing regulations are to blame for a lot of homelessness. But at the same time, we must acknowledge the impulses that make people want to intervene in the housing marketplace.

About a year ago, I spent a few days in San Francisco's Market Street district, a notorious skid row. Although not particularly dangerous, the surroundings were decidedly unpleasant. Weatherbeaten young men, each of whom seemed to have his entire worldly belongings wrapped in a sleeping bag, lounged along the sidewalks. Ragged holdovers from the sixties perched on public monuments, performing drunken imitations of rock singers. Veterans of motorcycle gangs weaved past timid pedestrians, carrying on garrulous arguments with their equally disheveled girlfriends. Along the side streets, tattoo parlors jostled with cheap cafeterias, pornography shops, and the inevitable flophouse hotels.

It was easy enough to imagine some ambitious politician surveying the scene and deciding that it was time to "clean up Market Street." Such campaigns have occurred all over the country and have inevitably produced the disjuncture that we now find between the supply of housing and the price that poor people can afford to pay for it.

Yet distasteful as it may seem, skid rows play a crucial role in providing the poor and near-poor with cheap housing. Not everyone can live in suburban subdivisions or high-rise condominiums. To provide for everyone, we also need rooms for rent, fleabag hotels, tenements, trailer parks—and the "slumlords" who often run them. Although usually imagined to be rich and powerful, these bottom-rung entrepreneurs almost always turn out to be only slightly more affluent than the people for whom they are providing housing.

Build New Housing First

In the utopian dreams of regulators and "housing activists," such landlords are always eliminated. They are inevitably replaced by the federal government and the "non-profits," orchestrated by the city planners and visionary architects who would "tear down the slums" and replace them with "model tenements" and the "garden cities of tomorrow."

It is not wrong to have such visions. But let us do things in stages. Let us build the new housing *first*—and only then tear down the old "substandard" housing that is no longer needed. If we let the best become the enemy of the good—or even the barely adequate—the homeless will have nothing more substantial to live in than the dreams of the housing visionaries themselves.

"Shelter health clinics that offer routine health
care services are invaluable."

Providing Health Care
Would Help the Homeless

Barbara A. Blakeney

Because homeless people are regularly exposed to conditions associated with illness and injury, they suffer from a variety of
health problems, Barbara A. Blakeney argues in the following
viewpoint. Blakeney maintains that shelters should help the
homeless by providing health care services ranging from first
aid to the treatment of chemical dependency. Blakeney states
that too many of the homeless neglect basic health care needs
and that an aggressive outreach approach by shelter workers is
necessary to convince the homeless to take advantage of health
care facilities. Blakeney is the principal public health nurse for
the city of Boston, Massachusetts.

As you read, consider the following questions:

1. How can homeless persons' health care needs be met if a
   homeless shelter lacks medical facilities, according to
   Blakeney?
2. Why does the author believe that infectious diseases are a
   major concern in homeless shelters?
3. According to Blakeney, why must health care services be
   integrated with other homeless shelter services?

Historically, shelters [for the homeless] were not designed, funded, or identified as health care institutions. Nonetheless, the shortage of health care facilities serving indigent persons and the special difficulties that homeless persons encounter when using traditional health care services have led many shelters to enter the health care business. Most shelters offer basic first aid and some health screening; others offer substantially more.

Because their guests are exposed daily to conditions associated with illness and injury, shelter health clinics that offer routine health care services are invaluable. Shelter-based clinics range in structure from a nursing station in one corner of a shelter to fully equipped clinics staffed by full-time health care professionals. A nurse on-site, a clinic with basic supplies, and a visiting physician are reasonable goals for some shelters. In the absence of such a clinic, close relations are needed with a local hospital or visiting health care team. Provision should be made for staff to help guests maintain a schedule for taking prescribed medication and ensure that clinical evaluations occur when shelter guests appear to need them.

Preventing Health Care Crises

An ounce of prevention is worth every bit as much with homeless persons as it is with those who are housed. Health care crises disrupt shelter functioning and require inordinate amounts of resources. Providing routine checkups and maintaining patient records will help to reduce the incidence of such crises. Accompanying shelter guests on visits to hospitals or other off-site health care facilities should help to ensure that the care needed is obtained. Preventive care is even more important with expectant mothers; a connection with a prenatal clinic is essential.

The catalyst for many shelter-based clinics has been the Health Care for the Homeless project established by the Robert Wood Johnson Foundation and the Pew Memorial Trust. Health Care for the Homeless became one of the most innovative and effective programs targeted for homeless persons on a national basis. The two foundations designed the program to address directly the impediments to provision of health care to the homeless. Each local program was required to use locations for health care delivery where as many homeless persons could be served as possible; service teams were expected to include physicians, nurses, and social workers; service coordinators and mechanisms for making service referrals were encouraged; and welfare and housing agency representatives had to be included among the program sponsors.

Perhaps most importantly, cities were limited to only one application. All potential applicants within a city had to collaborate as part of a local coalition, including the mayor and representatives of religious groups, as well as representatives of public and private nonprofit groups. Nineteen cities were chosen after a competitive review.

A Public Health Crisis

As we witnessed the suffering of America's poorest citizens, we came to understand that the individual health care problems of homeless people combine to form a major public health crisis. We can no longer sit as spectators to the elderly homeless dying of hypothermia, to the children with blighted futures poisoned by lead in rat-infested dilapidated welfare hotels, to women raped, to old men beaten and robbed of their few possessions, and to people dying on the streets with catastrophic illnesses such as AIDS. Without eliminating homelessness, the health risks and concomitant health problems, the desperate plight of homeless children, the suffering, and the needless deaths of homeless Americans will continue.

Bruce Vladeck, *Issues in Science and Technology*, Fall 1988.

Boston's Stabilization Services for Homeless Substance Abusers project, funded by the National Institute of Alcohol Abuse and Alcoholism Community Demonstration Program, also showed that it is possible to deliver effective health services to guests who are in residence at shelters. The project provided extensive recovery services for randomly selected shelter guests, all of whom had histories of alcohol and/or other drug problems. The project demonstrated that despite histories of multiple addictions and prior treatment, lack of social and economic supports, and psychiatric problems, many homeless clients can be stabilized by providing intensive services in shelter settings.

Respite Beds for the Sick

Respite beds are an important component of a comprehensive clinical services program and can be used to enhance health care in many shelters. Essentially, respite beds are set aside in the shelter for persons recovering from some type of illness. Usually, these beds are in one area within the shelter. Persons allotted a respite bed typically are allowed to keep the same bed as long as they are ill and can remain in the shelter during the day. In addition, they receive more comprehensive care, including nurse practitioner and physician visits. Providing this modicum of stability in the otherwise chaotic life of homeless persons can substantially improve the recovery process, but because of the illness involved, more support also is needed.

The necessary support arrangements for persons in shelter respite beds include help with obtaining and taking prescribed medications and regular visits from clinical personnel. A shelter-based respite unit also must develop clear policies concerning admission and discharge. There should be a clear understanding with local hospitals about the type of patients who are appropriate for the respite unit so as not to tax unreasonably the shelter's resources and to discourage hospitals from rushing their indigent patients too quickly to the shelter. Support services also must be planned to facilitate the discharge process and to aid discharged respite guests to adjust to a new schedule and to new surroundings.

While making health care and ancillary services available in shelters is critical, it is not enough. Too many homeless persons neglect basic health care needs because of overriding problems with substance abuse, mental illness, or immediate survival. Aggressive outreach may be required to make homeless persons, even shelter users, aware of health care facilities and convince them of the benevolence of those who provide the health care. It was the commitment of Health Care for the Homeless teams to set up clinics within shelters, rather than waiting for homeless persons to come to off-site hospitals or clinics, that made the HCH approach so successful. Within shelters, an outreach-oriented approach also is necessary to maximize success.

An outreach mentality should pervade the approach of those staff members who provide health care for persons with physical as well as mental problems who are in shelters. Health care workers should be prepared to offer services in different ways to different guests, respecting a desire to withhold information or to refuse care entirely, except in emergencies, and yet continuing to build a relationship through low-demand contacts—saying hello, checking on how people are doing, asking about the quality of the food.

Health Problems Among the Homeless

Many basic issues of health care need to be addressed by the shelter community. Infectious diseases, such as tuberculosis, hepatitis, lice and other infestations, herpes and the so-called childhood illnesses, such as measles, mumps, and chicken pox are public health issues that every shelter, both adult and family, will face. In addition, health issues secondary to drug abuse and alcoholism will be prevalent.

HIV infection is rapidly becoming a major health issue for the homeless population. In fact, some reports estimate that as many as one third of the homeless population are HIV-positive. Therefore, it is important that the shelter community be aware of these issues and be prepared to address them within their own facility. The first step in addressing these issues is a sound knowledge base.

Health problems function as both antecedents and consequences of homelessness. Evidence from health care studies and clinical observations point to substantially higher morbidity rates among homeless people, compared to other populations. Thus, responding to the health care needs of the homeless should be seen as a cornerstone of policy and human service solutions to the crisis of homelessness. Yet, while homeless persons' health care needs are acute, it is not easy to separate health care from other urgent survival needs—income, employment, and housing, in particular. For this reason, it is vital that health care and treatment providers integrate as closely as possible the provision of health services with the other segments of the local service network—the Health Care for the Homeless approach. Shelters can play a critical role in linking homeless people with health care opportunities and in providing directly essential emergency services.

"I see a very strong relationship between the weakening of the family through a variety of forces and an increase in homelessness."

Strengthening Families Would Reduce Homelessness

Richard W. White Jr., interviewed by *The Family in America*

Richard W. White Jr. is a research scholar at the Institute for Contemporary Studies, a public policy research group in San Francisco, and the author of *Rude Awakenings: What the Homeless Crisis Tells Us*. In the following viewpoint, White is interviewed by *The Family in America*, a monthly publication concerned with family issues. White argues that in the past, tight-knit families have always been able to come to the aid of a family member and prevent that person from becoming homeless. White maintains that families today lack this cohesiveness and that many of the homeless are comprised of single-parent families and single fathers. White asserts that government should strengthen families by encouraging self-reliance and supplementing lower-income workers' pay, rather than trying to solve problems for them through programs such as welfare.

As you read, consider the following questions:

1. Why does White believe that blacks have suffered most from family disunity?
2. In the author's opinion, how can Americans benefit from the family traditions of immigrant groups?

"The Homeless and the Confused," by Richard W. White Jr., interviewed in the August 1992 issue of *The Family in America*, copyright 1992 by The Rockford Institute. Reprinted with permission.

FIA: What has your extensive research taught you about the relationship between homelessness and family life?

White: I see a very strong relationship between the weakening of the family through a variety of forces and an increase in homelessness. It has to do with people losing the kind of ties that used to keep them from falling into homelessness when everything else failed. There was always a family there to catch them.

FIA: More people lack these ties now than twenty-five years ago?

White: I think that's so. The combination of declining availability of low-skilled, but well-paying jobs in the central cities and of an increase in the availability of welfare for people make it so that we have in inner-city communities a new kind of culture: a single-parent family, nobody works, and the family itself is no longer a place where values can effectively be communicated. That's the worst version, the central-city version, that is characteristically black families. Black families used to be rather strong when there was an attachment to the labor force and strong and extended families who kept everything together through terrible times. In the last twenty-five years or so, that's all changed. So the black family is now seen as something pathological, where 30, 40, or 50 years ago it was, in fact, the main strength of that [ethnic] group.

The Family and the State

FIA: Some researchers have written about formation of the mother-state-child family. Is that what you're talking about?

White: Yes, that's it. The mother-state-child family. The mothers never marry. In effect, they are marrying the state. The state is not a very good father. When you look at family homelessness, it is primarily these single-parent families. You also look at growing homelessness among singles. I think that a great many of those new single homeless people are the fathers who are not in those families. I think it's a new phenomenon because it is the people who would have been married and in those families had it not been for a combination of low, unskilled worker wages and the presence of a welfare system that enables the mother to make a decision to live independently with her children.

FIA: Do you see the same kind of pattern among some of the new immigrant groups? Some of these groups are relatively impoverished, yet they come with religious or cultural traditions that have emphasized the family. Are those traditions holding up?

White: They are under attack. Newly immigrant families from strong family traditions, like the Mexicans in particular, who come into this society actually have a longer life expectancy when they first arrive here than you and I do. The importance of family is so strong that somebody can come from a poor agricultural background, come to the United States—mother, father, and however many children—live here, have an average life expectancy of say 70 years or something, and have low problems on every health (not economic) kind of indice. They do fine, and then the next generation is worse, and then the next generation after that is worse. The ones who manage to make it in our society end up with about the same indices as we would have. The ones who fail to make it in our society end up with worse indices than we would have. The family is so strong that it seems to overcome practically everything else until it itself falls to the forces of mobility, modernism, secularism, economic strain.

Abandoning Families

"Angel" could not "stand being around her husband and child anymore" and so "made a choice to leave and become homeless." She smokes dope every day, takes speed three times a week, describes herself as "stubborn and rebellious," and says "being homeless is OK." "Foreman" abandoned his wife and four kids, sifts through garbage for food, and has spent 17 years in prison for shooting two police officers. "Alfred" chose to become homeless when he left his wife and kids because he "no longer wanted to be tied down" and discovered "he could make more money stealing." He mugs indigent women for their food stamps and "finds himself thinking about hurting other people."

Theodore Pappas, *Chronicles*, November 1991.

The most important lesson is that even the lowest-income immigrants coming to our society with a strong family tradition have advantages over those of us who are living this kind of modern-urban-secular existence. That's astonishing. If there were only some way for us to benefit from these waves of immigrants, instead of having their culture disappear, have it somehow strengthen ours, it would be a wonderful thing. But who has any idea how something like that could come about?

FIA: You have been involved in federal efforts to reduce poverty for some time?

White: Well, I was in the federal anti-poverty program from 1964-81, which is the entire lifetime of the federal OEO [Office of Economic Opportunity].

FIA: How many people anticipated corrosive effects of welfare on the family? Were there many people who saw this coming and tried to warn against it? Were most of the people taken by surprise? Or is there still a good deal of denial going on about the effects of the welfare system?

White: I think it's all three. I think the person who's most associated with having seen these things most clearly earliest was [U.S. senator] Pat Moynihan. You remember the flack he took? He's never recovered, I think.

FIA: You don't express much confidence in your book *Rude Awakenings* in the standard programs for helping the homeless.

White: I think that many of the standard programs for helping the homeless sustain homelessness. They sustain people in that pattern. They don't really help people to get out of that pattern.

A Home Is How You Make It

FIA: At bottom, isn't there some relationship between spiritual or emotional homelessness and the physical homelessness that receives all of the attention in the media?

White: That is really an excellent point, and I'm not quite sure how to put it across in the kind of discussion we have these days. It's true that so many families living together aren't really making a home with each other. There is all this talk about quality time. But where people are really committed to one another, that's the secret. You can imagine the family of a mother and father and three children living out of their car. They could be a happy family; it could be a home. And then you've got other people living in what they call today "dysfunctional families." Some people claim that 90 percent of families are dysfunctional, which of course is ridiculous, because people don't have to be always hugging each other to make it clear that they care. In real estate, they use the term "buy a home." I've always been bothered by that. You can't buy a home; you buy a house. You have to make a home.

FIA: There's been a lot of rhetoric in the media about the homeless. Can political leaders fix what is wrong with most American families or do we need to look to other sources?

White: Of course, what we do need to do is to look to other sources. But I think our political leaders can play an important role in that the government is a big resource for both good and ill. I really think that the government needs to be refocused. Instead of trying to substitute for what goes wrong in our society and set up something to take its place, we need to evaluate our government programs and policies so that they are aimed at strengthening the ability of our natural institutions to deal with social concerns.

FIA: Could you be a bit more specific?

White: For instance, when it comes to welfare, I think that David Ellwood's ideas on the subject make a lot of sense, that instead of having an AFDC [Aid to Families with Dependent Children] system where there are families that are supported by the government, we need to make sure that people who go to work can earn enough money to support a family. How do they do that? What I've recommended is that we actually put in the paycheck the money that . . . [now goes] into welfare and call it "social income." That is, the difference between what a person is worth to the employer and what we would pay them would be "social income." . . . The total would put every working family over the poverty level. And it would cost less than what we're now spending on welfare. We would be supporting families instead of supporting non-work and single-parent situations. The point is that the overall policy of the government . . . should be . . . to strengthen families, neighborhoods, small communities to manage their own lives rather than to set up bureaucratic structures that will manage for them.

The Homeless Need Roots

Homelessness increases as the family weakens and as greater numbers of individuals become alienated from their families and neighborhoods. These individuals do not need rights so much as they need roots. Reportedly, most of those released from mental hospitals in the early years of deinstitutionalization did not become homeless because they had families and friends to help them relocate and to see that they were cared for. Only when patients without supporting relatives began coming out of the hospitals in significant numbers did we begin noticing mentally ill individuals on the streets.

Richard W. White Jr., *Rude Awakenings*, 1992.

FIA: How are government officials to encourage such self-reliance?

White: One of my biggest surprises in doing my research was to discover that real social workers are nothing like what they teach at the university . . . and nothing like the stuff that the profession publicizes, which is all about advocacy and victimization and all this stuff. What happens with real social workers out in the field is they really do try to get individual clients to take responsibility for themselves. We need a lot more of that. And we need to get behind it and make it official that what we're doing is trying to help people to take as much responsibility as they can for their own lives, their own families.

FIA: But what of the government's promotion in recent decades of a gender-neutral ideology? What are the effects of that ideology on the family? Is it possible for government to strengthen the family and adhere to a gender-neutral ideology?

White: My biases are to say, 'No, it is not possible for government to do that.' But I don't think there is anything that you or I can do about that. The way the government is right now, it is undermining the best way for families to live. I think what we ought to be able to do, at least, is get it so the government really is gender neutral. It is not neutral now. You may think it is neutral, but what it is doing is funding the breakup of families and the wandering away of men.

FIA: You are saying that the government is not truly acting under a gender-neutral ideology now, that it is actually promoting the employment of women and undercutting familial roles of men?

White: Inadvertently. I can't honestly object to the policy that says that a woman's earnings are as good as a man's earnings when it comes to going to the bank and getting a mortgage. I can't honestly say that that's a bad policy. But I can say that the effect of the declaration in the middle of the 1970's—when they made it clear that you could no longer discount the woman's income in making those kinds of decisions at the bank—was immediately to have the price of housing rise to meet the availability of additional home-purchase income. So that was, more than anything else, responsible for the increased cost of housing in the mid-1970's. So it did no good. Whatever you want to say, there are such crazy unforeseen side effects to almost any of these presumed implementations of social justice.

Undermining Traditional Families

FIA: When you say it did no good, you mean it didn't really help families get into homes?

White: It didn't help families get into homes; it just raised the price. In fact, what it most profoundly did was to make it more difficult for a family that had decided—in whatever way—that only the male was going to go to work and earn money, it made the house more expensive for them so they couldn't afford to buy one anymore, because it drove up the price by making the dual-income family's second income part of the mortgage consideration. This was not the government intending in any way to come out against the traditional economic unit, but it did.

With welfare, it is the same way. They don't want families apart, but this is what happens. . . . We don't need to spend more or spend less on programs necessarily, but we need to spend money differently. We need to change the dynamics in our social policies. . . . I think we should rebuild the mental-illness system, again working with the families wherever possible. . . . There is a big debate among people who want to rebuild the mental-illness system between [those who] advocate listening to the patients and [those who advocate] listening to the patients' families. I think our government should come down on the side of working with the patients' families. We're trying to rebuild natural institutions. We need tough but kind policies. It's a lot like an effective family. In an effective family the father is tough but kind.

FIA: But in the absence of the personal virtues essential to strong family life, what hope is there of making progress through *public* policy?

White: We really can't directly make progress through public policy, because what progress is, is individuals making better decisions about their lives, and if the decisions are going to be made publicly, then that is a contradiction in terms. The government needs to make sure we have the kind of political economy within which we can responsibly work out our own lives. . . . [Currently,] government is devilish: it tempts us to do wrong all the time. It offers people inducements to do the wrong thing rather than supporting them in doing right. Government programs are undermining our natural institutions by providing all kinds of ways out of putting in the effort to make them work.

"People living on streets, especially many who are mentally ill or chemically dependent, cannot be expected to act on their own."

Treating Chemically Dependent and Mentally Ill Homeless Is Necessary

Gordon Berlin and William McAllister

Many homeless people are mentally ill or dependent on drugs or alcohol. In the following viewpoint, Gordon Berlin and William McAllister argue that medical treatment and shelter must be provided for such needy persons because they do not seek help on their own. Berlin and McAllister maintain that mental health and drug treatment centers should treat these homeless people prior to placement into permanent housing. Berlin is senior vice president of Manpower Demonstration Research Corporation, a social policy research group in New York City. McAllister is a visiting senior research fellow at the John Jay College of Criminal Justice Research Center in New York.

As you read, consider the following questions:

1. Why have so many mentally ill and chemically dependent people become homeless, according to Berlin and McAllister?
2. In the authors' opinion, how can permanent housing for these homeless people be ensured?
3. Why do the authors support laws against loitering and panhandling?

From Gordon Berlin and William McAllister, "Homelessness: Why Nothing Has Worked and What Will," *The Brookings Review*, Fall 1992. Reprinted with permission of The Brookings Institution.

"Homeless" used to describe people who were transient, poor, socially isolated, and living in the cheap hotels and flop-houses on skid row. They had housing, but they didn't have homes. Today, the homeless are "houseless"—they literally cannot expect to have even a flophouse roof over their heads.

They are also extraordinarily poor. The Urban Institute found that single homeless adults averaged less than $150 and families about $350 in reported monthly income from all sources, excluding food stamps. Families, usually a woman and two children, make up 20-30 percent of homeless people. About a third of the homeless suffer from severe and persistent mental illness. At least a third abuse alcohol or illegal drugs. Most have multiple disabilities, for example, mental illness and drug abuse. . . .

How Policy Changes Caused Homelessness

That state mental hospitals no longer cared for most severely mentally ill poor people caused many to end up on the street. Instead of the hospitals, a system of federally supported community mental health centers was to administer psychotropic drugs and otherwise care for mentally ill people, thereby allowing them to live independently. But fewer than half the centers were built, they were not connected to the discharge planning of state mental hospitals, and hospital admission standards were tightened. As a result, many mentally ill people were not served, as they would have been in the past, and some wound up on the streets. Also, many were able to live successfully in the community until the housing in which they resided, such as SROs [single room occupancy hotels], disappeared.

Around this time, the civil rights of alcoholics and the mentally ill were extended. Recognizing that alcoholism is a disease, local governments decriminalized public inebriation. Involuntary institutionalization now requires that a person be mentally ill and likely to harm himself or others. In an earlier era, street alcoholics would have been jailed and the mentally ill hospitalized.

The rise of crack may have increased and deepened the homeless problem. Compared with earlier drugs of choice, like heroin, crack causes more violent behavior, is more fiercely addictive, and costs as much or more, and so may be more likely to lead to homelessness. . . .

Serving the Drug-Addicted and Mentally Ill

Of all the problems complicating homelessness, none is likely to be more prevalent, persistent, and difficult to treat than drug abuse. To end homelessness for some who are drug dependent, a system of services and strict performance standards is essential.

After an initial 10 days to two weeks in detoxification, either in community-based "detox" centers or in the shelters themselves, clients would move to drug-free transitional residences to begin therapy. Some will be able to find their own housing and will require only short-term outpatient treatment; others will need long-term transitional housing and case management, possibly followed by "supported" housing, where they would be supported in dealing with their drug dependency.

Community Care

People in community living arrangements for the homeless mentally ill provided by New York City and State.

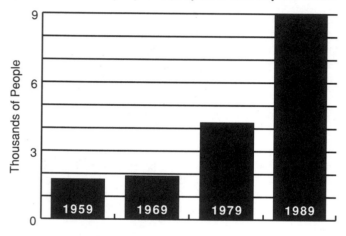

Source: New York State Office of Mental Health.

After meeting the goals set by the transitional shelter, clients would receive help finding work and permanent housing. Those unable to locate housing and who had lived in the shelters one to two years could be eligible to move into supported SROs.

Because many drug users will refuse treatment and others can function with their dependencies, not all homeless drug abusers will be treated. Drug treatment and daily living services for 71,000 people for an average of 12 months would cost $550 million.

The system for mentally ill people would be similar to that for other groups. Intensive outreach would bring people from the streets into small "safe havens" that would provide psychiatric assessment and care. Depending on their condition, people would move from the safe havens into permanent housing or into transitional shelters. These would monitor medication, train patients in daily living activities, and provide general medical services and psychiatric and psychosocial treatment. Stays could last from three months to a year. . . . .

To prevent the mentally ill from becoming homeless and to provide care for those who are, the charters of community mental health centers should require that their primary mission be to serve the severely and persistently mentally ill. Also, each state should be required to develop a comprehensive service plan linking the centers to state mental hospitals.

A presidential commission should be appointed to review laws determining whether to institutionalize individuals when they suffer from illnesses that impair their judgment. And demonstration programs for transitional housing and services should be started in preparation for statewide expansion of these initiatives over the next decade.

The annual cost of transitional housing and services for the homeless mentally ill would be $900 million. But if the government can redirect community mental health centers to serve the severely and persistently mentally ill, most of these costs would be offset.

Outreach and Legal Pressure

People living on streets, especially many who are mentally ill or chemically dependent, cannot be expected to act on their own to improve their situation. Successful outreach requires intensive, skilled, protracted effort. In one National Institute for Mental Health program, fewer than 20 percent of those contacted were actually connected to programs and services. Succeeding at outreach for drug abusers living on the street is even harder.

To encourage, or, in some instances, force people to take advantage of outreach, it will be necessary to enforce laws against sleeping in public places, loitering, and perhaps begging. The threat of jail may encourage addicts to remain in a therapeutic program or in transitional shelter or to get housing on their own. Such action, however, can and should be taken only if alternatives to jail actually exist.

This policy may seem retrograde for a society that has tried to move away from coercion and punishment and toward treating substance abuse and psychological problems as illnesses. And the legal ascendance of individual rights makes such a policy difficult to implement. Members of the psychiatric health community, however, have questioned whether the balance between these rights and the needs of mentally ill people has been lost. Moreover, the goal is not punishment, but the treatment required for the homeless to become housed.

106

Ranking Priorities to Reduce Homelessness

This activity will allow you to explore the priorities you think are important in reducing homelessness. A wide variety of people experience homelessness: young and old, male and female, parents and children. Many factors can lead to homelessness. These include the loss of a job, a lack of available housing, addiction to drugs or alcohol, family breakups, and mental illness. Because there are so many causes of homelessness, finding solutions is not always easy. Those who create programs to help the homeless must consider all of the various causes when they formulate policies.

The authors in this chapter discuss several strategies they believe would help the homeless. In this activity, you will rank the strategies you believe would reduce homelessness.

Part I

Imagine that you are the new mayor of a large city who has pledged to reduce homelessness. Below is a list of strategies that your advisors consider important. Working individually, rank the strategies. Decide what you believe to be the most effective strategy to help the homeless. Be ready to defend your answers. Use number 1 to designate the most important concern, number 2 for the second-most important concern, and so on.

_____ Increasing the supply of low-income housing.

_____ Identifying which homeless people are able and willing to work and helping them find jobs.

_____ Placing chemically dependent, homeless people into alcohol and drug treatment programs.

_____ Providing day care for young children of homeless parents so they can search for work and shelter.

_____ Hospitalizing mentally ill homeless people.

_____ Establishing job training and placement programs for the homeless.

_____ Strengthening homeless people's family relationships through family counseling.

_____ Offering counseling sessions that teach the homeless to become more self-sufficient.

_____ Giving emergency food and shelter to the homeless.

_____ Helping homeless people to reenter school and further their education.

_____ Shifting the burden of homeless services from government to private groups.

_____ Encouraging pedestrians to be charitable to the homeless and to give them spare change.

Part II

Step 1. The class should break into groups of four to six students. Students should compare their rankings with others in the group, giving reasons for their choices. Then the group should make a new list that reflects the concerns of the entire group.

Step 2. In a discussion with the entire class, compare your answers. Then discuss the following questions:

    1. Did your opinion change after comparing your answers with those of other group members? Why or why not?

    2. Consider and explain how your opinions might change if you were:

      a. homeless

      b. a taxpayer

Periodical Bibliography

The following articles have been selected to supplement the diverse views presented in this chapter.

James N. Baker   "Don't Sleep in the Subway," *Newsweek*, June 24, 1991.

L. Christopher Awalt   "Brother, Don't Spare a Dime," *Newsweek*, September 30, 1991.

Robert James Bidinotto   "Myths About the Homeless," *Reader's Digest*, June 1991.

Don Feder   "Buchanan Is Right About the Homeless," *Conservative Chronicle*, January 15, 1992. Available from PO Box 11297, Des Moines, IA 50340-1297.

Mary McGrory   "A Shelter with a Mission Succeeds," *Liberal Opinion*, April 27, 1992. Available from 108 E. Fifth St., Vinton, IA 52349.

Jay Mathews   "Rethinking Homeless Myths," *Newsweek*, April 6, 1992.

Katie Monagle   "Desperate Measures? The Homeless: Should Cities Evict Street People from Public Places?" *Scholastic Update* (teachers' edition), January 10, 1992.

Daniel Radosh   "Instant Empathy," *The New Republic*, May 18, 1992.

Eric Rubenstein   "Homelessness and Values," *Vital Speeches of the Day*, April 15, 1992.

Lynne Sharon Schwartz   "Beggaring Our Better Selves," *Harper's*, December 1991.

Betsy Streisand   "Gimme Shelter," *U.S. News & World Report*, February 3, 1992.

USA Today   "Homelessness Is Harmful to Health," April 1992.

David Whitman   "Exodus of the 'Couch People,'" *U.S. News & World Report*, December 23, 1991.

How Can Urban Crime Be Reduced?

Chapter Preface

In September 1992, two car thieves forced a successful Maryland chemist, Pamela Basu, out of her BMW. As Basu tried to rescue her young daughter from a rear car seat, Basu caught her arm in the car's shoulder harness. As the criminals sped away, Basu was dragged to her death. The suspects then stopped the car and threw Basu's child on the side of the road. They were arrested after crashing one hour later.

The crime that caused Basu's death is known as "carjacking." In 1992, America's cities witnessed a rash of these previously rare crimes in which thieves use guns, knives, or brute strength to force drivers to give up their automobiles. The Basu case generated so much outrage that Congress deemed carjacking a federal crime. Besides carjacking, other types of serious crime—murder, rape, armed robbery, and assault—continue to plague cities. Indeed, in 1990, according to the *Christian Science Monitor*, "More than a dozen U.S. cities—from Boston to New Orleans to Oakland—have broken homicide records."

The Basu case illustrates that poor urban residents are no longer the only victims of urban crime. People from all classes are being victimized. According to *Newsweek* writers John McCormick and Bill Turque: "The capricious brutality of big-city crime has metastasized to smaller communities long envied for their relative safety and civility."

The spread of crime has Americans more concerned than ever about how to protect themselves. While some people call for more police protection and tougher laws, other more frustrated residents believe that a stronger response is necessary. Consequently, they are acquiring guns or patrolling their neighborhoods to safeguard their homes and themselves. The following viewpoints consider these and other possible solutions to the high rate of urban crime.

"When uniformed officers patrol drug markets on foot, customers and dealers are reluctant to do business."

Enforcing Drug Laws Reduces Urban Crime

Roger L. Conner and Patrick C. Burns

A combination of effective drug law enforcement and community intervention can eradicate drug dealing and drug-related crime from cities, Roger L. Conner and Patrick C. Burns argue in the following viewpoint. Conner and Burns contend that traditional police strategies have failed to reduce drug sales. Police should instead eliminate whole street drug markets, the authors believe, with the help of civilian patrols, whose presence can force drug dealers and their customers out of neighborhoods. Conner and Burns are, respectively, executive director and assistant director of the American Alliance for Rights and Responsibilities, a Washington, D.C., organization concerned with the interests and legal rights of communities.

As you read, consider the following questions:

1. Why are current street drug markets more violent than private drug markets in the 1970s, according to Conner and Burns?
2. Why do the authors believe that police "buy-and-bust" campaigns have failed to reduce drug dealing?
3. According to Conner and Burns, how can the use of telephone beepers by police reduce drug sales?

Roger L. Conner and Patrick C. Burns, "The Winnable War: How Communities Are Eradicating Local Drug Markets," *The Brookings Review*, Summer 1992. Reprinted with permission.

Over the years the "war on drugs" has been fought on many fronts, both international and domestic. Policymakers have tried to attack the "root of the problem" by launching assaults on border traffickers, spraying defoliants on South American drug crops, sending Drug Enforcement Agency teams to destroy jungle cocaine labs, seizing boats on the high seas, attacking money laundering schemes, and even by invading a foreign country. At home, politicians have called for more jails, better drug education, federally funded drug treatment, improved schools, and a return to basic family values.

The combination of all these tactics appears to be slowly working. Although marijuana was openly smoked in Lafayette Park across from the White House in the 1970s, it is now rare to see anyone smoking marijuana on the street. And although drug use steadily increased during most of the 1970s and early 1980s, the *National Household Survey on Drug Abuse* reports a 50 percent decline in monthly drug use between 1985 and 1990.

Neighborhood Concern

Yet community concern at the grass roots level has escalated consistently. The reasons for this are as current as this morning's headlines. Into once thriving neighborhoods has crept a culture of fear, with children sleeping in bathtubs to avoid stray bullets, old people afraid to walk to the store, and parents afraid to send their children to the park because of the litter of crack vials and spent syringes.

In hospitals across the nation thousands of drug-damaged infants languish in neonatal wards. Brazen street drug dealers, with gold chains on their necks and telephone beepers affixed to their side, make a mockery of every anti-drug message our children hear in school, at home, in church.

Though public policy generals cite statistics to show we are winning the war on drugs, the foot soldiers on the front lines are cynically skeptical. For them, the issue is not the number of drug users in America, but the proximity of drug dealers to their bedrooms, school rooms, and board rooms.

The number of street drug markets has exploded since the introduction of PCP and crack cocaine in the early and mid-1980s. Combined with the entry of new ethnic and youth gangs, these street markets have become pervasive, unstable, and violent. The result has been a rapid deterioration in law and order in America's largest cities. A whole new set of pathologies, unimaginable just 10 years ago, has risen to the forefront of the national consciousness: drive-by shootings, generalized community terror, and a rapid decline in urban property values.

Although illegal drug use, at some level, is here to stay, there is nothing inevitable about street drug markets. They scarcely existed 15 years ago. In the mid-1970s drug users relied on a private referral market where sales took place indoors between people who had at least a passing acquaintance with each other. These markets were (and still are) rarely violent, do not tempt children or recovering addicts, and do not depress local housing markets.

By eradicating street drug markets, communities can go "back to the future," when drug sales resulted in little collateral damage to residential neighborhoods.

Drug Markets: How They Work

The open-air drug market or crack house is the 7-Eleven of the drug trade, making up in quantity of transactions what it misses in size of sales. While a drug dealer in the private referral market may make just a few sales a week, a drug dealer operating in a street market or crack house may make dozens of sales in a single day.

To make so many sales, street drug dealers must have many customers and make sales quickly. They must effectively colonize specific locations so that customers can, with some degree of confidence, keep returning to buy drugs. Dealers know that if they change location they cannot easily advertise the move and so will lose customers.

Street drug markets are also highly specialized. By selling just one drug at a known price (such as vials containing $20 rocks of crack cocaine), dealers can make sales without making change or even much conversation. A street drug sale can be completed in less than 10 seconds.

Most neighborhoods, including poor, urban, minority neighborhoods, are not plagued by flagrant drug dealers. The reason is simple: a thriving street drug market operation requires a particular kind of neighborhood, usually one that has four distinct characteristics.

First, drug dealers are not interested in setting up shop in clean, well-lighted neighborhoods with strong community associations. They know such communities will not tolerate their activities. Instead, dealers gravitate to neighborhoods with poorly maintained yards, abandoned cars, overgrown lots, and poor street lighting—obvious signs that a community is poorly organized to defend itself against street dealers and has already accepted a certain level of disorder.

Second, drug dealers need a legitimate cover for their presence on the street. It can be a bar, a restaurant or convenience store, a school or housing development, or even a car wash. When people are naturally coming and going from an area, drug dealers are better able to blend into the crowd and post a legal defense if arrested.

Third, drug dealers are drawn to poor communities that frequently have large numbers of poorly supervised children. These children, hungry for money, are easy to recruit as lookouts and salesmen. If arrested, they are likely to get off with little more than probation.

Winning the War in Tampa, Florida

During June 1989, about three months after the QUAD [Quick Uniform Attack on Drugs] Squads went into action, drug arrests were more than double what they had been that month the year before. In the first year, QUAD officers arrested 1929 sellers and 543 buyers; uniformed officers nailed another 2522.

From 1987 to 1990 robberies dropped 15 percent, burglaries 14 percent and larceny 24 percent. Of the 150 dope holes identified, about 140 showed little or no activity, while volume at the ten remaining was greatly reduced. . . .

Tampa's example shows what police action with community support can do for drug-infested neighborhoods. "We're well on the way," says mayor Abe Brown. "With cooperation from the community, churches and law enforcement, we can clean up street drug sales in this city. Many dealers have packed up and gone elsewhere. People can sit on their porches and walk the streets. And Tampa is once again a decent place to raise children."

Eugene H. Methvin, *Reader's Digest*, July 1991.

Finally, drug markets are dependent on a steady stream of customers and a means of quick escape. Markets are usually accessible by car, with dealers naturally gravitating to locations where police patrols can be spotted at least a block away. When the police show up, dealers want to exit quickly—into nearby housing developments, bars, or other hard-to-reach areas.

If a neighborhood has these characteristics, a drug dealer will probably test the local business waters. If not, he will probably pass on by.

Why Conventional Enforcement Is Not Working

The traditional police response to street drug markets is to send in undercover officers to buy drugs and arrest the dealers. But despite their popularity, buy-and-bust operations alone almost never break the back of an entrenched drug market. As long as customers keep coming to a known drug market location, the market is able to recruit new dealers.

Buy-and-bust arrests present the same kind of minor logistical problems a suburban shopping mall faces when labor force turnover is unusually high. As long as customers keep coming, both the drug market and the shopping mall will attract new workers and continue to do business with scarcely a hitch. Even if arrested, street dealers will, as a rule, suffer nothing more than inconvenience. Because of court and jail overcrowding (in part due to buy-and-bust arrests), most street dealers will receive little or no jail time even if they have previously been arrested for misdemeanor drug sales.

Yet despite its ineffectiveness, surveys indicate that the buy-and-bust operation is the only anti-drug-market technique used regularly by big-city police departments. Its continued popularity stems from both internal and external police evaluation systems. Individual officers regularly visit "drug holes" to make arrests in much the same way a fisherman will visit a proven fishing hole. In addition, highly visible buy-and-bust campaigns show public, press, and politicians that "something" is being done to counter the epidemic of drugs and violence in the streets. Like generals in a conventional war, police use "body count" statistics to show that the war on drugs is being won and that more officers and bigger budgets will be needed to wage an even more effective campaign.

Getting the police to abandon buy-and-bust techniques will require changing the way police are evaluated. One step, which some cities are beginning to take, is to stop grading officers and units on the number of arrests made and instead hold them accountable for the number of street drug *markets* in their area of patrol. For Tampa, Florida, this simple step helped cut drug markets 95 percent.

Other Cities' Successful Efforts

Tampa is not alone in its success. A Charleston, South Carolina, program designed to cripple the mechanics of street drug sales drove dealers out of town—and into nearby North Charleston, where local police cling to the old ways of doing business. In Chicago, drug dealers were systematically denied access to public housing, and gang-plagued high-rise developments began to turn around after more than two decades of combat-zone conditions.

These examples of success are islands in a sea of generalized failure. In the nation's 15 largest cities police report more than 1,500 flagrant or open-air drug markets. Three-quarters of responding police departments report that their local drug market problems are getting no better or are getting worse. Yet failure is not universal. What are successful communities doing that the others are not?

Police action can temporarily clean up a neighborhood. But to drive drug dealers and buyers away from an entrenched market,

116

the community must show it is willing to pick up where the police leave off. Drug dealers must believe that they are fighting not just the police, but an entire community.

Organized community patrols, identified by a common hat or T-shirt, and armed with walkie-talkies, clip boards, video cameras, and bull horns, have successfully broadcast community intolerance for drug sales in Washington, D.C., New York City, Philadelphia, and dozens of other cities. Citizen patrols use positive moral force, backed up by the implied threat of police action, to drive drug dealers and their customers out of residential neighborhoods. When citizen patrols record license plate numbers and videotape drug sales, dealers and their drive-through traffic generally beat a hasty retreat.

Community clean-up programs are also important. By removing abandoned cars, installing street lights, clearing abandoned lots of brush and trash, and sweeping streets and alleys, a community signals that it is willing to defend its space. In Tampa more than 80 tons of trash were hauled out of a single community in one day, thereby depriving dealers of places to stash drugs. Noted one amazed resident, "Getting rid of drug dealers is just like getting rid of rats: once you put the trash in barrels and haul it away neither one feels comfortable anymore."

Neighborhoods Can Reclaim Marketing Space

Street drug markets and crack houses require a stable location. If they move, they cannot advertise their new addresses to existing customers, and so market efficiency declines. The more often the market must move, the less likely it is to return a profit and stay in business.

As many as four steps may be necessary to force dealers to move. First, community leaders should examine the sales location itself. Can it be abolished through eviction, a property closing, a property seizure, or by razing an abandoned and unsalvageable building? If so, they should talk with local property managers, housing inspectors, the city council representative, or the city attorney responsible for property seizure.

Second, leaders should examine customer and dealer entrance and escape routes. If the drug market is in a public housing development, the aim is to keep nonresident dealers and customers out of the buildings. In Chicago, legislation requiring residents to be listed on the lease and to carry a photo-ID card to gain entrance helped prevent nonresident customers and dealers from entering the buildings and using them to conduct business and escape police.

Third, it may be necessary to enact legislation to outlaw the mechanics of street drug sales. In Tampa and in Tacoma, Washington, local anti-drug-related loitering laws proscribe a narrow band of activity common to street drug sales but uncommon to legitimate activity: loitering in a drug market area, waving to passing cars, engaging in multiple brief meetings with passing motorists and cars, and covertly exchanging small packages for money. When these activities are seen together, police can enforce local laws that make it a crime to loiter with the intent to sell drugs.

Fighting Crime in Public Housing

Our efforts to improve public housing and to close down open-air drug markets have yielded unintended benefits for Charleston. As the success of our crime-reduction strategies has become more widely known in South Carolina, areas around Charleston have petitioned to become part of our city. . . .

We found that simply by targeting specific neighborhoods we could have an immediate and lasting reduction of street-level drug dealing and the victimization associated with it. We also proved that it was possible over time to reduce significantly the incidence of crime in public housing.

Reuben M. Greenberg, *Policy Review*, Winter 1992.

Finally, it may be necessary to remove existing drug market "enablers." These enablers may range from public telephones used by dealers to conduct business, to bars, dance clubs, and convenience and liquor stores that serve as restocking and meeting places for drug market activity. Pay telephones can be removed or altered so that they no longer receive incoming calls or make beeper calls. Bars and stores can be forced to cooperate either through pickets and rallies or through liquor and business license revocation.

The overt message of open-air drug markets is that both dealers and customers can conduct business with virtual impunity. As a result, drug dealers have little trouble recruiting youths to sell drugs or buyers to buy them.

One way to remove that sense of impunity is to increase the visible police presence in the neighborhood, particularly around the drug market. When uniformed officers patrol drug markets on foot, customers and dealers are reluctant to do business. When the dealers move, police should move with them, shadowing their activities and hampering their trade.

The efficiency of police patrols can also be increased. In Tampa, local anti-drug-market officers make sure that local citizens know their telephone beeper numbers. A citizen who witnesses street drug sales can page an officer and get an immediate response by phone. The result has been improved citizen-police cooperation and a dramatic citywide decline in street drug activity.

Drug buyers and sellers must face penalties. Because 40 states are now under court order to reduce prison overcrowding, penalties must be found that do not involve incarceration. One particularly effective penalty is seizing cars used by drive-through drug customers. Putting seized cars on display at local malls, schools, and recreation centers, and posting banners across selected streets ("Car Seizure Program in Progress: Drive In for Drugs and Walk Out") can reduce drive-through drug sales to a standstill.

Successful community-based anti-drug-market efforts use a variety of techniques, laws, and methods, but all work to break the back of drug market *mechanisms* rather than merely to maximize dealer arrests. By focusing on that objective, while eschewing the larger issues of reducing generalized drug use and solving deep-seated social problems, most individual neighborhoods manage quickly to achieve measurable success. . . .

Individuals Make a Stand

Successful anti-drug-market efforts begin with specific individuals standing up and accepting responsibility for solving their community problems. In Charleston, it was the police chief; in Tampa, a Baptist minister; in Chicago, the chairman of the local housing authority; in New York City, the leader of a local community association.

Each of these individuals, independent of the others, crafted his own anti-drug-market program whole-cloth. What they had in common was not race, religion, or job description, but a commitment to action and the conviction that their communities were worth fighting for. From Tacoma to Fort Lauderdale, diverse communities have shown that freedom from street drug markets is possible if individuals will take responsibility for finding local solutions. As one member of a Bronx clergy group put it, "Change starts when you stop talking and start walking the streets. It's dangerous if you fight them because they'll threaten you, maybe rob you. But if you don't do anything, they'll take over your street and rob you too. You're a prisoner no matter how you look at it. The only question is, how do you want to serve your time."

*"'Drug-related crime' has become the single
largest result of the War on Drugs. "*

Enforcing Drug Laws
Escalates Urban Crime

Sam Staley

Many Americans believe that the war on drugs has failed to
both reduce the supply of drugs and the demand for them. In
the following viewpoint, Sam Staley agrees and argues that the
prohibition of drugs is responsible for an increase in urban
crime and violence. Staley maintains that many crimes are committed by drug dealers who use violence to protect themselves
and their illegal trade, and by drug users who commit crimes to
get money for drugs. The author believes that helping drug
users end their addiction would be a more effective way of reducing drug-related crime. Staley is president of the Urban
Policy Research Institute, a Dayton, Ohio, organization that
studies urban issues.

As you read, consider the following questions:

1. Why do drug dealers regard many customers as potential
   enemies, according to Staley?
2. In Staley's opinion, how can restrictions in drug supplies lead
   to more violence among drug dealers?
3. How does crime prevent investment in inner-city
   neighborhoods, according to the author?

From Sam Staley, *Drug Policy and the Decline of American Cities*, © 1992 by Transaction
Publishers, New Brunswick, NJ 08903. Reprinted with permission.

The criminal justice system is but one of many urban institutions being crushed under the weight of the War on Drugs. Almost every local government service, including schools, health care, juvenile services, and neighborhood development and job training, is underfunded because billions of dollars are being syphoned off to pay for a failed national drug strategy. That money would be much better spent if it were invested in public education, Head Start, prenatal care, and other services designed to help children grow up healthy, smart, and full of self-esteem. Such an investment would also be a giant step toward fairness and justice. There are now more African-American men under the control of the criminal justice system than there are in college. There is something profoundly wrong with a policy that leads to such an unjust outcome. The fact of the matter is, those with the least hope, the least education, and the least chance of achieving economic opportunity are bearing most of the burden of drug addiction, incarceration, and drug-related crime. . . .

Drug-related killings currently make up substantial proportions of all homicides in major American cities. In Washington, D.C., an estimated 60 percent of all homicides were considered drug related. In Dade County, Florida, officials estimate that over one-third of the homicides were connected in some way to the drug trade, while one-fourth of homicides in New York City were classified as drug related.

Indeed, most law enforcement officials blame the recent rise in urban violence on the drug trade. "In much the same way that the traditional Mafia uses professional contract killers to settle its disputes," notes author Steven Wisotsky, "cocaine traffickers also require private methods of security, discipline, and punishment."

Drug Laws Send Mixed Messages

American drug laws send mixed and confusing signals to unemployed, undereducated inner-city teenagers. On one level, the legal system is set up to protect the right of citizens to do what they want as long as they do not harm others in the process. The legal system supposedly protects the right of people to engage in voluntary exchanges as long as the transactions respect their respective individual rights (as stipulated in the Constitution and the legal code).

On the other hand, the most visible part of the criminal justice system is geared toward an activity that, in addition to being one of the few lucrative employment activities, does not directly harm others. Drug sales are completely voluntary. No one can be forced to buy drugs. In addition, street-level sales rarely involve violence. In fact, if a dealer developed a reputation for violence among his normal customers, he would likely be out of business quickly as his customers found more passive suppliers. Yet, the legal system does not protect those contracts. Contract enforcement is left to the specific needs and individual judgement of the dealer.

In the absence of the peaceful dispute resolution available through the legal system, contract enforcement inevitably becomes violent. Violence is also becoming an accepted part of drug dealer behavior because the trade is inherently constrained by uncertainty, deception, and theft. A dealer often does not know if his customer is an undercover policeman, a rival drug dealer moving in on his territory, or a normal customer. In order to protect his market and reduce the likelihood of being arrested, the drug dealer is forced to consider anyone a potential enemy and demonstrate a willingness to take whatever means necessary to protect his business. . . .

Governments on all levels have mounted an impressive campaign against illicit drugs for decades. Earlier enforcement efforts, however, paled in comparison to that mounted in the 1980s. In 1982, the federal government allocated a mere $3 billion to the War. By 1990, federal expenditures had ballooned to over $10 billion. To help finance state, local, and federal drug law enforcement efforts, over $1 billion in assets were seized by law enforcement personnel from 1985 to 1990. These efforts represent the most recent version of the nation's commitment to the War on Drugs. . . .

Drug-Related Crime

Unfortunately, the effects of the War on Drugs are not neutral. Many consider efforts to enforce drug prohibition as a zero sum game, where any reduction in the supply of drugs should be considered a social benefit weighed only against the resources spent to control drug use and distribution. Attempts to arrest users and traffickers may be, in reality, a negative sum game.

If the demand for drugs continues unabated, restrictions on supply will simply increase the profits to entrepreneurs willing to take the risks necessary to produce and supply drugs on the black market. The higher the potential profits are, the more likely drug markets will become violent and socially disruptive. Of course higher profits also represent the increased risks associated with the drug trade, but this simply suggests that the suppliers are less risk-averse than previous participants.

The cost of crime as a consequence of America's drug problem is well-known although misinterpreted. The standard approach is that drug users commit crimes and, therefore, drug users cause crime. Bernard A. Gropper, an experimental psychologist and specialist on the relationship between drug use and crime, concluded a review of research on crime and drug abuse by observing,

> perhaps the foremost finding is that heroin abusers, especially daily users, commit an extraordinary amount of crime. These studies reveal a lifestyle that is enveloped in drug use and crime. The major impetus for most of their criminal behavior is the need to obtain heroin or opiates.

In fact, there is a wide body of literature linking trends in drug use and the amount of crime committed. As drug users move into an addictive stage in their life, they tend to commit more crime. Further, daily users and addicts tend to earn the vast majority of their income through crime to sustain their habit.

Yet the correlation between drug use and crime does not establish causality. There is an important intermediate stage in the analysis that is left out of the standard perspective. If the drug user is capable of sustaining his or her habit through a legitimate income source, participation in illegal activities is restricted to those required to purchase illegal drugs (not the commission of non-drug-related crime). The root of the criminal activity stemming from drug use flows from users' inability to afford their habit.

The Costs of Drug Abuse

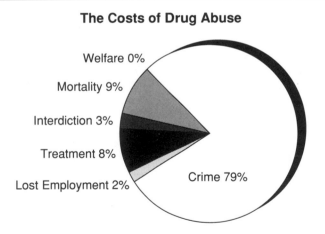

Welfare 0%
Mortality 9%
Interdiction 3%
Treatment 8%
Lost Employment 2%
Crime 79%

Source: James Ostrowski, "Thinking About Drug Legalization," *Policy Analysis No. 121,* Washington, DC: Cato Institute, May 1989.

Ironically, the War on Drugs, which is aimed at reducing the supply of illicit drugs, will if successful drive up prices and increase crime by drug users. According to data compiled by scholars at the Research Triangle Institute in North Carolina, the costs of drug abuse in the United States amounted to $60 billion in 1983, although $33.3 billion was attributed to marijuana. While the data is outdated, the breakdown of costs is useful for understanding the importance of crime as an inherent part of America's drug problem.

James Ostrowski revised the costs of drug abuse in the Research Triangle study, excluding the costs for marijuana for methodological reasons. Based on total costs of drug abuse of $26.4 billion in 1983, almost 80 percent of the discounted costs are attributable to crime alone. All other categories pale in comparison to the importance of crime in understanding the drug problem in the United States. The emphasis of law enforcement personnel on arresting and incarcerating criminals is understandable in this context. But, to the extent current policy artificially raises prices, making the acquisition of illicit drugs expensive, criminality is an artifact of drug prohibition rather than drug use.

Drug Supply and Demand

Attempts to reduce the supply of illicit drugs may also be contributing to the demand side of the drug problem. A survey of 13,711 inmates in state prisons conducted in 1986 by the U.S. Bureau of Justice Statistics found that most had first used a major drug *after* their first arrest. While only 9 percent reported first use of a major drug in the year preceding and succeeding their arrest, 43 percent reported their first drug use one or more years after their first arrest. Incarceration may be associated with increased drug use rather than reduced drug use.

Moreover, the War on Drugs appears to have had little effect on drug availability. According to the National Institute on Drug Abuse's ongoing survey of high school seniors, the availability of all major drugs increased throughout the 1980s. The proportion of high school students indicating cocaine was "very easy" or "fairly easy" to obtain increased from 47.9 percent in 1980 to 58.7 percent in 1989. Crack, a late arrival to the drug scene, also increased in availability: 40 percent of seniors polled in 1987 found easy access to crack compared to 47 percent in 1989.

Not only does the criminal justice system run the risk of increasing drug use, the current strategy is undermining the institutional foundations for peaceful and progressive community development. By encouraging the breakdown of the rule of law and the respect for private property rights, current drug policy may promote poverty by increasing drug-related crime. Most inner cities suffer because their residents are victims of crime. Most people, for example, are killed or victimized by people within their own neighborhood ("predatory street criminals"). Crime prevents investment in inner-city neighborhoods by threatening property values, endangering lives, and increasing the costs of doing business in the city. . . .

Consensus does not exist on the proper drug control strategy on any level of government. While most people are convinced that drugs are inherently "bad" and should not be encouraged, large numbers of Americans routinely use them. In the case of alcohol, consumption is so ingrained in American culture that few argue for alcohol prohibition.

Several different drug control strategies are possible. The current strategy focuses on complete prohibition of select drugs for recreational use. These drugs are determined, for the most part, politically, with little concern for medical opinion on their mentally or physically damaging qualities. A policy of prohibition is virtually impossible to implement successfully. The prohibition policy is even harder to maintain given the lack of consensus among the public and the law enforcement agencies responsible for drug law enforcement on the overall importance of the drug problem. . . .

Some insights from the experience of national and state-level alcohol policy may help provide insight in determining the proper role of public policy. The most extreme policy option, prohibition, was attempted briefly in the 1920s and repealed in 1933. Alcohol prohibition was repealed, however, not because public policy was unable to affect consumption or the alcoholic beverage industry. Alcohol prohibition was repealed because the effects of a prohibitionist policy outweighed the costs of allowing alcohol to be consumed through a regulated policy framework.

Effect of Prohibition on Alcohol Consumption

Indeed, a recent analysis of alcohol consumption before, during, and after Prohibition reveals that legalization did not significantly increase consumption levels. While the initial effect of Prohibition was to reduce alcohol consumption by two-thirds, consumption levels rose to between 60 and 70 percent of pre-Prohibition levels throughout the 1920s. Consumption rose to 65 percent of pre-Prohibition levels by 1925 and to 71 percent by 1929. A comparison with alcohol consumption in the 1920s to the period 1937 to 1940 reveals that alcohol consumption levels remained approximately equal. Thus, Prohibition had an immediate, but not enduring impact, on the level of alcohol consumption.

Another twenty-five year study of alcoholic beverage restrictions on the state level between 1955 and 1980 reveals more important information with respect to the role of public policy. The researchers found that the price of the beverage had the strongest impact on consumption during the period studied. They also found that certain regulatory variables such as the number of outlets and the method of licensing could impact consumption levels within states. More traditional variables such as advertising, hours of the day, and the drinking age had little or no effect.

Problems with Prohibition

This evidence shows that prohibition may not work if the goal is to eliminate drug use altogether. While proponents of alcohol prohibition may point to the *relative* success of the laws in their first years, the long-term effect was substantially weaker. *Public policy was unable to eliminate the market for alcohol*. Similarly, public policy has been unable to eliminate the market for illicit substances such as heroin, cocaine, and marijuana. Moreover, public policy was able to influence consumption largely through its impact on price.

The lesson from this era is not that public policy is ineffective. On the contrary, public policy has a significant impact on black markets for illegal products. Prohibition allowed alcohol distribution to become more concentrated in the hands of organized crime and allowed distilleries to avoid careful regulation of their product's quality.

Higher Drug Prices Equal More Crime

Florida's police devoted a growing share of their resources to drug law enforcement during the 1980s. Drug arrests rose 90% between 1982 and 1987, while total arrests increased only 32%. But instead of subsiding in the wake of the stepped-up war against drugs, property crimes also escalated. Between 1983 and 1987, for example, robbery rates climbed 34% and auto theft rates jumped 65%.

In the past, economists have explained such increases in crime by noting that drug users have an inelastic demand for drugs. Since greater enforcement of drug laws presumably drives up drug prices, addicts have to step up their criminal activities to pay for their habit.

Business Week, December 2, 1991.

Thus, what is important is *the way* public policy influences the market for illegal products. Policy has important implications for determining the structure and characteristics of an industry. A prohibitionist policy explicitly rejects any regulatory role for the industry even though a regulatory strategy appears to have the most profound impact on the consumption and structure of the industry. . . .

Drug prohibition, however, is unlikely to solve what now constitutes the nation's drug problem. The drug problem is no longer simply the costs of drug addiction and resulting behavior. Rather the costs associated with the trappings of prohibition—crime and violence—have eclipsed drug addiction as the central problem with drug use in the nation. As a result, continued efforts to use law enforcement to stop the flow and distribution of drugs into domestic markets and reduce demand for drugs by arresting users is likely to compound the problem rather than solve it.

This does not mean that drug prohibition will not reduce the aggregate consumption of illicit substances. Indeed, current law enforcement programs may be able to increase the cost of using drugs sufficiently to deter some from experimenting with drugs. The consequences of these policies, however, are to raise the prices to addicts and nonaddicts willing to pay the price for recreational drug use.

The result, as the events of the 1980s have demonstrated, is a highly profitable and violent drug trade. "Drug-related crime" has become the single largest result of the War on Drugs. Eliminating drug crime will only be accomplished by pursuing policies that are more sensitive to the problems of the drug user rather than to the entrepreneurial desires of drug traffickers.

"Community policing is essential to insure both the perception and reality of the public safety and quality of life in the city."

Police-Community Partnerships Reduce Urban Crime

Lee P. Brown

Lee P. Brown is a former president of the International Association of Chiefs of Police and served as New York City police commissioner from 1990 to 1992. In the following viewpoint, Brown argues that police-community partnerships, or "community policing," can reduce urban crime, primarily through increased police officer foot patrols. Brown contends that these regular neighborhood patrols heighten officers' visibility, thus deterring crime and making residents feel safe. This strategy, Brown maintains, fosters contact and cooperation between the police and neighborhood residents and encourages residents to report drug dealing and other criminal activities.

As you read, consider the following questions:

1. What criticisms does Brown make of police car patrols?
2. According to Brown, how can police departments use personnel more efficiently to increase foot patrols?
3. Why does the author believe that civilians are important in formulating police strategies?

Lee P. Brown, "Bring the Community into the Battle Against Crime," a lecture given at Long Island University, New York, NY, March 11, 1992.

We examine tonight what I consider to be one of the leading, if not *the* paramount issue concerning public administration for the 1990s, and well into the 21st Century. And that is the way we police urban America in the face of social stratification, economic uncertainty, family break-up, and other issues which have consequences the police must deal with, but over which the police have little control.

The public becomes acutely aware of the consequences when they are dramatized by a particularly horrific act, like the shooting deaths of students by a student *inside* a school. But the less dramatic incidents and the wide-spread availability and use of guns and drugs and alcohol . . . all of these lead to numbing statistics.

One that is particularly compelling for the African American community is that homicide is now the leading cause of death of young black men. Low level street crime and nuisances also combine to make life in many urban neighborhoods *feel* as dangerous as actual life-threatening situations. Collectively, street disturbances, vandalism, prostitution and the like create a hostile environment that invite more serious crime, and at the very least, intimidate law-abiding citizens.

An Essential Crime Strategy

Ultimately, a safe environment and the *perception* of a safe environment are important to the long-term health of the city. I believe that community policing is essential to insure both the perception and reality of the public safety and quality of life in the city. And I also believe that community policing is the future of policing in America. In New York, we have adopted community policing as dominant philosophy and operational style, and we are now actively implementing it throughout the five boroughs.

What is community policing? It is a working partnership between the police and the law-abiding public to prevent crime, arrest offenders, find solutions to repeat problems, and ultimately to enhance the quality of life in the city, particularly in its residential neighborhoods where we are bringing back the old-fashioned cop on the beat, but in a modern way.

My vision of community policing is to have a police officer or a group of officers and their supervisors responsible for every street or group of streets in the city. I want police officers to know the community well. I want them to form partnerships with clergy, community leaders, merchants and others to find solutions to recurring crime-related problems.

In New York City, community policing means getting more police officers out of the patrol car, on foot and into the community. The conventional way to police a city has been to deploy officers in radio-equipped patrol cars, randomly patrolling a given area until they are dispatched to the scene of a 911 emergency. The officers respond to emergencies, but they never get to know a community well. They keep responding to the same situations, over and over again. With the advent of the radio-equipped patrol car, police officers in city after city become incident responders, not problem solvers. It was thought to be an efficient way to police a large city. It also discouraged familiarity with the people we serve. The concern a few decades back was that familiarity bred the kind of corruption that was uncovered in the Police Department by the Knapp Commission. But there are ample safeguards against corruption now in place in the Police Department. So we can encourage close contact with the community without the fear of corruption.

Police Patrol Studies

As to the efficiency, a landmark study showed that conventional, routine motorized patrol was never the efficient deployment of resources that many assumed. Known as the Kansas City Preventive Patrol Experiment, and conducted by the National Police Foundation, the Kansas City study found that traditional routine patrol in marked police cars did not appear to affect the level of crime. Nor did routine motorized patrol affect the public's feeling of security. Most importantly, the study demonstrated that urban police departments could test various deployment strategies without jeopardizing public safety. Another study was the Fear Reduction Experiment, carried out simultaneously in Newark and Houston. It showed that increased communication between police and community reduced fear of crime, and, in some instances, crime itself.

The result of these studies over the years pointed to community policing. The questioning of total reliance on radio car patrols . . . the positive community response to foot patrols . . . the importance of improving police-community communication and cooperation. They all pointed to community policing. Much like the goal of the cops of a by-gone era, the goal of the community police officer is, ultimately, to have nothing happen on his beat. Instead of measuring police success by the number of arrests, we should measure it by the absence of crime . . . by the peace and stability on the street.

New York City is particularly well studied for community policing because of the density of its population, and its history with community policing programs. New York City's history with foot patrol goes all the way back to the Dutch in 1625, and the original "night watch," which was a foot patrol assigned to citizens as a civic duty. New York City also created the original cop on the beat. In 1970, the Police Department introduced a program called Neighborhood Police Teams, designed to operate in a problem-solving mode. But the teams were disbanded in the city's fiscal crisis of the mid-1970s.

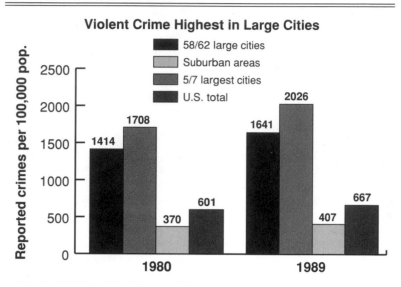

Violent Crime Highest in Large Cities

- 58/62 large cities
- Suburban areas
- 5/7 largest cities
- U.S. total

Reported crimes per 100,000 pop.

Source: FBI Uniform Crime Reports, 1990.

In 1984, the Community Police Officer Program, or CPOP, was introduced in the 72nd Precinct in Brooklyn, and expanded as a limited program in all precincts in 1988. But now, instead of a program, we are making problem-solving, community policing the dominant style and philosophy of the entire department. The introduction of community policing is coinciding with a significant expansion in the uniformed strength of the Police Department.

Police Efficiency

One of my first acts as police commissioner was to undertake a study of the New York City Police Department to determine whether its staffing configuration was adequate to meeting mounting demands of the last two decades. It was the first such study of the New York City Police Department in a quarter century. And we discovered, yes, we needed more cops. But we also found we could be a lot more efficient. We discovered we had become over-specialized. We found we could consolidate and eliminate some specialized units, and free up more police officers for patrol. We also found that police officers were doing jobs that civilians could handle, so we could free up police officers for patrol and other enforcement duties by using civilians for non-enforcement tasks.

That staffing study was one of the key elements in the Mayor's "Safe Streets, Safe City" program, which was passed in 1991 by the City Council and State Legislature. Funds for "Safe Streets" were put into a dedicated fund. They may *not* be used for any other purpose. The plan provides for an overall increase of 23 percent in our uniformed headcount, from a 1990 base of 25,465 uniformed personnel, to 31,351 as of July 1, 1995.

While this overall increase is certainly significant, we will experience a 50 percent increase in uniformed officers assigned to precincts through the new hires and by taking every opportunity to put police officers back in uniform. Even before the "Safe Streets, Safe City" program was approved, we devised and implemented ways to increase police visibility. For example, in Operation All Out, we required Headquarters personnel and other officers performing non-patrol duties to return to patrol, in uniform, on foot, for an average of one tour a week.

Increased Police Coverage

As a result, we have added 150,000 tours of duty since April 1990. That is the equivalent of hiring 350 additional police officers. Similarly, by refining the way we dispatch 911 calls in non-life-threatening cases, that do not require police presence, we are reducing 911 responses by an estimated 450,000 radio runs annually. That is the equivalent of 752 police officers. It means we can devote all the time once consumed by this 911 coverage to policing the neighborhoods in ways that give the police officers a chance to get out of their cars and into the community to better understand the people and their problems.

Police visibility and neighborhood contact are at the heart of the community policing philosophy. So are partnerships.We want to build partnerships that bring community people into the decision-making process to combat crime.

As part of community policing in New York, we have created precinct management teams in each of the city's 75 precincts. The teams are comprised of the precinct commanding officer and other key precinct personnel, along with the local community board district manager, and the precinct community council president. This is something new. This is the first time in the history of American policing that civilian members of the community are being directly engaged to regularly develop police strategy at the ground level.

Once the problems have been identified and a strategy is developed and implemented, the team regroups to measure the effectiveness of the strategies they chose. And once a problem is evaluated as either "corrected" or "significantly improved," the management team replaces it with another problem on the list of precinct priorities.

Let me give you an example of how community policing and precinct management teams were used to fight a chronic problem in Brooklyn's 72nd Precinct, which also happens to be the precinct we are using as a model to develop a number of community policing strategies. On three blocks of just one street— 49th Street—we had made 418 arrests in 1991, mainly for various drug offenses. Still, the street was under the virtual control of a few area drug dealers who operated with a significant degree of impunity due, in part, because of the fear of law-abiding people.

The people were afraid that cooperation with the police would be met with retaliation as long as the dealers had their freedom. 49th Street became the number one priority of the precinct management team. With support from the precinct's Special Operations Unit, the Major Case Team of the Brooklyn South Narcotics Division, the District Attorney's office, and the courts which issued the warrants, eight major dealers were identified, arrested and charged with various felonies, including murder. This sweep happened one night with the deployment of various Department resources, including helicopters to frustrate any attempt by the targets to flee.

Cops and Citizens

The goal of community policing is to transform big-city policing into a community-oriented game of "cops and citizens." The image of policing it beckons is of cops on foot patrol, listening to community residents, working with community leaders and groups, coordinating problem-solving activities with other government agencies, and using their authority and resources in ways that the public understands and approves.

John J. DiIulio Jr., *The Brookings Review*, Fall 1992.

Within hours, community members who had been afraid to come forward, were reporting to the police about the effect of the sweep on lower level associates of those arrested. They reported, in short, that the bad guys were panicking, and law-abiding people had their confidence restored. However, at its next meeting, the management team recognized that once the panic in the drug underworld subsided, there would be a rush by other dealers to fill the vacuum.

The management team recommended continued street level enforcement and high uniformed visibility along 49th Street, and that adjoining areas be targeted for increased drug enforcement. The civilian members of the management team also maintained contact with the district attorney's office to emphasize the importance of seeking long prison sentences or deportation for the defendants in the case.

As neighborhood residents themselves, the civilian members of the team recognized how devastating it would be psychologically to people now coming forward to cooperate with the police if any of the dealers were seen back on 49th Street. The team also discussed sentencing, and how a livery service in the area had volunteered to transport neighborhood residents to court for the dealers' sentencing. They wanted the judge to see for himself how important it was to the law-abiding people of 49th Street.

No one believes that a sweep, no matter how effective, is a permanent cure unless there is follow up. And that's exactly what the precinct management teams are focusing on. They are also tapping other-than-police resources. Community policing, with management teams as one of its vehicles, recognizes something that can-do organizations like the police sometimes won't readily admit. It acknowledges that the people most affected by crime may be the best people to help us attack the problems and find the solutions. That's what's happening in New York City today. It is something worthy of your own involvement.

"Don't even think this [community-based policing] has anything to do with 'stopping crime.' It doesn't. It's about control. It's about clampdown."

Police-Community Partnerships Are Racist and Unjust

Revolutionary Communist Party

Many inner-city residents believe that the police abuse their power and discriminate against minorities and the poor. In the following viewpoint, the Revolutionary Communist Party agrees and argues that rich and powerful members of society have devised police-community partnerships to further oppress poor inner-city residents. The RCP asserts that the police, under the guise of these partnerships, seek to control poor neighborhoods and instill order by harassing innocent civilians. The RCP is a political party based in Chicago.

As you read, consider the following questions:

1. According to the RCP, how are members of the lower class exploited?
2. Do you agree with the author that the police discriminate against certain groups? Why or why not?
3. Why are police experts worried about increased immigration, according to the RCP?

Excerpted from "Community-Based Policing: Program for Police-State Communities," from the September 20, 1992, edition of the *Revolutionary Worker*, the weekly newspaper of the Revolutionary Communist Party, U.S.A. The article has been retitled and subheadings and inserted quotations added by Greenhaven Press editors. Reprinted with permission.

A specter haunts the powers-that-be. It's been building over the past few years. It lurks in the heart of every major city in this country. It busted out for a few, sweet days in April-May 1992 in L.A.—spread to a dozen other places—and changed the scene all over the country, jacking things up to a whole new level. Ever since, the powers have been desperate to push it back down and lock it up tight.

What is it that spreads fear in the hearts of the rich and powerful? The danger that the rip-off society they rule might rip apart. The prospect that they might not be able to control the millions of nobodies who are daily treated like dirt. The vision of this class of people who have nothing to lose—but their chains—rising up against the system that means nothing but misery for them.

But those who run this country have a plan to hold their tattered social fabric together and deal with the dangerous element that threatens their domination. They call this operation *community-based policing*. And in L.A., in the wake of the rebellion, they're putting key parts of the program under the direct control of the federal political police, like the FBI—those cops who specialize in suppressing the people they think are a threat to the established order.

Gestapo-Style Control

This is a big jump-up in repression against the people. The powers have visions of Gestapo-style control over the neighborhoods where the basic people live and hang out. They want barricades to separate off and isolate particular 'hoods. They want to have the police run everything—from schools to sports to social programs. They want to have the police know everything—who everyone is, what they do, and where to find them. They want to turn the places where we live into concentration camps.

Since the rebellion, the powers are really desperate. They see the people holding their heads up higher. They see the people even angrier today than when that racist [Rodney King] verdict came down. They see the effort to stop fighting amongst ourselves and get together to go up against them. All this gives the authorities the shivers. All this puts them in a frenzy to put this police-state program in full effect.

This is the real deal. After the rebellion, the powers want the people back down on our knees. They're going full speed ahead with community-based policing. If they get over with it, the oppressed people will be put in lockdown. It will be much harder to resist and rise up against all the abuse the powers bring down. But if the people unite and fight against this police-state program, if we deal *defeats to their plans*, it will be a whole different ball game. We will have taken a giant step toward the total change we need.

The powers and the media have dressed up community-based policing nice and pretty, like it's some kind of "reform." They say that the cops will mostly be acting like Officer Friendly. They've even got a new Black police chief, Willie Williams, to sell us on how sincere they are. He's running all over town offering to meet with anybody and everybody, always smiling sweetly while the cameras roll. And community-based policing is supposed to be Willie Williams' "bible."

Who Friends and Enemies Truly Are

Community-based policing is not about stopping crime. But the cops want to use the fact that street crime is heavy in the oppressed areas to get people to work with them. Some people are so uptight about it they forget to think clearly about who are our friends and who are our enemies.

Revolutionary Worker, September 20, 1992.

The powers are not about to openly admit that they've got a plan to pen us in, lock us up, hammer us down and kill us off. Instead, they're trying to trick the people, especially those who don't face Rodney King-style brutality all the time like some middle class people who've been getting hip lately to how the people on the bottom are treated. They're trying to build a barricade wall between the people in the middle and the people who know why police are called "pigs" because they experience it every day. They're trying to get some people to think community-based policing will make things better. The powers want the people in the middle to support the clampdown and make it seem legit.

Don't believe the hype! Community-based policing isn't cops being nice to the people, it's cops being on top of the people—all the time. It doesn't mean a better life in the neighborhood, it means all life in the neighborhood is run by the police. It doesn't mean cops helping the people, it means some people helping the cops mess with the people. Community-based policing doesn't mean community control of police. It means police control of communities. . . .

A Police Clampdown

It's been advertised as all about getting the cops out of their patrol cars and putting them on the scene on the ground, walking a beat or riding a bike or going door-to-door or setting up a storefront mini-station right in the 'hood. What's so bad about all that?

There's a method to this madness. First, all this means a heavy police presence and a lot more pigz in the hoodz. That's why one of the first things Willie Williams did when he became chief was to stump for a thousand more cops to rampage through our neighborhoods. He says that's what's needed to make community-based policing a success. And all the top politicians agree with him.

Next, the plan is for the cops to get to know the area and the people in them. They want to find out who the "law-abiding-citizens" are. That means anybody who's willing to work with the cops.

Don't even think this has anything to do with "stopping crime." It doesn't. It's about control. Its about clampdown.

Police experts spell it out when they talk to each other in their magazines and conferences. These professors and bureaucrats—whose whole careers are dedicated to figuring out how the system can control the people it oppresses—admit that what they're trying to prevent is not crime but "disorder."

What do they mean by "disorder"? One article by an expert on community-based policing says that "law-abiding citizens . . . are afraid to go out onto streets filled with graffiti, winos, and loitering youths. . . . (W)hen disorderly behavior—say, rude remarks by loitering youths—is left unchallenged, the signal given is that no one cares." In a report for the federal No-Justice Dept., another expert warns against "signals" like "untended property, disorderly persons, drunks, obstreperous youth." (According to Webster's New 20th Century Dictionary, "obstreperous" means "noisy" and "unruly, especially in resisting or opposing.")

The So-Called Criminals

This is what community-based policing is about. The fed who runs "weed and seed" says programs like "bicycle patrols, recreational activities, and mobile substations" will make it easier for the cops to "rely on the residents" to help them get rid of "criminals." Who are these "criminals?" Rude youth. Homeless people. People who aren't in step with the ORDER demanded by 1990s America. People who have nothing to lose. They are all "criminals" to the powers-that-be.

When they target the people on the bottom like this, the powers reveal—in spite of all their efforts to hide it—a great deal about the role of the police in this society. The people need to learn what they're teaching.

The police are enforcers of an oppressive social order. A class society. A society that has to keep millions and millions of people in a situation where there is literally a gun pointed at their head all the time.

Why? Because this is a system based on robbery, on massive looting. The ruling class of wealthy capitalists steal from the working people who produce all the wealth. And they oppress all kinds of people to keep that thievery growing.

That's where the police come in. They serve and protect the class of criminals. The police are their enforcers, their hired hitmen. They are the first line of defense for this brutal system. They make sure that the robbery continues. That's why they've got guns and helicopters and billy clubs.

RCP Chairman Bob Avakian says: "In short, the armed force of the bourgeois state exists for the purpose of suppressing, by force of arms, the proletariat and all those who would step out of line and challenge this 'great way of life' founded on robbery and murder, not only within the U.S. itself but throughout the world. And that, simply, is why pigs are pigs, and will always be pigs—until systems that need such pigs are abolished from the earth. A hard truth—but a liberating truth."

A History of Fluff and Failure

The history of earlier interactive policing programs in New York City is largely a sobering record of fluff and failure. And the limited applications of community policing going on know highlight more of the possible pitfalls. Identifying a community problem is a far cry from solving it, and members of the Community Patrol Officers Program—the 10-officer neighborhood teams now operating in all the city's 75 precincts—often find themselves battling the city and police bureaucracy for months for things as simple as a streetlight for a dark corner.

Ralph Blumenthal, *The New York Times*, February 24, 1991.

That's why having a Black or Latino police chief or more Black and Latino cops won't help at all. It won't stop the pigs from singling out Black and Latino people for especially brutal treatment (as the movie "Boyz 'n the Hood" accurately showed). Because the oppression of Black, Latino and other nationalities is built into this capitalist system. Would this country even exist as it does today if it hadn't ripped off land from the indigenous peoples, slaves from Africa, 40 percent of Mexico, murdering literally millions of oppressed people and viciously suppressing their cultures in the process? Can anyone even imagine the U.S. without racism and discrimination against Black and Latino people and other oppressed nationalities? Be real! The system demands that the Black and Latino masses be oppressed. And the job of the police is to help make sure that this system keeps on keeping on. So, they've got to mess with the Black and Latino masses, no matter who the Chief is.

Schemes like community control of police or civilian review boards—or any plan to "involve the community" in keeping watch on the activities of the police—won't work either. All that these propositions, proposals and pipe-dreams do is spread illusions about the possibility of reforming the system. They mislead the people. We need to get rid of these harmful fantasies and realize that it's only the struggle of the masses—fierce and uncompromising—that can deal with this miserable society and its brutal enforcers.

A Police Strategy for a Dying Empire

There are calculations involved in the change to community-based policing—desperate calculations. This police-state program is not a sign of strength. The authorities see big trouble ahead. They know they're in deep crisis. They know they have no alternative but to bring down a ton of misery and oppression on the people. And they know the people won't just sit there and take it.

Some police experts are pretty open about all this, at least when they talk to each other. An issue of the FBI's magazine worried about "troublesome trends" in economics and the make-up of the population

The experts worried that America is getting less white. By the year 2010, Black, Latino and Asian children are expected to be the majority in California, New York, Texas, Florida, Louisiana, New Mexico and the capital, Washington, D.C. And children of the oppressed nationalities will make up 25 percent in another 19 states. So, those who the system brings down racism, discrimination and national oppression against are becoming an increasingly large part of the population.

The experts worried about immigrants in particular. They were concerned that "immigrants account for an ever-increasing share of the U.S. population and workforce." They worry that up to 300,000 immigrants without papers are added to the U.S. population every year. Most of these people have been forced to leave countries dominated and propped up by the U.S., only to be treated like animals by the U.S. once again when they get here.

Most importantly, the experts worried that the U.S. is dividing in two and that "the gap between the 'haves' and the 'have nots' is widening. . . . An underclass of Americans—those who are chronically poor and live outside society's rules—is growing." Around the country, 880 "underclass neighborhoods" (which tend to have more Blacks, Latinos and Asians than other areas) have been identified by these experts. It is these "underclass neighborhoods" where community-based police-state programs will be concentrated.

Fears of the Leaders and Police

Why does this massive increase in the number of people on the bottom of society upset the powers so? The FBI magazine article says that people on the bottom look at "government as the 'bad guy,' and many of the underclass see police as the ultimate symbol of oppression. . . ."

Or, as Bob Avakian has said, "The slave always wants to kill the slavemaster, and the oppressed always wants to eliminate the oppressor. This is the knowledge that instills fear and desperation in exploiting classes everywhere."

And the powers fear where this is leading. The police experts say, "Urban unrest and civil disorder are likely possibilities. . . . The long-term risks of ignoring critical shifts in the population and the economy pose a serious threat to the internal security of the Nation."

That's why the powers have turned to community-based policing. Because they're scared shitless of the masses they oppress. They're afraid that whole society will be out of control. They're afraid that as their crisis worsens, their old police methods won't be good enough any more. They need "innovative, nontraditional approaches" to maintaining their gangster rule. They need to get ready for the roundups.

But the same conditions that fuel their nightmares and drive them to new leaps in repression also reveal the possibility of a different outcome, a revolutionary one. They show that there will be storms of upheaval ahead. They show that objective conditions may well develop very favorably for a mass revolutionary uprising that can overthrow this monstrous system and take the first step towards a bright new future for humanity. We saw a glimpse of that future in the rebellion. WE WON'T GO BACK!

Recognizing Stereotypes

A stereotype is an oversimplified or exaggerated description of people or things. Stereotyping can be favorable. Most stereotyping, however, tends to be highly uncomplimentary, and, at times, degrading.

Stereotyping grows out of our prejudices. When we stereotype someone, we are prejudging him or her. Consider the following example: Mr. Smith believes all poor people are lazy and irresponsible. Whenever he sees a poor family, he assumes the parents have done something to cause the family's poverty: they are lazy, ignorant, or have no desire to work or study. He disregards the possibility that the parents are working but are still unable to make ends meet, or that circumstances beyond their control have forced them into poverty. Instead, he assumes that if they really wanted to get out of poverty, they could. Why? He has prejudged all poor people and will keep his stereotype consistent with his prejudice.

Part I

The following statements relate to the subject matter in this chapter. Consider each statement carefully. *Mark S for any statement that is an example of stereotyping. Mark N for any statement that is not an example of stereotyping. Mark U if you are undecided about any statement.*

S = stereotype
N = not a stereotype
U = undecided

1. Police officers hate poor minorities and harass them whenever possible.

2. Hardcore drug addicts often commit thefts to obtain the money needed for drugs.

3. Inner-city police officers witness more serious crime than police in the suburbs.

4. Minorities in poor neighborhoods will not cooperate with police in criminal investigations.

5. Black youths are raised in homes without their fathers and lack the guidance that others get in two-parent homes.

6. Inner-city youths are violent criminals who prey on innocent victims.

7. Police departments in large cities are not interested in solving less serious crimes such as petty theft and burglary.

8. Drug dealers are not really hurting anyone.

9. Many inner-city residents turn to drugs because of peer pressure or a sense of despair.

10. Police departments in cities such as New York or Los Angeles are understaffed and cannot respond immediately to minor crimes.

11. Most minorities do not trust the police.

12. Teenage drug dealers believe that they will not be punished as severely as adults if they are arrested.

13. Street drug dealers earn a small fortune before retiring after a short period of time.

14. Inner-city youths become drug dealers because they hope to emulate the success of some veteran dealers.

15. Police officers are likelier to brutalize the poor.

Part II

Based on the insights you have gained from this activity, discuss these questions in class:

1. Why do people stereotype one another?

2. What are some examples of positive stereotypes?

3. What harm can stereotypes cause?

4. What stereotypes currently affect members of your class?

Periodical Bibliography

The following articles have been selected to supplement the diverse views presented in this chapter.

Business Week	"How Cracking Down on Drugs Can Foster More Crime," December 2, 1991.
John J. DiIulio Jr.	"A Limited War on Crime That We Can Win," *The Brookings Review*, Fall 1992. Available from the Brookings Institution, 1775 Massachusetts Ave. NW, Washington, DC 20036.
Terry Eastland	"Weed and Seed: Root Out Crime, Nurture Poor," *The Wall Street Journal*, May 14, 1992.
Reuben M. Greenberg	"Less Bang-Bang for the Buck," *Policy Review*, Winter 1992.
Carl F. Horowitz	"An Empowerment Strategy for Eliminating Neighborhood Crime," *The Heritage Foundation Backgrounder*, March 5, 1991. Available from 214 Massachusetts Ave. NE, Washington, DC 20002.
John McCormick and Bill Turque	"Big Crimes, Small Cities," *Newsweek*, June 10, 1991.
Michael Massing	"What Ever Happened to the 'War on Drugs'?" *The New York Review of Books*, June 11, 1992.
Eugene H. Methvin	"Tampa's Winning War on Drugs," *Reader's Digest*, July 1991.
Tom Morganthau	"The War at Home: How to Battle Crime," *Newsweek*, March 26, 1991.
Eloise Salholz	"Blacks and Cops: Up Against a Wall," *Newsweek*, May 11, 1992.
William S. Sessions	"Law Enforcement and the Community," *Vital Speeches of the Day*, May 15, 1991.
Sam Staley	"The War on Drugs Escalates Urban Violence," *The Wall Street Journal*, August 13, 1992.
Joseph B. Treaster	"Police in New York Shift Drug Battle Away from Street," *The New York Times*, August 3, 1992.
Gordon Witkin and Ted Gest	"Street Crime: An Agenda for Change," *U.S. News & World Report*, October 5, 1992.

What Measures Would Improve Urban Housing?

Chapter Preface

In October 1992, a seven-year-old Chicago boy was killed by a sniper in the Cabrini-Green public housing project, the third child shot dead in the development that year. Cabrini-Green has long been infamous for gangs and crime and is often considered the epitome of urban public housing failure. Many housing projects such as Cabrini-Green have become dilapidated and dangerous.

Public housing projects were started in the late 1930s by the federal government as temporary housing for low-income Americans. Today, however, they have become permanent housing for generations of many poor families. In addition, many of the projects are in run-down, crime-filled neighborhoods.

Experts differ on how these conditions can best be improved. Former Akron, Ohio, public housing director Paul H. Messenger believes government has been a negligent landlord, allowing tenants to damage buildings, sell drugs, and commit crimes. He favors privatizing public housing. As Messenger states, "Under private management these public nuisances would almost surely go." Peter Dreier, head of the Boston Redevelopment Agency, also encourages private ownership but believes government involvement is also crucial. "Without public funds, self-help efforts are doomed to fail," he writes. Dreier states that government should fund residents' child care and job training and repair apartments and facilities.

While the government plays a primary role in the quality and availability of housing, other factors are also involved. The authors in the following chapter discuss these factors.

"Properly run, [public housing] remains one of the best options for housing the poor."

Increase Public Housing

John Atlas and Peter Dreier

For the most part, government public housing programs work well and provide decent, affordable units to the poor, John Atlas and Peter Dreier write in the following viewpoint. Atlas and Dreier maintain that public housing can be improved by more funding, stronger tenant management, and improved applicant screening. Atlas is executive director of a legal services agency in New Jersey. Peter Dreier is housing director for the Boston Redevelopment Authority in Massachusetts.

As you read, consider the following questions:

1. Why do Atlas and Dreier contend that public housing comes under much public scrutiny and criticism?
2. In the authors' opinion, how has public order decreased in housing projects?
3. According to Atlas and Dreier, how can training and social programs for tenants improve public housing?

After a quick visit to riot-torn Los Angeles in May 1992, George Bush dusted off an old plan to privatize public housing and offered it as part of his face-saving plan to show he cares about America's cities. In fact, public housing represents less than 2 percent of the nation's housing supply, yet it looms large in public debate about national housing policy: Should we sell apartments to tenants? Demand better-behaved tenants? Evict drug dealers (and their families) from projects? Give tenants a stronger voice in management? Tear down developments? Replace them with housing vouchers?

In the midst of the broadest housing crisis since the Depression—declining home-ownership, scarce affordable rental housing, rising homelessness—why does public housing command so much attention?

A Metaphor for Failure

In a conservative era, public housing seems to many Americans a metaphor for the failures of activist government. The conservative attack on public housing is part of a larger privatization agenda to reduce government and discredit public endeavors of economic uplift.

But unless defenders of activist government address public housing's real dilemmas, it will continue to serve as a decrepit symbol, mocking aspirations of public improvement. Restoring public housing's integrity will require not just programmatic reform but ideological and political revision as well.

The first thing to appreciate about public housing is that it has become the housing of last resort for the very poor—often those without jobs, skills, or hopes. Thus the dilemma is partly circular: public housing is likely to remain socially and politically unattractive until we alleviate poverty itself. To that end, one might imagine new public expenditure—on job-creating public works, human capital programs of training and education, as well as health care and child care. But such an agenda will not likely receive majority support unless the voters believe their tax dollars will be well spent. And there stands public housing, our most visible symbol of well-intentioned government gone awry.

Politically, public housing encompasses several voter backlashes—against crime, drugs, illegitimacy, violent youth, minorities, the "undeserving" poor, and government itself. Joining Ronald Reagan's welfare queen and George Bush's Willie Horton is the public housing drug dealer protected by the American Civil Liberties Union.

Where to break into the circle? There is today a broad consensus among social scientists, policy experts, and politicians that public funds by themselves will not cure the current epidemic of drugs, gangs, and violence in America's slums. Conservative

Housing and Urban Development (HUD) Secretary Jack Kemp, liberal sociologist William Julius Wilson, and the Rev. Jesse Jackson all argue for self-help—that ghetto residents themselves must change the moral environment in which they live. But bootstrap lectures alone will not restore the physical, economic, and moral well-being of the ghettoes. Without public funds, self-help efforts are doomed to fail.

Public Housing for the Working Poor

We can and should enrich residents of public housing communities with the qualities of those who work and dream of bettering themselves. Their example will inspire other tenants.

We can develop opportunities for the working poor to enter public housing by increasing the amount of money that those applying for public housing may earn and remain eligible. These working poor are "low-income" people who earn 80 percent of an area's mean income. At present, "low-income families," that is, the "working poor," are excluded from public housing. . . .

By changing the income eligibility rate to allow more "low-income people" to become tenants, housing authorities would receive more rent revenue and thus require less HUD subsidies. With this increase in money available for other purposes, HUD could again add to the "new housing fund," and provide more needed housing for both "low-" and "very low-income" families.

Frederick Brown, *Journal of Housing*, November/December 1990.

As we shall see, there are workable strategies to turn subsidized housing into livable communities. But they will require a revision of cherished beliefs across the political spectrum. Conservatives will have to abandon the idea that the marketplace, by itself, can provide affordable housing for the poor. And progressives will have to acknowledge that the rights of residents must be balanced with responsibilities to communities.

Most Public Housing Works Well

The best-kept secret about public housing is that most of it actually provides decent, affordable housing to many people. Properly run, it remains one of the best options for housing the poor. There are 1.3 million public housing apartments and about 800,000 families on the waiting lists of the nation's 3,060 local housing authorities. Public housing developments often are no worse than privately owned, low-rent apartments; most, in fact, are better, which is why the waiting lists continue to swell. But because public housing involves tax dollars, it is more visible and open to public scrutiny.

Many projects, especially racially isolated high-rises in big cities, have indeed failed. These represent less than one-quarter of the nation's public housing, but they cast a giant shadow. The projects isolate and concentrate minorities dependent on welfare, suffering from high unemployment rates, teenage pregnancy, single parenthood, and a climate of serious crime. Some projects, like St. Louis's infamous Pruitt-Igoe homes, virtually ceased to function as viable communities. Pruitt-Igoe was eventually dynamited by the city not because of structural flaws but because it was an unlivable environment. . . .

By the late 1960s, the housing industry convinced Congress to replace public housing with privately owned, subsidized housing (known by their statute numbers: Sections 236, 221d, and 8) that gave private developers tax breaks, low-cost mortgages, and rent subsidies to house the poor. These inefficient and costly programs led to widespread political abuses and eventually to the HUD scandals of the 1970s, which were repeated in the 1990s.

Social Problems Persist Elsewhere

Tellingly, Jack Kemp has not focused on the troubles of privately owned, subsidized projects, despite the fact that there are more of these developments (1.9 million apartments) than there are public housing projects (1.3 million units). But while Kemp has usually spared private slumlords the antidrug and empowerment rhetoric that he directs at the public projects—a tactic that fits into neoconservatives' government-bashing agenda—the crime, drug, and social problems in these privately owned projects are as bad as, if not worse than, the problems plaguing government-owned projects. The tenants of privately owned, government-subsidized developments deserve the same attention and resources as their public housing companions.

Conservatives like Kemp address the need for self-help but not the need for resources, an approach that appeals to taxpayers who want solutions that cost no money. To reframe the conservative-dominated housing debate and to make public housing successful both for residents and in the eyes of the public, we must alter some basic assumptions.

First, we must turn developments into livable communities. That means insisting on better screening of applicants and tougher treatment of abusive tenants. It also means giving residents a stronger voice in management and, ultimately, ownership.

Second, social housing should not be for only the very poor. The homeless and the welfare poor deserve decent housing, but

150

not at the expense of the working poor, who can help stabilize housing developments.

Third, public housing needs more money—for repairs, maintenance, and security, as well as social services, child care, and job-training programs that can help residents move into America's mainstream. But that money won't be forthcoming until America decides that public housing is worth saving.

Finally, traditional public housing needs to be one strand of a broader social housing strategy that relies more heavily on a new generation of competent and dedicated community nonprofit developers.

Law and Order Once Prevailed

Though today they stand as symbols of lawlessness, public housing projects until the 1960s were places of almost excessive law and order. Indeed, project managers nearly ruled with an iron hand, as Harry Spence, the court-appointed receiver of the troubled Boston Housing Authority from 1979 to 1984, described in a *Working Papers* interview ten years ago:

> Until the late 1960s, public housing . . . worked on a theory of despotism. The project manager was the despot. Longtime tenants will tell you there was a day when if my kid walked across the lawn, the manager came out and said you either stop that or you're out. That's now looked at almost nostalgically. And it depended almost entirely on the caliber of the manager. For much of the community, that unrestrained power was being used to enforce community norms. But often, it was abused, because there was a class gap between the manager and the tenants. It was a highly personalized and often vicious order.

The managerial despotism Spence recounts was finally overturned on grounds of both civil rights and civil liberties. Until the 1960s, public order in the projects was preserved partly through a system of fines for minor infractions such as littering, loitering, and petty vandalism. Tenants objected that the fines were both a hardship for struggling families and—equally important—a source of sometimes arbitrary management. . . .

Resident management and ownership are not panaceas for poverty. But where tenants are well-organized and exercise power, both physical and social conditions improve. Self-reliance replaces dependency. Residents stop being victims. What's more, experience suggests that ultimately, tenant-managed or -owned developments save funds because tenants have a greater stake in their homes and are less tolerant of destructive and costly behavior.

Kemp's 1990 initiative, the Homeownership Opportunities for People Everywhere (HOPE) program, is far too limited in scope and implementation. . . .

Revitalize Public Housing

Many housing authorities are far from model landlords, to be sure; financial weaknesses structured into the public housing program nationally and the use of agency jobs as political patronage have led to poor operations in several cities. But there are also some excellent local housing authorities in cities and towns—New York City being perhaps the outstanding example—that run exemplary programs, given severe financial, locational, design, and social impediments. A revitalized social housing program would do much to restore the sense of mission and dedication that characterized the early public housing movement of the 1930s and 1940s. These agencies and other nonprofit groups exist to serve the housing needs of particular sub-populations, providing housing at the lowest costs in the most user-responsive fashion.

Chester Hartman, *Winning America*, 1988.

HOPE will raise hopes but end in hopelessness because it does not provide the resources needed to fulfill its worthy goals. To work, HOPE must incorporate criteria that guarantee its residents a chance for real success:

- Congress must provide adequate funds so that tenants can organize—with the help of experienced organizers—to address day-to-day concerns (crime, for example, or maintenance) as a prelude to ownership.

- Tenants must be given the initial and ongoing training necessary to participate in management effectively, to create resident-run management corporations, and eventually to own their own developments.

- Congress must provide adequate subsidies so that the new owners can meet both the long-term and the day-to-day costs of homeownership. Better yet, working with tenant groups, HUD should repair the complexes before they are sold.

- The developments should be sold only as limited-equity cooperatives, not as single condos, to guarantee that this housing will continue to be available for low-income residents after the initial owners have left.

- Beyond bricks and mortar, HOPE should include funds to provide social programs—such as job training, child care, drug treatment, and community-based health care—and hire tenants for management and construction jobs.

- HOPE must ultimately become an entitlement program for all public and subsidized housing developments in the country, not a "demonstration project" for a lucky handful of people.

An expanded tenant-ownership program should not be a substitute for an ongoing federal commitment to expand the supply of affordable housing through a variety of approaches. One alternative is private, nonprofit housing sponsored by community organizations, churches, unions, and tenant groups. With the support of many private foundations, local and state governments, and business groups, these nonprofit developers patch together resources to create low-income housing.

Problems Remain for Nonprofit Developers

Such groups now have an enviable track record of constructing and rehabilitating housing for the poor. According to a survey sponsored by the National Congress for Community Economic Development, about 2,000 Community Development Corporations (CDCs) have produced 87,000 housing units in the past three years. Some housing experts view these CDCs as the next wave of housing reform; in 1991, Congress recognized this success by enacting the first federal initiative—the Community Housing Partnership program—to target funds for the nonprofit sector. . . .

Like every revolution, public housing has had its victims—in some cases the very people it was intended to help. In public housing projects, destroying arbitrary authority without replacing it with democratic authority left residents prey to overlords of the underclass, to criminals, and to drug abusers. In the new climate, where drug use was held to be a victimless crime and purity of procedure took precedence over community safety, residents of projects who had once been shackled by the inequity of law were now trapped by the absence of law.

Salvaging public housing will not, on its own, solve our housing crisis. Less than one in five low-income households receives any kind of federal housing assistance—the lowest level of any industrial nation. Just providing rent subsidies for all of them would cost over $25 billion a year. But Congress is unlikely to appropriate funds for rent subsidies, housing repair, or new construction by nonprofit community-based groups. As long as public housing remains a quagmire, providing the resources that will give the residents of these developments a greater voice in management and the skills to make their environment more livable will be a major step forward in helping the poor to help themselves. Admittedly, this will not substitute for a macroeconomic program to eradicate poverty. Admittedly, too, it will touch only a small percentage of America's 33 million poor, leaving the majority to fend for themselves in the private housing market. But if it works, it will help restore the public's confidence in activist government and in public and community enterprise.

"Conversion of the entire public housing program to a private, voucher-paid enterprise would have a number of specific advantages."

Eliminate Public Housing

Paul H. Messenger

In the following viewpoint, Paul H. Messenger argues that the public housing administration should eventually be eliminated and turned over to private management. Messenger believes private ownership would be more competitive, efficient, and effective than government at providing low-cost housing. Messenger directed public housing authorities for more than twelve years, most recently in Akron, Ohio, and is now a private citizen there.

As you read, consider the following questions:

1. In Messenger's opinion, how has the absence of working families hurt public housing?
2. Why does the author believe that public housing authorities should streamline the services they provide to residents?
3. Messenger has worked in the public housing administration. How might his experience influence his viewpoint? Do you think his experience makes his viewpoint more credible? Why or why not?

From Paul H. Messenger, "Please Abolish My Job, Mr. Kemp," *Policy Review*, Winter 1990. Used by permission of the Heritage Foundation. All rights reserved.

On the knuckle of my left forefinger is a small scar. I got it from the lid of the pot-bellied coal stove that heated our public housing unit in Hammond, Indiana, back in the '40s. Families had to pay their own way in those days—there was no welfare— and I don't know how my mom managed. She had me, her mother-in-law, and my baby sister to handle on the allotment from my father's Army pay; and she had to pay the rent every month or we would be out, to make room for another working-class family on its way up the ladder. But she did manage, and in 1951 my dad put down the first payment for a house of our own.

For the past 10 years, I have run public housing authorities in Springfield, Ohio, Little Rock, Arkansas, and again in Ohio, in Akron. Often I wonder whether the time for these institutions hasn't come and gone. Back in Hammond, dads were off at the war, like mine, or working in the steel mills. Public housing was a temporary way station for people saving every penny to get a leg up. Now, rather than onward and upward, we have the spectacle of two and three generations of public assistance in tenancy, even under the same roof. We have 17-year-olds, already with three children, on welfare, waiting for their own public housing unit. Many tenants openly mock the notion that they should be working and saving so as to be able to get off public assistance. In the project outside my office window in Springfield I once watched a dozen able-bodied men and women grilling T-bone steaks and pounding Budweisers on a weekday afternoon.

Housing Projects Today

The project where I once lived was rough but safe. I played soldier with the other kids and was proud of my toy pistol, a couple of clothespins that my mother had clipped together. Children at the projects I run today carry MAC-10s, breakstock shotguns, and 9mm automatics. Real ones. Recently a 15-year-old was picked up carrying a shotgun, an auto-mag, and a long knife. He was holding vials of crack and a couple of thousand dollars. At another Akron project, there was a fatal shoot-out between two men, neither of whom lived there. We can sympathize with public housing tenants terrorized by the drug gangs, but we also have to face up to the unpleasant reality: the dealers are there because the users are. One reason there's so much gang warfare in projects is that the market opportunities are enormous for the dealer who wins a monopoly there.

To restore public housing to its original design, liberal as it was then, would now be viewed as a reactionary conservative proposal. You mean people have to be employed to receive the benefit? You mean they have to be married? You mean they have to abide by the rules without five layers of due process?

And they have to pay the rent on time every time? What an old-fashioned idea. It wasn't too long ago, though, that public housing mainly served low-income working families who needed a boost along the way and who paid their way in the meantime.

Welfare Colonies

In the '50s and '60s, welfare clients were made eligible and the influx began. In the '70s the Brooke Amendments artificially limited rent to 25 percent of adjusted tenant income, later 30 percent of income, and very nearly bankrupted public housing until some genius figured out that public housing authorities could not manage and maintain property without income. Thus began the era of "operating" subsidies, running now at almost $2 billion a year. Add to this the nearly $2 billion a year for capital improvements since Brooke wiped out most public housing reserve accounts. Most recently, the Reagan "safety net"—limiting benefits to the lower income people—has for all its good intentions wrung out all but the last few working (and rent-paying) families from the program. We have created an enormous network of welfare-dependent government housing colonies, for which most working families are no longer even eligible.

Many tenants actually "pay" negative rent: in very low-income families, after the rent calculation and deduction for utilities under the Brooke formula, we arrive at a minus number. That amount goes to the family each month in the form of a check for occupying the apartment. In HUD [Housing and Urban Development] Newspeak we call this a "Utility Adjustment Payment." In our public housing program here in Akron we have nearly 700 tenants living rent-free in addition to receiving monthly checks totaling $1.7 million annually. In our Section 8 program, more than one-third of the accounts carry negative rents. As just one example, we have a mother with six children on welfare living free in a $612-per-month, five-bedroom unit, receiving in addition a check from us each month for $66.

Public housing is now just an extension of the welfare system, and like other aspects of this system, the benefit structure has become too attractive for many people to try to work themselves out. . . .

It's no wonder the projects are so popular: Public housing authorities provide many services that have nothing to do with housing. And this raises a fundamental question of equity: How do we explain that one family gets housed, has very low rent or gets a check each month, has access to meals programs, recreation programs, community facilities, child care, training programs, and a range of other services provided or sponsored by the housing authority; while another family, equally eligible and equally needy, pays 70 or 80 percent of income for rent, lives in overcrowded housing or in their car, or bounces from one shelter to another waiting for a call to say they have been selected for housing? The standard answer is that the government should build more housing. Wrong. The government should make some sense out of the way it provides housing assistance.

Housing Vouchers

The linchpin of a simpler and more equitable method of providing housing assistance is the housing voucher. The voucher, properly implemented, would put the purchasing power directly into the hands of the needy family. Since assisted housing is already part of the welfare system, it would be appropriate to issue the vouchers through the existing welfare agencies rather than to continue supporting separate agencies such as public housing authorities. This step alone would remove a large part of the bureaucracy associated with the administration of subsidized housing. . . .

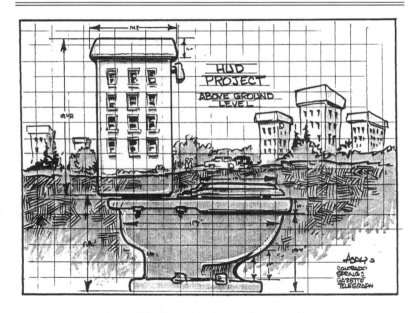

Chuck Asay, by permission of the *Colorado Springs Gazette Telegraph*.

The conversion to vouchers would focus on the two major housing subsidy programs. The first is the Section 8 Certificate program for existing housing, in which there are about a million units now. In this program the tenant is issued a Certificate of

Eligibility, which he takes to a private landlord, who agrees to sign a contract and is then paid directly by the public housing authority to subsidize the family. Sounds simple enough, but it is choked by paperwork. The leading vendor of training for the program conducts three-day seminars and provides two loose-leaf binders, each six inches thick, of rules, regulations, policies, forms, do's, don'ts, and maybes.

The Section 8 Certificate program has two major flaws. First are so-called Fair Market Rents (FMRs), which put a cap on what may be paid to subsidize a given sized apartment. The FMRs are determined nationally based on data from various market areas, and are supposed to follow the local rental market. In fact, they give landlords an incentive to drive up the rents, which in turn drives up the subsidies.

The second flaw in the Section 8 Certificate program is the Housing Quality Standards (HQS). These standards represent the hoops a landlord must jump through to get a property approved for the program, all contained in a multi-page booklet. Often a family satisfied with a property is denied assistance with the unit until it meets our standards. To understand how HQS works, imagine a bureaucrat at the end of every grocery checkout analyzing food stamp purchases and sorting out what the family can and cannot be permitted to buy.

Incidentally, there is already a Section 8 "Voucher" program, but it is subject to the same bureaucratic red tape as the Certificate program. Rather than Fair Market Rents we have Housing Payment Standards (HPS), and the units are still subject to Housing Quality Standards.

The answer to the Section 8 program is conversion to a true housing voucher with the elimination of HQS, HPS, and FMRs. Remove Big Brother as a costly middleman and let rents settle where the market would have them. Let tenants and landlords manage their lease arrangements as is done in the real economy, and let local government meet the responsibility for housing code enforcement.

Privatize the Projects

The other major candidate for conversion to vouchers is the public housing program itself, which now includes about 1.5 million units. This is the current, codified program for public construction and management of low-income housing, with the Public Housing Authority (PHA), a local citizen board, presumably in charge for each jurisdiction.

Conversion would require disbanding the PHAs and their associated bureaucracies, and putting the responsibility into private management. Current tenants would be issued housing vouchers. Many would take the opportunity to vote with their feet and get out of public housing at the first chance, especially when the projects are stripped of non-housing services and nearly automatic continued tenure. However, the (formerly) public housing units would also remain in use, if only as a residual resource, and tenants could use vouchers here as well. . . .

Tenant management should be encouraged and implemented where it will work. But we cannot put all our eggs in that basket and expect to turn public housing around in the near future. The alternative is private management companies, and the objective is to remove the housing from the public domain.

Public Housing Exacerbates Poverty

Most commentators agree that public housing has been a failure in the United States. The federal program has come to exacerbate rather than alleviate poverty. It has contributed to the growth of an urban underclass that now perpetuates itself across generations, in a kind of culture of poverty in isolation. It is a major contributor to urban community disintegration. Big-city housing projects epitomize the modern slums. Social pathologies associated with public housing are legion. . . . Such pathologies are spawned by debilitating social contexts. For the under-class warehoused in central city public housing, escape becomes increasingly difficult. Social disabilities are systematically sustained. Self-help values come not to apply. Poverty and despair come to constitute a norm.

John A. Jakle and David Wilson, *Derelict Landscapes*, 1992.

Conversion of the entire public housing program to a private, voucher-paid enterprise would have a number of specific advantages:

•*Demolitions.* Thousands of public housing units currently stand vacant, vandalized, boarded up, and useless. Many are centers for drug trade, prostitution, gang activity, and garden-variety street crime. The HUD rules keep them that way. It is surprising that in some of these cases city mayors have not simply gone in with their own wrecking balls and bulldozers; the cities are theirs to run, not HUD's. Under private management these public nuisances would almost surely go. . . .

•*Tenant Assignment Plans.* Freedom of choice ends at the doors of public housing. Once families have completed the application process and are deemed eligible, they are placed on a consolidated waiting list (with all its nuances). When finally called, they are "assigned" to units based more on the needs and rules of the housing authority than on their housing needs: take it or leave it. Under private management they could apply at the developments of their choice and the management would have an incentive to be competitive. . . .

•*Evictions.* The normal process in the private sector takes a matter of days, or a couple of weeks at most. The public housing administrator is faced with three-day, 14-day, or 30-day notices, two levels of administrative "due process" and then the judicial process with Legal Aid scratching tooth and nail each step of the way. To his credit, Jack Kemp has moved to simplify things by using a previously ignored provision in the housing legislation. Even at that, too many local judges and referees view us as the housing of last resort, and bestow rights on public housing tenants far in excess of those available to working families in private housing. As a housing administrator, I probably spend half my time dealing with arcane rules and policies from HUD, the state and local bureaucracies, and courtroom litigation gone bonkers. In 1989, we lost a case in arbitration over denying a transfer to someone who claimed a hardship because of her child's asthma. The arbitrator ruled we should provide her a dust-free environment. I don't know where we will move her; we don't have any cocoons for rent. . . .

No More Diversions

•*Tenant Services.* What started as a simple effort to teach people how to clean house and use flush toilets has grown to the point where the public housing authority is expected to serve *in loco parentis* for its tenants. The range of services the PHA is supposedly responsible for includes day care, literacy training, law enforcement, drug abuse programs, nutrition, job training, employment, tenant councils, gerontology, psychology, homemaking, budgeting, transportation, recreation, travel tours, and whatever somebody thinks up tomorrow. We don't do a very good job at this. Under private management we would get back to managing housing without the diversions of time and resources to managing tenants' lives.

•*Public Employee Unions.* Work rules make twice as many people necessary. David-Bacon wage floors make twice the wage rates necessary. Under private management, neither would be necessary.

•*Performance Funding System (PFS).* After the Brooke Amendments, when operating subsidies hit the big time, HUD dreamed up the PFS. It did little more than codify the inefficiency and inflated costs that already existed, and they have been carried forward through subsequent HUD administrations. There has been some marginal tinkering with PFS, but the attitude at HUD seems to be that the system is so screwed up it is better to leave it alone. One of the anomalies of public housing is that the worse a public housing authority has done, the more money it has attracted from HUD. Under private management, the good managers could manage and the rest could pay the price.

How do we pay for vouchers and private management of public housing? Private management operates on the rents it collects. The voucher money comes from several sources. First is the $2 billion a year we currently spend for operating subsidies (PFS). Second is the $2 billion a year we currently spend for modernization and rehabilitation of properties (which, incidentally, helps only those currently in occupancy—not those outside waiting.) Third is the $6 billion to $7 billion a year it will take to renew the old Section 8 Certificates that will expire. Bear in mind, here, I am not necessarily talking about saving money; I am talking about a more rational use of the funds we already have. The appropriations mentioned should provide a tidy sum for start-up. . . .

Clearly it is time for a reappraisal of taxpayer-subsidized housing. We need to stop turning relatively normal people into "clients." We need to reach more of the actually needy, minimize the overhead of running the current programs, substitute market transactions for public directives, restore some sense of responsibility and motivation to those helped, and remove the consultants and developers from any direct role.

The best way to achieve these goals is to convert current subsidized housing programs into voucher programs. This is not a new idea, but it might be a bit unusual for one who has spent over 20 years in the government housing industry to suggest we throw the whole thing out and start over.

Given my own provenance, the question has to occur: what happens to all of us housing bureaucrats when our jobs are eliminated by vouchers?

The answer, I guess, is that we form our own private management companies. If we are as good as we claim we are, business should be brisk.

"Rent control seems in many cases to be the most efficient technique so far known for destroying cities."

Repeal Rent Control Laws

William Tucker

Rent control laws are often criticized by housing experts and others for inducing tenants to live in the same apartments for many years, thus reducing the availability of apartments and creating a housing shortage in many cities. William Tucker, the author of the following viewpoint, agrees and argues that cities without rent control laws have more vacant apartments available to new renters than cities with rent control. Tucker contends that these laws discriminate against new tenants who must pay higher rents than they would in the absence of controls. Tucker is a former Hoover Institution fellow and the author of *The Excluded Americans: Homelessness and Housing Policies*.

As you read, consider the following questions:

1. According to Tucker, why is the housing crisis a result of local, rather than federal, action?
2. In the author's opinion, how can rent control laws create a black market in which some renters pay unfair, higher prices?
3. Why does Tucker believe that rent control is a violation of owners' property rights?

From William Tucker, "The Source of America's Housing Problem: Look in Your Own Back Yard," *Policy Analysis*, February 6, 1990. Reprinted with permission of the Cato Institute.

The housing problem—particularly the shortage of housing for the poor—emerged as one of the major domestic issues of the 1980s and threatens to continue well into the next decade. The signs are everywhere. Homelessness has been a major concern for nearly 10 years. Rents have been absorbing ever-increasing portions of poor people's incomes. In some cities, the rental vacancy rate has reached a dangerously low 3 percent or less. . . .

It is obvious that housing markets have varied widely from city to city. Some cities have been plagued by high abandonment rates and high vacancy rates. Other cities have had little abandonment and extremely low vacancy rates—and have scrambled to find every available space. Still other cities, particularly New York, have had high abandonment rates *and* low vacancy rates.

It is also obvious that the undesirable conditions in such vastly different housing markets have not resulted from federal actions. They have varied according to the housing policies pursued by local governments. The housing crisis is not a national phenomenon. It is a local problem brought about by local regulations.

Local regulatory ordinances generally fall into two categories: zoning and rent control. . . .

Rent Control in America

Rent control plays a surprisingly large role in the nation's housing affairs, essentially dominating the markets on the East and West coasts. The reason rent control receives so little national attention and is rarely recognized as a prevalent pattern is that it is almost always perceived as a local issue.

Rent control, of course, is a pure price control. It is axiomatic among economists that price controls produce commodity shortages. As Assar Lindback, chairman of the Nobel economics committee and an avowed socialist, warned the American New Left in 1971,

> The effects of rent control have in fact been exactly what can be predicted from the simplest type of supply-and-demand analysis—"housing shortage" (excess demand for housing), black markets, privileges for those who happen to have a contract for a rent-controlled apartment, nepotism in the distribution of the available apartments, difficulties in getting apartments for families with children, and, in many places, deterioration of the housing stock. In fact, *next to bombing, rent control seems in many cases to be the most efficient technique so far known for destroying cities*, as the housing situation in New York City demonstrates.

Over 200 American municipalities have rent control. More

than half of them are small communities in northern New Jersey, which significantly affects the already-overregulated New York metropolitan area. Most of the large suburbs of New York City, including Yonkers, White Plains, New Rochelle, Garden City, and Mt. Vernon, have rent control. Such principal New Jersey cities as Newark, Paterson, and Jersey City also have rent control.

Boston, Brookline, and Cambridge, Massachusetts, have rent control, as do Hartford and several smaller Connecticut cities. Washington, D.C., has it, as does Takoma Park, Maryland, a 19th-century suburb just beyond the District of Columbia's border.

Los Angeles, San Francisco, Oakland, and San Jose as well as Berkeley, Santa Monica, West Hollywood, Palm Springs, and several other small California cities have rent control. San Diego and Sacramento are the only major cities that have rejected it.

Rent Control Causes Housing Shortages

Remarkably, in 1984 every American city with rent control had a vacancy rate of less than 3 percent, whereas every American city without rent control except Worcester, Massachusetts, had a vacancy rate of more than 4 percent. Apologists for rent control argue that the vacancy rates were already low when it was imposed, but census results indicate that Boston, Washington, Newark, Los Angeles, and San Francisco all had much higher rates in 1970.

The Inequity of Rent Control

Rent control favors existing tenants by holding down their rents, but it tends to reduce the availability of housing to all prospective new tenants and raises the rent of uncontrolled housing. Although it helps low-income renters who stay in the same apartment for many years, its principal long-term effect is to reduce the profitability of rental housing and thereby to encourage its provision by government.

Richard W. White Jr., *Rude Awakenings*, 1992.

In fact, housing shortages were not an issue during the 1970s, when rent control was imposed. The principal purpose of such legislation was to control inflation. Boston, Washington, and Newark acquired rent control by extending President Nixon's general wage-and-price freeze of 1971. California cities adopted it in the late 1970s, after Howard Jarvis promised tenants a rebate from Proposition 13; when the rebate didn't materialize, a statewide rent control movement developed. More than half of

California's population now lives under rent control.

Economists' routine prediction that rent control would produce housing shortages, then, has been borne out by the low vacancy rates in rent-controlled housing markets. What has not been generally recognized, however, is that a large percentage of a tenant population—perhaps even a majority—can reap considerable long-range benefits from rent control. In fact, a tenant who is willing to stay put, even as living conditions deteriorate, can obtain what amounts to a lifetime annuity. Many New York City tenants with modest incomes are able to buy homes in the country, do part-time work, or pursue artistic avocations because they have rent-controlled apartments. Only when tenants move do they experience the adverse consequences of rent control. Until then the problems are diverted to newcomers, outsiders, and minorities.

The reason is once again the long life expectancy of housing. As Ludwig von Mises pointed out, every form of socialism is capital consumption. In the case of housing, however, there is a great deal of capital to be consumed. A community's housing stock usually represents its principal capital investment. As a result, tenants living in a well-built apartment house can pay below-market rents for as long as 30 years before the building begins to fall down around their ears.

When price controls are placed on a relatively short-lived commodity such as gasoline, the ensuing shortages are evenly distributed. Such shortages result in general dissatisfaction and may even produce pressure for deregulation. But rent-controlled apartments can be consumed by the same people for decades. Tenants who are protected by strong leases—almost always an adjunct of rent control—can achieve virtual lifetime immunity from market forces.

Rent Control Exemptees Fare Worse

On the other hand, tenants who were outside the market when rent control was imposed and tenants whose apartments are not covered by the rent control regulations do much worse. In practice, rent control is rarely imposed on all apartments. Instead, the government leaves a "hole in the market" through which excess demand can escape. Ironically, the rents of apartments in the deregulated sector will rise higher than they would if rent control laws were not in effect. (Imported oil was the hole in the market through which Americans' excess demand for oil escaped, and U.S. price controls raised world oil prices to unsurpassed levels.)

Under rent control, the deregulated sector is likely to include small buildings whose mom-and-pop owners are not regarded as "real" landlords. Many cities also practice vacancy decontrol, which usually consists of allowing apartments to reach market value the first time they are vacated, then reregulating their rents. Other cities exempt new construction, although they are often forced to repeal that exemption when tenants of new buildings become a powerful political faction.

Such exemptions create a secondary market in which prices are higher than they would be if rent control laws were not on the books. Supplementing the secondary market is a black market in which regulated apartments change hands by means of "key money" and other bribes. Anyone who tries to break into the primary market or move from apartment to apartment is funneled into those submarkets and ends up paying higher-than-market prices.

Rent Control Creates Shortages

Rent control makes it hard for investors to build, renovate, and operate rental housing profitably. Worse, it encourages landlords to remove existing apartments from the market by deliberately keeping them vacant, by converting them to condominiums and cooperatives, or even by abandoning them. Rent control thus creates rental shortages.

According to a 1987 study for New York City, Michael Stegman, of the University of North Carolina City and Regional Planning Department, found that if all of New York City's apartments held deliberately empty because of rent control were put back on the market, the city's 2.5 percent rental vacancy rate would rise to a little over 5 percent. A higher vacancy rate would mean lower rents.

Carl F. Horowitz, *The Heritage Foundation Backgrounder*, August 26, 1991.

As a result, under rent control a transfer of income from one tenant to another is just as likely as a transfer of income from landlord to tenant. A 1985 study of the Los Angeles rental market found that while longtime tenants of rent-controlled apartments were paying about $18 a month *less* than tenants of comparable unregulated apartments in neighboring communities, relatively new tenants of rent-controlled apartments were paying $15 a month *more*. The study concluded that the biggest transfers of income were from tenants who moved frequently to those who stayed put.

Repealing Rent Control Exemptions

Because so many people are disadvantaged by rent control, it might appear that the losers could be mobilized into a constituency for its repeal. Unfortunately, they are more likely to argue that the regulations should be extended to include them as well. That argument is also likely to prevail. San Francisco eventually abolished vacancy decontrol. Toronto exempted new construction when it established rent control in 1975, but the gap between the haves and the have-nots became so wide that the city repealed the exemption, recapturing thousands of apartments for regulation. In New York, the tides of regulation, deregulation, and reregulation have ebbed and flowed so many times that the current housing laws are almost incomprehensible to everyone except the most practiced specialists. New York now has two different forms of rent control plus ordinances covering a bewildering variety of special cases.

The regulation of rents, of course, is a blatant violation of property rights. Moreover, as [the Brooking Institution's] Anthony Downs pointed out, rent controls would be unconstitutional even if they were benefiting only the poor and hurting only the rich (which is clearly not the case).

> Presumably, rent controls are adopted to serve a basic public purpose: the protection of tenants from experiencing unfair rent increases. . . .

> However, as a general principle, it is undesirable for government to protect one private group against undue injury attributable to circumstances beyond its control by forcing another private group to transfer resources to the first one. If protection is indeed in the public interest, taxpayers should pay for such protection through normal means of taxation. Reliance on rent controls comes perilously close to—and may even amount to—a government taking of one group's resources to aid another group, without compensating the first group.

In sum, there can be very little doubt about where the housing crisis originates—it is a function of local, not national, politics. If General Motors had to negotiate with every municipal planning board in the nation to get permission to sell automobiles in that municipality, we would be experiencing a car shortage as well as a shortage of affordable housing. . . .

It can also take decades for large numbers of people to experience the adverse consequences of rent control—although that is now on the verge of happening in New York City. A community with rent control can essentially go on subsidizing tenants until their buildings start to fall apart.

An Opportunity for Solutions

Thus, one can legitimately ask, Is there any hope of solving the housing problem? Strangely enough, the debate touched off by the Housing Now! march on Washington may offer an opportunity to start doing so. Now that concerned citizens have been willing to bring the issue to the nation's capital, perhaps it will finally be discussed honestly there.

Rent control is obviously ripe for a national debate. Most of its benefits are bestowed on the middle class, and it allows cities to wall themselves off and become virtually impenetrable to outsiders. In a study issued by the Manhattan Institute, Peter Salins and Gerard Mildner argued that the whole nation is suffering because cities on the East and West coasts restricted their housing markets while their job markets were expanding. Salins and Mildner suggested that community development block grants be awarded only to cities that had submitted plans for phasing out rent control. (Paris and London are getting rid of their much older rent control systems in order to join a unified Europe.). . .

It seems at least remotely possible that people of good will in every community may eventually be brought to the realization that solving the housing problem requires something far more difficult than just complaining about federal policies or sending angry demonstrators to Washington. It means making the most difficult adjustment of all: accepting change in their own back yards.

Rent Control Laws Must Remain in Force

Margery A. Turner

Advocates of rent control laws argue that such laws protect many poor families, lower-income renters, and others from repeated rent hikes. In the following viewpoint, excerpted from a study of rent control in Washington, D.C., Margery A. Turner argues that these laws provide long-term, affordable rents for many D.C. residents. Turner states that in spite of low rents, housing conditions in D.C. apartments have improved and apartment building owners can still profit from these units. Turner is director for housing research programs at the Urban Institute, a Washington, D.C., research organization that studies social and economic problems in America.

As you read, consider the following questions:

1. In Turner's opinion, why are cities under increasing pressure to provide more affordable rental housing?
2. According to Turner, why are the elderly and families with children less likely to move from one apartment to another?
3. In addition to rent control, how can cities maintain an adequate supply of low-income housing, according to the author?

From Margery A. Turner, *Housing Market Impacts of Rent Control*. Washington, DC: The Urban Institute Press, 1990. Reprinted with permission.

Affordability has become the most serious housing problem confronting renter households. With the shrinking federal resources allocated to housing assistance, and the less than full replacement of lost federal funds by state programs, local governments are under increasing pressure to make rental housing more affordable. Rent control offers the promise of making housing more affordable at virtually no cost to the public sector. But it also runs the risk of restricting profits to such an extent that the housing stock deteriorates.

The D.C. [District of Columbia] rent control system was established in 1975. About two-thirds of the rental stock is subject to controls, with the following categories exempt: small units, new and substantially renovated units, units in continuously vacant buildings, co-op units, and subsidized units. Even the controlled units do not have fixed rent levels. A complex system regulates both the frequency and amount of rent increases. Properly licensed and registered units can increase rents annually by the Consumer Price Index. When a unit is vacated, its rent can be increased by 12 percent or up to the rent ceiling, whichever is higher. Landlords can petition to increase rent ceilings to reflect certain cost increases. And landlords can negotiate voluntary agreements with tenants to increase rents. . . .

Rent Control: No Detriment to Housing

D.C. rent control has kept rents lower than they would have been in its absence. The monthly rent for the average unit would be at least $50 higher and possibly $200 higher without rent control.

These benefits are not spread equitably or efficiently. By targeting benefits to long-term stayers, D.C. rent control provides greatest benefits to lower income renters, elderly households, and families with children. But affluent renters also obtain direct benefits if they stay in a unit for an extended period. And poor renters, if they move, pay rents just as high as those that would prevail on the open market.

Rent control has not eliminated profitability. After accounting for appreciation gains and tax benefits, investment in D.C. rental housing today compares favorably with alternative investment opportunities.

Whether rent control is responsible for housing deficiencies in the District's rental stock is unclear. About one in five rental units is physically deficient. Without controls, gross rent revenues would have been 33 percent higher. Landlords say they would have used the increase for better maintenance. But even with rent control the proportion of units that are physically deficient in the District has declined from a total share of 26 percent to one of 20 percent, and the rate of deficiencies is *higher* among the *exempt* units.

The size of the rental stock declined precipitously during the period of rent control in the District, but many cities without rent control have witnessed similar declines. The relative attractiveness of home ownership, expansion of suburban housing opportunities for minorities, and the basic costs of rental housing production appear to be the critical determinants of the number of units added and lost to the rental housing stock. This conclusion is supported by the fact that the supply of rental housing in the District has begun to respond to renewed demand pressures. . . .

Rent Costs Without Controls

Estimating what rent levels would have been in the absence of controls constitutes the critical first step in analyzing the impacts of controls on the rental housing market. Our 1987 survey of renter households provides a wealth of information about the characteristics of units on the rental market today, but it obviously cannot tell us what rent levels would have been if rent control had not been implemented. . . .

Rent Control: No Housing Shortage Effect

A study of multifamily construction between 1980 and 1986 ranked Santa Monica second among seven coastal cities in the Los Angeles area in multifamily construction per square mile, undermining real estate industry claims that rent control leads to shrinking construction and therefore more severe housing shortages than a regulation free atmosphere. . . .

To answer the question "Who benefits?" then, the evidence points to low- and moderate-income tenants and to the fact that urban space is made more accessible to mixed-income groups as a result of strong rent controls.

Stella M. Čapek and John I. Gilderbloom, *Community Versus Commodity*, 1992.

At a minimum, we estimate that average rents in the District would have increased at a rate of about 8.8 percent annually—half a percentage point higher than the rate for the surrounding suburbs. In other words, in the absence of controls, the relationship between rent inflation in the District and its suburbs would have been more typical of other metropolitan areas. However, given the rates of rent inflation that prevailed in other central cities over the period, we consider it more likely that rents would have increased faster—at a rate of 9.5 percent annually. This "best estimate" of 9.5 percent annual rent inflation corresponds to the average rate experienced by the uncontrolled central cities and by U.S. central cities generally.

Finally, given the above-average rate of income growth that occurred among D.C. renters in the 1970s and 1980s, it is possible that in the absence of controls, the pressure on rents would have been considerably higher here than in the comparison cities. Median rent levels consistently increased at a faster pace than the median incomes among renter households in both central cities and suburban jurisdictions. In fact, among the uncontrolled central cities, the annual rate of rent inflation averaged about four percentage points higher than the average annual rate of income growth among renter households. If the District had experienced this pattern in the absence of controls, rents would have increased by as much as 11 percent annually.

The task of estimating what rents would have been in the absence of controls is fraught with uncertainty. There is no unimpeachable source of evidence. Using the best available method, we estimate that, in the absence of controls, average rent levels would be significantly higher than those that prevail today. Even given the lower-bound estimate of an 8.8 percent annual rate of rent inflation, rents in the District today would average about $50 more in an unregulated market. And at the upper-bound estimate, unregulated rents would exceed today's levels by more than $200 on average. Our best estimate of a 9.5 percent annual rate of rent inflation implies that, in the absence of controls, D.C. renters would be paying between $95 and $100 more per month in rent (including utilities) than they do today.

Rent Control and Affordable Housing

Without question, the rent savings generated by controls in the District moderate the problems of housing affordability faced by D.C. renters. At our "best estimates" of uncontrolled market rent levels, the share of households paying more than 30 percent of their income for rent would increase from its current level of about 43 percent to more than 50 percent. Thus, while affordability problems in the District are severe today, a much larger number of renter households would pay excessive rent burdens in the absence of rent control. In fact, the median rent burdens would be much more typical of other central cities in the U.S. at these estimated market rent levels.

However, the rent savings generated by controls are not evenly distributed among all D.C. renters. In fact, not all households would be paying more in an uncontrolled market than they do today. About one-quarter of all D.C. renters probably pay rents as high—and perhaps higher—than the "market" rents that would prevail in the absence of controls. And, among those who experience rent savings, about one-third pay rents that are within $100 of estimated market rents, another third pay between $100 and $200 less than they would in the absence of controls, and the remaining third pay rents that are more than $200 below market rent levels.

Those Who Benefit Most

The households who enjoy the greatest rent savings are those who have remained in their controlled units for several years. The vast majority of households who occupy controlled units and who have remained in their units for six or more years enjoy substantial rent savings, while roughly half of those who are recent movers pay rents as high, or higher, than they would in the absence of controls. Our estimates suggest that, when controlled rental units are vacated, landlords sometimes raise rents to levels *above* those that would prevail in the absence of controls, to compensate for the fact that, if the new tenant stays for more than a year or two, rents will be constrained from rising as rapidly as they would in the absence of controls. Thus, the turnover history of controlled units plays an important role in determining the level of rent savings—with units that turn over frequently much more likely to charge rents at or above market levels than units that have experienced only occasional turnover.

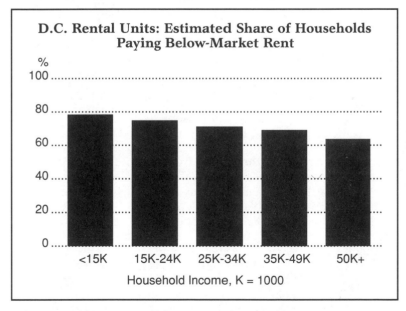

D.C. Rental Units: Estimated Share of Households Paying Below-Market Rent

Household Income, K = 1000

What types of households benefit from a system of controls that provides the biggest savings to long-term stayers? In general, elderly households and families with children are the groups most likely to enjoy rent savings from the existing system of controls, while younger and more mobile singles are those most likely to pay rents that are as high or higher than those that would prevail in the absence of controls. Moreover, poor and moderate-income households are more likely to enjoy direct rent savings than are those with higher incomes. Specifically, as shown in the figure, about 80 percent of poor households (annual incomes under $15,000) pay below-market rents, compared to 65 percent of high-income renters (annual incomes over $50,000). This pattern stems from the fact that the most affluent segments of the District's renter population consist of young singles and groups of unrelated adults, who are more likely to be recent movers and to occupy the newer, more expensive, and larger units that typify the exempt portion of the District's rental stock. . . .

Strong Support Among Renters

District renters—including those living in both controlled and exempt units—strongly approve of rent control. For virtually all segments of the renter population, sentiment runs at least three to one in favor of rent control. Although D.C. renters are enthusiastic about rent control, many do not really know whether or not the units in which they live are controlled. Specifically, almost 40 percent either do not know or answer incorrectly when asked to identify the control status of their units. Tenants in controlled units are more likely to know their control status than those who live in exempt units, and the share of households with accurate information increases systematically among those who have remained in the same units for several years. But the fact remains that two out of every five D.C. renters are either uninformed or misinformed about their status.

The primary benefit of rent control, as perceived by residents of controlled units, is that it makes rents more affordable. Roughly 90 percent of those who live in controlled rental units indicate that rent control has made their apartments more affordable. But tenants also value the sense of security provided by the existing system of controls; about 80 percent of those who live in controlled units say that rent control provides them with the security to stay in their apartments if they want to. Most of these households (almost 75 percent) also indicate that rent control increases their incentive to stay in their existing apartments even if they might prefer to move. Thus, D.C. renters recognize that continuous occupancy of a controlled unit is what generates the greatest monetary savings under the existing system of controls, but this impediment to mobility does not appear to outweigh the benefits of controls in the minds of most.

Most tenants in controlled rental units (80 percent) believe that building maintenance is as good or better than it would be in the absence of rent controls, and a substantial share (61 percent) report that the protections offered by rent control make them more willing to insist on building repairs. Low-income households were particularly likely to include this as a benefit of the District's rent control program. . . .

Little Impact on Investment and Supply

Advocates often advance rent control as a panacea for problems of housing affordability, while opponents blame controls for the poor quality and dwindling supply of low-cost units. In the District of Columbia, neither of these extreme positions is supported by the facts. Rent control appears to have moderated the housing affordability problem, but has by no means solved it. And there is no convincing evidence that controls have significantly deterred investment in either maintenance or new construction, although the profitability of rental housing would be higher in the absence of controls.

Economic theory suggests that, certainly over the long term, any substantial price effect (reduced rents) must yield a supply effect (lower quality or fewer units). As a result, most economic analyses argue that the benefits of rent control—more affordable rent levels—are ultimately outweighed by the costs—deferred maintenance and limited availability of units. Our evidence, however, suggests that rent control in the District of Columbia has had little or no supply effect, despite over a decade of moderated rent increases. . . .

No system of rent control can ensure the availability of decent and affordable housing for low- and moderate-income renters. Whether or not cities regulate rents, more direct remedies are clearly required, including programs that supplement the rents that low- and moderate-income tenants can afford to pay, that preserve existing low-rent properties, and that induce the production of additional low- and moderate-cost rental units.

"Employer-assisted housing programs constitute a cost-effective strategy for the improvement of urban areas."

Encourage Employer-Sponsored Housing Loans

Richard Ferlauto

Employers should grant housing benefits to their workers to re-vitalize urban neighborhoods, Richard Ferlauto argues in the following viewpoint. Ferlauto contends that employers can act individually or in partnerships to provide benefits such as low-interest mortgage loans or loans requiring no down payment. These attractive loans would promote home ownership and im-provement in areas where employers and employees are located, thus improving real estate values, preventing urban blight, and developing community spirit. Ferlauto is the director of the Center for Policy Alternatives' Public Capital Program in Washington, D.C., and coauthor of the book *A New Housing Policy for America: Recapturing the American Dream*.

As you read, consider the following questions:

1. Why does Ferlauto believe it is difficult for a city to revitalize neighborhoods on its own?
2. In the author's opinion, how can partnerships between local employers and nonprofit housing developers benefit both sides?
3. Why should employers encourage workers who rent nearby to purchase neighborhood homes, according to Ferlauto?

Richard Ferlauto, "New Way to Affordable Housing," *The Christian Science Monitor*, May 4, 1990. Reprinted with permission.

With the cutback in federal funds for community development, and escalating state budget deficits, urban neighborhoods face the grim reality that they must rely on their own limited resources for revitalization. Since 1980, urban decay and the declining quality and quantity of affordable shelter has grown, according to the Joint Center for Housing Studies at the Massachusetts Institute of Technology. In that same period, Community Development Block Grant funds shrank by over 30 percent (adjusted for inflation) and the budget for the Department of Housing and Urban Development dropped from $36 billion in 1980 to $15.3 billion in 1990.

Bud Kanitz, executive director of the National Neighborhood Coalition, believes that employee housing benefits targeted to older urban neighborhoods could provide an important new resource for community revitalization and investment. According to Mr. Kanitz, "City halls and government planning agencies should encourage local employers to provide benefits to low- and moderate-income workers so that they can become first-time home buyers in neighborhoods that have not seen new investment in many years. By building partnerships with community-based nonprofit housing developers, employers could reinvigorate the previously stagnant neighborhoods."

Some cities have established housing partnerships, linkage fees for affordable housing, zoning-density bonuses to stimulate housing activity, and urban enterprise zones. But few cities have sufficient tools to spur ongoing investment in the revitalization of low-income communities.

Improving Urban Neighborhoods

Employer-assisted housing is a new tool that could spur increased investment in urban neighborhoods. More and more, cities and local companies are coming to realize that employer-assisted housing programs constitute a cost-effective strategy for the improvement of urban areas (by helping workers to afford homes in targeted neighborhoods). Across the country, employers are discovering that by helping employees buy homes they are stabilizing and enhancing real estate values, strengthening and maintaining residential property-tax bases, protecting the integrity of the local labor force, infusing local institutions with new vigor, and developing community spirit.

The role of businesses in funding low-income housing has grown with the new opportunities to earn a return on low-income housing investment made available in the Tax Reform Act of 1986. Since 1986, $9 billion in low-income housing tax credits, which earn a 15 percent return, have been sold to corporations. Employer-assisted housing programs involve the same business interest in a return on investment by linking return on investment to savings in employee training and retention, labor-force availability, productivity, and real estate appreciation.

A prime example of an employer-assisted housing partnership is revitalizing a low-income area in Chicago. Greater North Pulaski Development Corporation, Neighborhood Housing Services, and Fannie Mae [Federal National Mortgage Association] in association with local employers are rehabilitating a 50 square block low-income neighborhood with mixed industrial and residential uses in the northwest side of Chicago with an employer-assisted housing initiative.

A Competitive Edge

Employer-assisted housing strategies can help municipalities gain a competitive advantage in high-housing-cost areas. Economists and business leaders are increasingly blaming the lack of affordable housing for the slowdown in major regional economies across the United States. In New England, the Mid-Atlantic States, the Southeast, California, and portions of the Pacific Northwest, high housing costs have been shown to be causing or contributing to labor shortages. Housing costs contribute to labor shortages by encouraging outmigration from high-cost areas and discouraging migration to these areas; diminished productivity due to lateness and absenteeism caused by long commutes as workers seek housing affordability far from developed worksites; and unacceptable recruitment, retention, and wage rate distortions.

Richard C. Ferlauto, Daniel N. Hoffman, and David C. Schwartz, *Public Management*, January 1991.

Known as the Chicago Walk to Work Program, participating companies make investments based on the size of their workforce into a revolving loan fund. Firms include Pioneer Bank and Trust Company, Finzer Roller Company, Universal Allied Imaging Company, Helene Curtis Inc., and Pride Container Inc. Participating employers earn a return of 5 percent per year, payable at the end of the term.

Employees of enrolled companies are eligible to borrow up to $8,000 at 6 percent interest for a term of seven years. Funds can be used as home-improvement loans or to supplement funds needed for a down payment. Loans are bought on the secondary market by Fannie Mae.

Attractive Home Loans

The University of Pennsylvania has offered a mortgage-guarantee program for 20 years to its employees that has successfully stabilized the west Philadelphia neighborhoods in which the university is located. Because the university guarantees 100 percent of the mortgage value, no down payments are required. The program has given moderate-income employees who could not otherwise afford to buy a home because they were unable to save the down payment access to home ownership. Since the late 1960s, more than 1,000 loans have been made.

Cities with strong or emerging nonprofit housing developers will find that promoting partnerships between nonprofits and local employers for the creation of affordable units is much more efficient than the current system of patchwork financing. Rather than relying on corporate philanthropy, nonprofits would benefit by entering contractual arrangements to deliver low-cost housing for low-income employees. A nonprofit with a steady stream of financing on a contractual basis could develop an ongoing capacity to deliver many times the number of units they now provide.

For nonprofits, employer partnerships hold the promise of political stability, continuing financial capacity, and long-term institutional support that will help attract lenders, mortgage insurers, and other important financial players.

Employers may find that their employees are renters in neighborhoods adjacent to their facilities. Moving those employees into home ownership through group mortgage insurance programs and mortgage guarantees would stabilize real estate values in areas where local industry has a substantial investment. Just as important for local employers, a stable neighborhood helps insure that workers would be willing to work in an area not plagued by crime, drugs, and blight.

For low-income renters in urban neighborhoods, employers can use employer-assisted supply programs that subsidize housing to affordable levels even for these modestly paid workers. Employers could participate by providing surplus land to a land trust in return for some priority being given to employees. Or employers could join mutual housing associations, participating as a partner in financing and managing affordable units. Whatever method is used, targeted housing investment by employers in low-income areas will leverage private investment.

Help for Public Workers

In addition to private employers, cities and public institutions could use their human-resource budgets as part of a community development strategy. Municipal workers tend to be modestly paid, but to be stable long-term employees. With current strains on municipal finance, city administrators may find that they could offer housing benefits, at little or no cost to their budgets, that public workers would eagerly accept. A coordinated approach to revitalization that included a housing benefit targeted for use in low-income neighborhoods can have a greater impact on urban communities than limited dollars in community block grants.

Neighborhood developers across the country are building new partnerships with employers, nonprofit developers, and public institutions, rethinking the uses of their benefit packages to make available millions of new investment dollars in declining neighborhoods. These innovative public private partnerships may hold the key to saving our cities from blight.

"Anti-capitalist politics and direct action provide the best strategies for mobilizing working-class tenants and winning long-term gains."

Encourage Tenant Activism

John May

Tenant activist groups should organize to protect renters' rights and improve their living conditions, John May argues in the following viewpoint. May asserts that these groups can help tenants in disputes with landlords by informing them of their legal rights and locating legal services for them. Activist groups can also stage public protests to demand repairs of units, fight unjust tenant evictions and rent increases, and petition cities to protect affordable housing, May contends. May, a photographer and writer, is a volunteer organizer for City Life/Vida Urbana, a Boston-based activist group that promotes the rights of low-income tenants and homeowners.

As you read, consider the following questions:

1. How have many landlords neglected inner-city neighborhoods and deprived working-class tenants of decent, affordable housing, in May's opinion?
2. Why does the author believe that housing should be based on a socialist system rather than a capitalist system?
3. According to May, how do tenant-owned co-op apartments ensure affordable housing for future tenants?

From John May, "City Life/Vida Urbana: Rebuilding the Housing Movement." This article is reprinted from the Resist newsletter (April 1990). Resist is a nonprofit foundation funding grassroots social change projects since 1967. For more information, write: Resist, One Summer St., Somerville, MA 02143.

A battle is being fought for the roofs of America. Over the past 15 years the housing shortage reached a terrifying peak, with disastrous effects on American cities. As real estate speculation and gentrification drove housing costs in a dizzying upward spiral in the '70s and '80s, displacement and homelessness exploded. The hostile takeover of lower income neighborhoods by real estate profiteers in the name of "revitalization" tore apart communities, leaving them less able to confront the persistent problems of drugs, crime and decay in their midst. Land and housing development form the foundation of urban economic life. Gentrification, robbing working class neighborhoods of control, is a foreclosure on the future of entire communities.

The housing movement has struggled to respond to the challenge. In the past few years, a number of progressive housing groups have moved toward strategies based on a comprehensive view of the housing crisis and an understanding of its connections to larger political and economic issues. These strategies utilize neighborhood-based organizing to promote a socialist housing agenda; an agenda that calls for an end to real estate speculation, community control of housing and economic development, guaranteed affordable housing for all that is both decent and secure, and the removal of housing from private market control.

Committed to Lower Income Groups

City Life/Vida Urbana, founded in the Jamaica Plain neighborhood of Boston in 1974, was one of the first organizations in the affordable housing movement to develop this model. Committed to working directly with lower income tenants and homeowners at the street level, and using a class analysis of housing issues, City Life represents the marriage of traditional neighborhood activism with progressive, anti-capitalist politics. City Life's founders were veterans of the popular movements of the '60s and '70s. Its members consider anti-racism, feminism and democratic socialism the foundations of a just and equitable society, and neighborhood organizing and direct action the tools for building a broad, inclusive progressive movement.

City Life came on the scene at a time when the shortage of decent affordable housing in Boston was becoming critical. Working class neighborhoods, suffering from years of disinvestment, were under attack, both from traditional slumlords and a new breed of "investors." While the former made their money through rent-gouging, neglect and arson-for-profit, the latter used housing purchases as speculative investments to be resold later at the highest possible profit. They were both the promoters and beneficiaries of gentrification.

The failure of the private market to provide for the basic housing needs of so many people offered an opportunity to build a progressive movement that addressed an issue everyone cared about. The real estate industry represented one of the worst examples of the profit system gone wild, ransacking neighborhoods and depriving people of control over land and resources. At the same time, a relatively decentralized pattern of ownership (primarily smaller local landlords rather than huge, distant corporate owners) presented numerous, accessible targets to organize against.

Taking to the Streets

As an organization primarily founded by women, and based on feminist principles, City Life recognized that organizing low-income tenants meant building a movement led by women. The group's interest in working with the "tenant most in need" meant involving, in leadership positions, low-income African-American and Latino community members. City Life promoted direct action as a tactic in building neighborhood campaigns. We helped organize tenant unions to confront landlords over bad conditions, rent increases and evictions. When landlords ignored tenant demands, we helped organize rent strikes and eviction blockings. In one case, for example, City Life and dozens of neighborhood supporters physically prevented the retaliatory eviction of a Latina woman who had been working with tenants in her building to get basic repairs.

Tenant Activists Wield Power

Tenant groups exist in every major city and many suburbs. Groups usually begin in one building, primarily to monitor and improve building conditions. In some cases, tenants in different buildings owned by the same landlord will come together to wield their collective strength, and in other cases, tenants will organize on a neighborhood basis.

John Atlas and Peter Dreier, *Shelterforce*, August/September 1988.

Larger and more powerful landlords, including the City of Boston, were met with forceful and creative campaigns; we brought demonstrators directly to landlords' homes and offices, or to meetings and hearings. In the case of one landlord, who was trying to evict tenants for condo conversion, City Life circulated "Wanted" posters city-wide, with his picture and a list of charges against him. As landlords began clearing buildings and cashing in on them by using arson fires in the late '70s, City Life organized arson watches to identify properties at risk, monitor suspicious activity and expose those landlords responsible for the danger.

When the City of Boston began selling vacant municipal buildings to private for-profit developers, City Life urged that the buildings be developed for affordable housing. The effort culminated in a week-long "tent city" outside one such building, drawing hundreds of activists from around the city. (Recently, after a seven-year fight, the building was developed as a 45-unit rooming house for formerly homeless people.)

Tenant Advocacy

City Life also provided advocacy: going with tenants to meet with landlords, lawyers and the rent board; helping tenants locate legal services; holding educational meetings about tenant rights; and distributing a monthly neighborhood newspaper with information of interest to tenants and progressives. We spoke out at community meetings supporting tenant struggles and demanding affordable housing. While eschewing direct lobbying or electoral work, City Life lent its voice to efforts to preserve and expand rent control laws and other pro-tenant legislation.

To address non-housing concerns of the people we worked with, City Life formed committees on education, welfare rights, women's issues and international issues. A Workplace Committee was established to network and educate among progressive-minded union members and to publish a separate newsletter, *The Labor Page*. City Life's efforts throughout the '70s and early '80s brought together tenants, tenant unions and community organizations in three neighborhoods. While building a solid base of hundreds of supporters, we successfully defended individual tenants and tenant associations, and won important victories against some of the most powerful landlords in Boston.

In the process, we pushed the agenda for the housing movement far beyond that advanced by more mainstream organizations. Our "Housing Platform for Boston" called for stiff taxes on speculative profits, a ban on condominium conversions, recognition of collective bargaining rights of tenants, takeover of the properties of absentee landlords who repeatedly violated the law, an end to the sale of subsidized and city-owned properties to for-profit developers, an end to housing discrimination and extension of full rent control to cover all units.

Despite significant gains, however, City Life made little progress toward our goal of building a larger socialist housing movement that would change the balance of power between landlords and tenants in the city. Our work in the first 12 years was largely reactive, helping defend tenants who sought us out. Our short-term victories did not often lead to enduring tenant unions, or sustain ongoing activism among large numbers of tenants.

As a way of expanding our community base, City Life, along with the local Legal Services Center in neighboring Roxbury, conceived of the Eviction Free Zone (EFZ) project. It was designed to take the initiative in an area hard hit by another wave of gentrification, prompted by the construction of a new mass transit line through the center of the two neighborhoods. Using door-to-door outreach, we built contacts with tenants in certain targeted areas, and linked individual tenant cases with the larger organizing effort. As door-knocking brought in information about specific cases, we gathered a database on real estate activity in the target areas, enabling us to intervene around landlords and buildings before these situations became critical. At the same time, we received several grants and were able to hire additional paid staff, improving the level of services offered to tenants.

The effort resulted in many tenants becoming better informed about their rights, and a number joined City Life as organizers. We established a Spanish-speaking housing committee which has grown to include 15 active members and has taken the lead in City Life's work in Latino neighborhoods. The English and Latino committees hold bilingual meetings together to develop a cohesive agenda and plan overall strategy, but also meet separately to facilitate the political involvement of new members.

Building on Success

The EFZ has successfully intervened in dozens of tenant cases and frustrated the abusive practices of several notorious local speculators. We mobilized a demonstration of 125 community residents to prevent the auction of a 16-unit building and secure it for low-income housing. City Life led a slate of affordable housing activists who won control of the Jamaica Plain Neighborhood Council in 1987 by an 80% majority, and won again in 1990. (Neighborhood Councils were established by Boston Mayor Ray Flynn as advisory bodies on neighborhood issues and have been successfully used by activists in some neighborhoods as vehicles for community participation in development decisions.) City Life has also built strong links to several other community organizations, and helped establish a separate community group in the largest Latino neighborhood.

Most importantly, we have brought our activism to the attention of a larger segment of our neighborhood, and, through systematic and consistent contact with residents, have established a lifeline to the working class community. Landlords, developers and city and state officials now see us as a force to be reckoned with. Other tenant organizations have adopted our model in their own areas, as part of a growing network of progressive groups organizing in low-income and minority communities. . . .

Lack of resources and high tenant turnover, however, have made it difficult to establish lasting networks of street level activists. While the EFZ strategy has drawn considerable attention among housing activists, and has been adopted by other tenant organizations in Boston, fragmentation within the movement has impeded the formation of the city-wide network of EFZs that we originally envisioned. Working-class, community-based organizing remains a heterodoxy in a housing movement dominated by liberal reform organizations. These groups continue to treat housing as a single issue, best addressed by preserving and expanding existing rent control laws, housing code regulations and government subsidy programs. Ordinary tenants are limited to the role of client; the groups concentrate on lobbying on behalf of tenants in legislatures, courts and government agencies.

Activism Spurs Tenants' Rights Laws

Tenants had significant successes during the late 1970s and early 1980s. More than 200 cities—including Boston, New York, San Francisco, Washington, D.C., Los Angeles—and more than 100 communities in New Jersey have some form of rent control. Hundreds of cities and some states have adopted laws protecting tenants from condominium conversions: Some provide a notice period, some require relocation expenses, some place a ban on evictions, and some regulate the rate of conversion. Most states now have a "warranty of habitability" written into their laws, requiring landlords to provide decent, sanitary apartments in exchange for rent. A few cities have adopted versions of "just cause" eviction laws.

John Atlas and Peter Dreier, *Shelterforce*, August/September 1988.

Electoral victories during the '80s on the part of pro-tenant city councilors and the mayor have brought more attention to working-class neighborhoods, and provided some mechanisms for community input—i.e. the neighborhood councils. Although these officials have made some commitments to affordable housing, they have been unwilling to devote sufficient resources to offset the large number of units lost during the speculation boom, and they have yet to expend the political capital required to restore rent control protections lost in the '70s. While affordable housing may be on their agenda, empowerment of working-class neighborhoods is not. Community control of housing, though embraced by more and more housing groups, still faces entrenched opposition from City Hall and the real estate cartel.

Many tenants in Boston remain untouched by the housing movement; most are still unaware of what legal protections they have.

A New Opportunity to Act

A slump in the real estate market has slowed the march of gentrification somewhat. Taking advantage of this moment, and utilizing the network established by the EFZ, City Life is developing new strategies. Along with other progressive groups, we have begun promoting limited equity co-ops, a "third stream" of housing that is neither part of the private market, nor government owned. The buildings are owned and controlled collectively by tenants. Since the units are restricted from individual resale for profit, limited equity co-ops take buildings out of the private market and ensure permanent affordability. Non-profit community development corporations (CDCs) oversee construction and rehabilitation, financing the projects through private loans, grants and rent subsidies.

In addition to working with a local CDC to develop co-ops in our neighborhood, City Life is working with the Hotel and Restaurant Workers Union (Local 26) and other groups on a city-wide strategy. Local 26 negotiated a contract that includes a trust fund to provide housing assistance for its members, many of whom are low-income people of color. We are working to strengthen our existing ties to the union with an eye toward bringing together disparate labor and community organizations in a strong coalition around housing.

Despite their mass membership base, the liberal housing groups lack an organizing approach capable of mobilizing active tenant support. And many more progressive housing activists are reluctant to put forward a socialist analysis of housing, fearing that tenants will not accept it. But the need for a radical response by the community is evident in the bitter legacy of the Reagan years—six million people without homes, devastated school systems, communities ravaged by drugs and a horrifying resurgence of racism and violence. Seventeen years of organizing in working-class neighborhoods has shown us that inclusive, anti-capitalist politics and direct action provide the best strategies for mobilizing working-class tenants and winning long-term gains.

As in the events in Eastern Europe, where the cheerleaders of capitalism see socialism discredited, we see the resurgent potential of popular power and real democracy, ideas which form the foundations of City Life's vision. Now is the time to bring this power home. We have the opportunity to create a broad-based socialist housing movement that can build both housing and power for working-class tenants. Using the tools we have developed, we can begin to chip away at the profit system in housing, and build a new life for our neighborhoods.

Distinguishing Between Fact and Opinion

This activity is designed to help develop the basic reading and thinking skill of distinguishing between fact and opinion. Consider the following statement as an example: "The federal government allows public housing tenants to purchase their units." This is a factual statement because it could be checked by reading articles about public housing. But the statement "Tenant ownership of public housing is the solution to most urban problems" is an opinion. While some people support this statement, others would argue that the policy does not address private housing or other urban problems.

When investigating controversial issues it is important that one be able to distinguish between statements of fact and statements of opinion. It is also important to recognize that not all statements of fact are true. They may appear to be true, but some are based on inaccurate or false information. For this activity, however, we are concerned with understanding the difference between those statements that appear to be factual and those that appear to be based primarily on opinion.

Most of the following statements are taken from the viewpoints in this chapter. Consider each statement carefully. *Mark O for any statement you believe is an opinion or interpretation of facts. Mark F for any statement you believe is a fact. Mark I for any statement you believe is impossible to judge.*

If you are doing this activity as a member of a class or group, compare your answers with those of other class or group members. Be able to defend your answers. You may discover that others come to different conclusions than you do. Listening to the reasons others present for their answers may give you valuable insights into distinguishing between fact and opinion.

> *O = opinion*
> *F = fact*
> *I = impossible to judge*

1. The Department of Housing and Urban Development's budget dropped from $36 billion in 1980 to $15.3 billion in 1990.

2. Rent control laws deprive landlords of market-rate rental income.

3. The purchase and renovation of homes in inner-city neighborhoods by the wealthy robs control from poorer residents.

4. Approximately 3.5 million Americans live in public housing.

5. Unless home ownership is encouraged among inner-city residents, they are doomed to continue living in poverty.

6. Welfare regulations discourage fathers from living with their families.

7. Most heads of households in public housing are unemployed.

8. Rent control laws protect poor tenants from price-gouging landlords.

9. Most poor families would prefer to purchase private housing units rather than those in public housing.

10. The U.S. government reports that in some cities most poor families pay more than half their income on housing.

11. Abysmal conditions in public housing projects have forced authorities to destroy some of them.

12. Conditions in public housing began to deteriorate as most of the working poor moved out.

13. Employers are obligated to help their workers find decent, affordable housing.

14. The federal government's budget for public housing reached a record $6 billion in fiscal year 1991.

15. More than two hundred communities in America have rent control laws.

Periodical Bibliography

The following articles have been selected to supplement the diverse views presented in this chapter.

Trevor Armbrister	"How Government Makes Housing Unaffordable," *Reader's Digest*, March 1992.
John Atlas and Peter Dreier	"The Phony Case Against Rent Control," *The Progressive*, April 1989.
Julia Barnes	"A Celebration of Good Housing," *People's Weekly World*, July 4, 1992. Available from Long View Publishing, 235 W. 23d St., New York, NY 10011.
Tom Bethell	"Tenant Ownership: Will Anyone Bother to Buy?" *The Wall Street Journal*, January 10, 1990.
Frederick Brown	"Create More Dynamic Public Housing: A Modest Proposal," *Journal of Housing*, November/December 1990.
David S. Burgess	"Public Housing: A Cloud of Dust," *Christianity and Crisis*, July 20, 1992. Available from PO Box 6415, Syracuse, NY 13217.
Thomas J. Connelly Jr.	"Resident Initiatives: Hope or Hoax?" *Journal of Housing*, July/August 1991.
Christina Del Valle	"Low-Income Housing: Is There a Better Way?" *Business Week*, June 22, 1992.
J.S. Fuerst and Roy Petty	"High-Rise Housing for Low-Income Families," *The Public Interest*, Spring 1991.
Maggie Garb	"Saving the Inner Cities," *In These Times*, August 5-18, 1992.
James A. Maccaro	"The Folly of Rent Control," *The Freeman*, January 1990. Available from The Foundation for Economic Education, Irvington-on-Hudson, NY 10533.
John McCormick	"A Housing Program That Actually Works," *Newsweek*, June 22, 1992.
Michael Novak	"Barefoot Capitalism," *Forbes*, May 13, 1991.
Julia F. Siler	"The Odd Couple of Low-Income Housing," *Business Week*, October 28, 1991.

How Can Urban Conditions Be Improved?

AMERICA's
CITIES

Chapter Preface

Two events in April 1992 brought the woeful condition of many American cities to the public's attention. First, serious flooding occurred in Chicago when a river's century-old underground retaining wall collapsed due to neglect, causing more than $1 billion of damage. A similar amount of damage occurred later that month during the Los Angeles riots, which followed the acquittal of four police officers who had beaten a black man, Rodney King. Massive looting and violence brought international attention to the city's acute poverty and tense race relations.

While other cities may be spared such catastrophes, the majority are afflicted with racial conflict, poverty, decaying infrastructure, and high rates of crime and drug abuse. To improve these conditions, officials propose urban renewal projects and seek aid from federal and state governments and private organizations and businesses to provide more jobs, safer neighborhoods, and newer buildings and roads.

Clearly, as cities face greater problems with fewer funds, they will need to find ever more creative ways to improve conditions. Urban renewal proposals offer some solutions. The authors in the following chapter provide other ideas for helping cities regain their strength.

"It is very much in the national interest for the federal government to assist cities."

Federal Aid Would Improve Cities

Alan Beals

Many U.S. mayors call for an increase in federal aid to improve conditions in their cities. In the following viewpoint, Alan Beals argues that since most Americans live in urban regions, the United States cannot afford to ignore the mayors' plea and neglect its cities. Beals contends that because a symbiotic relationship exists between the cities and the nation, the success of the nation depends on the success of its cities. He opposes forcing states to shoulder the burden of urban programs. Beals is a former president of the National League of Cities and is now president of the Savannah, Georgia, chamber of commerce.

As you read, consider the following questions:

1. How have economic crises affected federal aid to cities, according to Beals?
2. In the author's opinion, why should the federal government pay for the enforcement of regulations it levies on cities?
3. Why does Beals believe that the federal government will need to provide continued job training programs?

From Alan Beals, "Federal Support to Cities Must Not Be Reduced," in *The Hidden Wealth of Cities*, Edward C. Hayes, ed. Greenwich, CT: JAI Press, 1989. Reprinted by permission.

American cities have been called "engines of the American economy" and "laboratories of social and economic experimentation." Cities are, in fact, the place where most people work, where most of the jobs are created, where most of the new businesses are born, and where most of the national wealth is created. According to the Census Bureau, in 1984 nearly three-quarters of the U.S. population was living in metropolitan areas, and the population of these areas was increasing at a greater rate than the population in rural areas. Some 85% of personal income is generated in metropolitan areas.

The Federal/City Relationship

The above mentioned statistics clearly indicate that there is a symbiotic relationship between the nation and its cities. Cities could not separate themselves from federal policies even if they wished to, and Washington cannot extricate itself from the problems of urban America. Because we are an urban nation, federal policy *ipso facto* becomes urban policy as well. The success or failure of our cities to create jobs, provide housing, and maintain the environment is the measure of our success or failure as a nation. Accordingly, it is very much in the national interest for the federal government to assist cities in carrying out broad national policy goals and in their efforts as incubators and sustainers of economic growth.

At the core of federal aid programs toward cities are the following current (or recent) well-designed programs:

- General Revenue Sharing (GRS)
- Community Development Block Grants (CDBGs)
- Urban Development Action Grants (UDAGs)
- Housing assistance programs for the low-income, the elderly, and handicapped
- Public Transit and Municipal Wastewater grants
- Job Training
- The use of tax-exempt financing for low-income housing, infrastructure investment, and industrial development

In its legislative advocacy it has been the policy of the National League of Cities (NLC) to preserve these programs at their present levels. Because of the cutbacks in Washington the NLC has directed its efforts toward maintenance rather than program expansion. This stance is consistent with the NLC's broad recommendation that expenditures across the entire federal budget be frozen, with the exception of entitlement programs and Social Security.

City finances have been hit hard both by occurrences in the economy and by federal cuts. Since 1975 cities have gone through two serious recessions, have been ravaged by a period of inflation that sent prices up 50% in 10 years, and are caught, in 30 states, by local or statewide ordinances limiting local tax revenues.

Message to Washington

ROTHCO

© Graham/Rothco. Reprinted with permission.

Within this context federal aid cuts have been more serious than they might otherwise have been. Federal aid as a percentage of state and local budgets peaked in 1979 and has been declining ever since. The Law Enforcement Assistance Administration (LEAA) and public-sector job training have disappeared entirely. Other programs, including Urban Development Action Grants (UDAGs), the entire Economic Development Administration (EDA), and General Revenue Sharing (GRS) were all targeted for elimination by the Reagan administration in FY [fiscal year] 1987. The first two programs were saved by Congress, at much reduced levels compared to their late 1970s levels; General Revenue Sharing was completely eliminated that year. UDAGs have survived as a shell, authorized as programs, but with a zero appropriation in 1989. Both the EDA and legal services for the poor have already been scaled back, as have the Community Services Block Grant (CSBG), wastewater treatment grants, the Community Development Block Grants (CDBGs) down to a $2.6 billion appropriation in 1989, and various health, education and nutrition programs.

One of the hardest hit programs is federal housing assistance. A research report commissioned by the National League of Cities chronicled a decline in reservations for additional low-income units under HUD [Housing and Urban Development] and Farmers Home programs. Reservations have dropped from 541,534 in 1976 to 395,000 in 1986. The President's proposed budget for FY 87 called for no additional authorizations. Meanwhile, housing starts from previous authorizations fell below 40,000 in 1985, and completion of new or rehabilitated housing from a backlog of previous authorizations was down to 100,000 units.

Federal aid to transit has likewise been closely cropped. Only the passage of a gasoline tax increase maintained urban transportation funding into the mid-1980s, and even those levels represented some reduction for cities. The administration sought and won municipal support for the gas tax increase while offering assurances that one cent of the new five cents per gallon tax would be dedicated to additional funding for public transit. Once the new tax had gone into effect, however, the administration's memory suffered a lapse, and it proposed a new round of cuts in federal transit assistance. In addition, the latest administration initiative is a state-administered transportation block grant that would incorporate both highway and transit functions, at lower combined funding levels and without stipulation as to use.

General Revenue Sharing, before its elimination, had lost half its real dollar value while frozen at the 1976 level of $4.6 billion for local governments. The state share of $2.3 billion fell under the budget axe in 1980.

More Aid to Nations than Cities

Some sharp-eyed observers of the federal budget have noted, with dismay, that the fiscal 1987 budget submitted by the administration contained more foreign economic development aid than economic development assistance for the nation's cities. To put this comparison directly, the administration is more prepared to come to the aid of Athens, Greece than Athens, Georgia.

Throughout all its budget cutting, the avowed goal of the administration and congressional leadership has been to restrain the growth of federal spending, to weed out special interest programs and to put the nation's fiscal house in order. This concern for the deficit is shared by the country's municipal officials. A NLC survey of 487 officials from 371 cities and towns, taken at the end of 1985, found that for 66% of these officials, deficit reduction was the foremost concern. Unemployment was a distant second with 18% of the tally.

But when the actual job of budget cutting began the performance of the administration was not as benign as its stated intentions, and it was cities that stood the gaff. In 1980, budget authorization for urban programs totaled $58 billion; the federal deficit was $73 billion. By 1986, annual deficits had exploded to around $200 billion while authorization for urban programs had been cut to $26.3 billion.

Over the same time period tax *advantages* for certain groups actually increased. A NLC analysis of the federal budget has found, for example, that accelerated depreciation for office buildings went from $10 billion in 1984 to $15 billion in 1986, while over the same two years Community Development Block Grants were slated for a 32% reduction. Special capital gains allowances for timber went up by 150% under new tax code provisions, while low-income housing was taking a 67% cut. The purchase price of a corporate airplane can be recouped entirely through tax credits and deductions, while public transit funding faced a 62% cut between 1986 and 1987. Corporate tax preferences and subsidies, including entertainment, gifts, and business lunches, cost the Treasury about $120 billion in 1986, the same time that General Revenue Sharing was slated for extinction.

Growth in Tax Loopholes

Indeed it is worth dwelling for a moment on so-called "tax expenditures," the tax deductions, tax credits, and other shelters provided for individuals and corporations by the federal code. Between 1982 and 1986, federal tax expenditures for state and local government grew from $38 billion to $47 billion, a 23% increase, while the total for all tax expenditures combined—all the "loopholes" for public and private individuals and corporations—grew from $200 billion (in 1979) to $439 billion in 1986, a 120% increase. In 1988, reflecting the influence of the 1986 Tax Reform Act, which tried to remedy tax inequities, total tax expenditures fell to $303 billion, still over 33% greater than the 1979 level.

If the federal government wished to solve its deficit crises, it would not have to put itself through the agony of Gramm-Rudman-Hollings legislation. Instead it could simply close off the large "loopholes," or tax expenditures, to an even greater degree than the 1986 Tax Reform Act, which still leaves $303 billion in loopholes in 1988. Yet all of the tax bills introduced in 1986 to foster tax reform, including the successful Tax Reform Act itself, were "revenue neutral"; they closed loopholes to varying degrees, but also reduced taxes on individuals and some business taxes to such a point that tax reform was of no assistance in budget balancing. Without raising revenue, the budget will not be balanced easily, and efforts to balance will make cities pay the price. . . .

The United States Must Support Its Cities

There are many reasons for the federal government maintaining a strong support role for cities. But there is one overriding reason for continuing this role: . . . No other level of government can handle the tasks of the national social agenda as well, and support that agenda at a level which is required.

Consider, first, the question of low-income housing. This is not a state or local problem in essence; it is a national problem, and one in which the federal government has been deeply, and successfully, involved since the Housing Act of 1937. Consider, also, the problems of maintaining the safety and purity of water, ground, and air. None of these substances are respectors of state boundaries; all lie on and across each of the 50 states. Fifty sets of differing regulations would guarantee no regulation at all of these basic national resources.

Consider the fact of federal mandates. The federal government does not set up its own bureaucracy to enforce its regulations; it works through existing state and local public agencies, requiring them to enforce mandates dealing with civil rights, housing, the environment, and many others. These mandates cost money to enforce. Unless the federal government puts up the money to pay for this enforcement, the result will be either, that state and local governments do nothing, or they groan and take the money from their own pocket. Neither result is fair to all concerned. Federal aid, including the defunct General Revenue Sharing, exists in part to avoid these negative outcomes.

Consider, too, the fact that federal money is really essential for most federal social, economic, and environmental programs to operate at all. If the federal government withdraws, it is very unlikely that state or local administrations will step in to fill the gap. A report to the Urban Institute in Washington, D.C., titled "Testing The Social Safety Net," closely examined the events in four metropolitan areas between 1981 and 1983 as cuts were made in federal assistance for abused and neglected children, the chronically mentally ill, and the low-income elderly. The study found that federal cuts led to parallel or modified reductions in San Diego, Boston, and Richmond, Virginia. Only

Detroit came close to offsetting the loss, drawing on state and local assistance. Local charities also helped. In general, studies on the subject show that "substitution" of local money for lost federal money does not occur. No feds, no program.

Reroute Foreign Aid to America's Cities

Why must our young folk go without jobs? Why must our mothers suffer the indignity of a low-down, dirty welfare system? Why must our elected officials keep turning their heads and sending our money all over the world rather than to our cities? I want some foreign aid for Washington, D.C. I want some foreign aid for Watts. I want some foreign aid for Chicago. I want some foreign aid up in the Bronx. I want America to invest in America's people.

Maxine Waters, *In These Times*, May 27-June 9, 1992.

Consider as well the facts of a study by the National Alliance of Business. This study concluded that there will be a significant growth over the next ten to fifteen years of the "less well-educated segments of the population that have typically been the least prepared for work." This growth of the less-educated worker will occur at the same time that the economy is demanding higher levels of skills in the workforce. Yet, in the words of the study, anticipated "pervasive mismatches between workplace needs and workforce capabilities" will require an enormous amount of general and vocational education money, a strong justification for the continuation of federal job training programs which specialize in exactly that kind of training.

And finally, consider the fact that many of the federal grants programs have gone to help private business, to keep the urban industrial machine running full speed ahead. The grants in this category include the now-defunct UDAGs and CDBGs, the still-functioning Small Business Administration, and others. If we take seriously the metaphor of cities as "engines of our economy" then we should also maintain a serious federal commitment to insure the machine is kept running well, a commitment that includes exercising federal, legal, regulatory, tax, and financial assistance powers.

Federal Shedding of Responsibilities

In 1982 President Reagan proposed, as a focus of his State of the Union address, a devolution of federal powers to the state and local levels. The outline of this proposal was received with initial enthusiasm by city officials. But the enthusiasm waned rapidly when it became apparent that little, if any, federal financial support would accompany this "shedding" of federal program responsibilities onto the states. In practice, the devolution anticipated by the administration was a devolution of program responsibility without devolution of program money.

In a 1985 report by the Advisory Commission on Intergovernmental Relations the subject of devolution and turnbacks was examined again. The report drew several lengthy and pointed dissents. In their dissent, Governor Ted Schwinden of Montana, Mayor Joseph P. Riley Jr. of Charleston, South Carolina, and Mayor William H. Hudnut III of Indianapolis stated:

> [The Commission's turnback recommendation] would result in a dereliction of responsibilities by Washington, particularly toward the nation's cities. This recommendation is not so much an effort to decongest the federal system as it is a philosophical desire by some to have our national government wash its hands of any concern for local needs and problems.

In his dissent, Senator David Durenberger (R-Minn.) expressed concern that the Commission's proposal "would seriously exacerbate fiscal inequities in our federal system, rather than reduce them." Representative Ted Weiss (D-NY) also dissented without submitting formal comments.

Can there be a constructive "devolution" proposal which does not sacrifice the cities? In the current deficit-cutting atmosphere of Washington, it seems unlikely. In the meantime the cities will rely on their own entrepreneurial spirit and fiscal abilities to promote economic growth and encourage innovation.

However, over the long haul, the development of cities will also require a strong fiscal presence by the national government, a presence that will have to include both direct programs of financial assistance and a judicious use of tax incentives.

"The expansion of federal assistance to local jurisdictions carried within it the seeds of its own destruction."

Federal Aid Would Not Improve Cities

Robert D. Reischauer

Robert D. Reischauer is the director of the Congressional Budget Office, which provides federal budget data and analyses to Congress. In the following viewpoint, Reischauer argues that financial aid to cities is ineffective because federal aid programs are traditionally inefficient. Reischauer maintains that the generous urban aid programs of the 1960s and 1970s were plagued by bureaucratic red tape and excessive regulations imposed on cities. Reischauer believes that these aid programs have failed to improve cities and that the federal government is unlikely to provide further direct aid.

As you read, consider the following questions:

1. Why does Reischauer blame Congress for trying to solve urban problems in as many cities as possible?
2. According to the author, why is the federal government targeting aid to needy persons rather than city governments?
3. Why does Reischauer believe that cities are losing their political clout?

From Robert D. Reischauer, "The Rise and Fall of National Urban Policy: The Fiscal Dimension," *The Future of National Urban Policy*, Marshall Kaplan and Franklin James, editors, pp. 225-234. Copyright 1990, Duke University Press. Reprinted with permission of the publisher.

Before the Great Depression the federal government provided little in the way of financial assistance to local governments either directly or through the states. Then in the mid- and late 1930s Washington responded to the erosion of urban tax bases and the widespread hardship of the era with a surge of support for local public works, unemployment relief, and public housing programs. Federal aid to local governments rose from $10 million in 1932 to $278 million in 1940. World War II brought a sharp reduction in this aid, but after the war a modest level of federal assistance was reestablished as the federal government acted to support airport construction (1946), urban renewal (1949), urban planning (1954), and education in areas affected by military installations (1950). From 1960 to 1978 a veritable explosion occurred in federal urban policy. The number of federal grants directed at cities and their problems increased dramatically, and, as a result, federal aid became an important source of money for many urban budgets for the first time. The period since 1978 has been characterized by a steady retrenchment, which, if continued, could return federal-local fiscal relations to the levels existing before the Great Society buildup. . . .

The Seeds of Destruction

The expansion of federal assistance to local jurisdictions carried within it the seeds of its own destruction. By choosing to deal directly with localities, the federal government became entangled in the complexity that characterizes local government in America. Different governments have different functional responsibilities and different taxing authority. Problems which might be dealt with effectively by the municipal government in New York might require a coordinated response from the county, the municipality, and several independent school districts in Dallas. In some areas the urban problems that concerned federal policymakers were exacerbated, if not caused, by various restraints state laws placed on cities. Examples of this include the limited annexation authority that most large cities had and their inability to tax workers in the city who commuted from the suburbs. In addition, few urban problems respected local jurisdictional boundaries. Thus, the recipient of a federal grant often had only a piece of the problem within its area of responsibility.

By choosing to deal with hundreds of localities, the federal government was confronted with jurisdictions of vastly different capacities, internal structures, and politics. Faced with this complexity, Washington had two options. One was to admit that no central government had the capacity to design and monitor programs that could accommodate even a majority of the different circumstances which would arise. Such an admission would have led to a block grant strategy. Under such a strategy, resources would have been given to jurisdictions for use in solving certain basic types of problems. But the recipient jurisdictions would have been allowed to choose which specific approaches would best address the problem in their particular area.

Beyond Government's Capacity

The Los Angeles riots have given renewed attention and debate to inner cities and their problems. What has yet to be acknowledged is that the most intractable problems of our cities and their minority residents are beyond the capacity of the federal government, and probably local governments, to solve.

Walter E. Williams, *Jobs and Capital*, Summer 1992.

The second option, which was the one taken, was to design programs in excruciating detail to try to anticipate every circumstance that might arise. This created a system characterized by red tape and regulation under which recipients were forced to submit plans, pre-proposals, proposals, and progress reports. Federal bureaucrats were charged with reviewing these submissions at every stage, thus maximizing the opportunity for conflict and contention. This approach reflected not only the confidence Washington's politicians and policy planners had in their own abilities, but also a political imperative. Loosely directed federal funds were more likely to end up misdirected, sometimes in scandalous ways. This might come back to visit political damage on the sponsoring agency, committee, or individual congressman.

Problems with Grants

The chosen strategy produced a reaction from both the grant givers and the recipients. The latter chafed under the red tape, excessive regulations, and delays imposed by Washington. The former were overwhelmed by the work load and stung by the criticism they received from what were supposed to be grateful beneficiaries.

The congestion created by the proliferation of grants spawned an intellectual backlash as well. Soon policy analysts were arguing that the intergovernmental fiscal system needed to be rationalized. Many experts came to question whether the needs being addressed by federal-local grants were truly of national importance. Calls for simplification and a sorting out of functions became more frequent.

The inherent inability of Congress to target local grants represented another destructive seed. Severe urban problems were not present in every, or even most, large cities. And yet, for a new grant program to be enacted or an existing one to receive a larger appropriation, the program had to spread its largess widely across as many congressional districts as possible. The incongruity between concentrated needs and dispersed federal aid helped to generate perceptions of inefficiency and waste.

The growing importance of federal-local fiscal relations caused strains with the state governments. Some cities were accused of being more attuned to the wishes and priorities of Washington than to those of the state capital. Some states, witnessing Washington's active interest in urban problems, slacked off their own efforts to deal with the problems of their large urban centers.

The Era of Retrenchment

In the past decade the conditions that contributed to the 1960-78 expansion of federal aid to cities disappeared and a new era of retrenchment began. The retrenchment drew strength from the turbulence that afflicted the economy in the late 1970s and early 1980s and from the growing perception that federal domestic programs were not working. The Reagan administration forcefully articulated these perceptions.

The most significant factor contributing to this retrenchment was the budgetary squeeze that the federal government found itself in starting in the late 1970s. With the tax cuts of 1981, the Reagan administration's defense buildup, and the 1981-82 recession, the squeeze was transformed into the crushing force of $200 billion annual deficits. The battle to reduce these deficits revealed that discretionary domestic spending, of which nonentitlement grants to state and local governments make up a significant portion, was not high on the nation's list of budgetary priorities. Over the 1978-88 decade nonentitlement federal grants were cut by 41 percent in real terms. General revenue sharing and Urban Development Action Grants were eliminated entirely. CETA [Comprehensive Employment and Training Act] was replaced by the Jobs Training Partnership Act at one-half the CETA funding level. On an inflation-adjusted basis grants for community and regional development were cut by two-thirds, and those for education, training, and social services fell by 45 percent. Under the strictures of the Gramm-Rudman-Hollings deficit reduction targets, continued pressure to reduce aid to cities should be expected. . . .

The long-run outlook for increased urban aid does not look bright. Relative to a decade or two ago, a much larger fraction of the federal budget is now devoted to relatively uncontrollable commitments such as Social Security, Medicare, debt service, farm price supports, veterans' benefits, and military and civilian pay. With the income tax indexed and reformed, there is no possibility that bracket creep or economic growth will generate a significant "fiscal dividend" that could be devoted to expanded domestic programs. Therefore, any significant expansion of domestic programs will require a tax increase, something that is not likely after the deficit issue is resolved.

In addition, the optimism about the effectiveness of government programs that existed in the 1960s has given way to an equally exaggerated feeling that little that the federal government tries works very well. As a mechanism for achieving federal objectives, categorical grants have fallen out of favor. Many programs are regarded as ineffectual; a few are accused of being positively harmful. For example, many analysts argue that federal mass transit aid has built uneconomical subway systems, led to excessive pay for transit workers, and distorted local transportation decisions. Others think that federal economic development efforts have heavily subsidized downtown development that would have occurred without this assistance. Even advocates of federal intervention are hard-pressed to document the programs that have generated dramatic, measurable results. The best they can do is to point to such programs as Job Corps, Chapter I (Compensatory Education for the Disadvantaged), Head Start, and WIC (the Supplemental Food Program for Women, Infants and Children), for which there is some evidence of modest positive impacts.

The Cities' Fall from Grace

Unlike during the earlier period, cities are no longer perceived as the most worthy or deserving level of government. Their relative status began to fade with the New York City fiscal crisis in the mid-1970s. The wave of municipal corruption, which was covered by the media in excruciating detail, accelerated this fall from grace. States have emerged as the new darlings of Washington policymakers. In large measure the rising status of state government reflects the genuine strengthening of this level of government since the early 1960s. State revenue structures have been strengthened considerably, and there has been a significant improvement in the quality of elected and appointed state officials as well as their staffs. Moreover, when the federal government began to relinquish its role as a policy innovator during the Reagan administration, the states stepped in. In the areas of health cost containment, education, work-welfare, the environment, economic development, housing, and tax reform, states have exhibited a good deal of leadership and innovation.

But Washington's renewed fascination with states also has a practical dimension. As long as retrenchment is required, the federal government will want to distance itself from the ultimate beneficiary of the programs it is cutting back. By channeling grants through the states and by transforming categorical programs into block grants, the political repercussions of federal cutbacks can be diffused. States may compensate for federal cuts by allocating more of their own money to the affected programs. If states choose to validate the federal cuts, some of the criticisms of the cutbacks may be directed at them rather than at Washington. But this is only the case when the aid is channeled through the state.

Not only have states replaced local governments as the focus of federal intergovernmental attention, but "people" have replaced "place" as the primary locus of policy concern in the 1980s. The limited success of the place-oriented strategies of the past and the mobility of the population have led policymakers to look more toward people-oriented approaches to solving the nation's domestic problems. New initiatives are more frequently shaped around individual entitlements, vouchers, or tax expenditures to individuals and businesses than around grants to governments. Housing vouchers, training and retraining payments, tuition tax credits, and tax incentives for economic development and historic preservation are some examples of this trend.

In addition, new actors have appeared on the local scene, actors that compete with and complement local governments. There are the nonprofit organizations and quasi-governmental organizations that often serve as the delivery agents of federal policy. Twenty years ago there were fewer such organizations, and cities had this niche almost entirely to themselves. Furthermore, public-private partnerships, a form of policy intervention which is not conducive to an active federal role, are playing an ever greater part at the local level.

An End to More of the Same

The biggest fallacy of all is the assertion that further increases in federal spending can solve the problems of poverty and dependence in our cities. As noted by HUD Secretary Jack Kemp, we have spent some *$2.5 trillion* on anti-poverty efforts since the 1960s, and the troubles of our cities are in many ways as bad today as they were back then. That record suggests that doing more of the same isn't going to make things better.

M. Stanton Evans, *Human Events*, May 23, 1992.

Finally, demographic and economic trends are working against a resurgence of federal fiscal assistance to large cities. The fraction of the population living in large cities continues to decline. Congressional redistricting has taken seats away from the areas of the country which contain the most distressed urban environments. A further reduction, based on the results of the 1990 census, will occur for the 1992 congressional elections. The relative economic position of the large urban centers also has continued to slip. As a result of these trends, the political clout of urban areas has eroded considerably since the mid-1960s, leaving them without the capacity to mount a successful legislative effort to expand federal aid to cities.

No Coherent Federal Policy

The conclusion that arises from this brief review of the past twenty-five years of fiscal federalism is that the 1960 to 1978 era was an aberration, one that is not likely to be repeated. There never existed a neatly defined or coherent national urban policy—a clear notion of what the federal government was attempting to achieve through its interventions to local governments. At first, federal involvement was portrayed as an effort to redevelop blighted neighborhoods. This was replaced by an emphasis on empowering underprivileged city residents and providing them with opportunities to better themselves. The next focus of federal policy was on ensuring that poor urban residents were provided with essential city services. Federal programs then focused on enhancing the fiscal health of cities and on the pursuit of federal antirecession objectives. The final federal thrust emphasized city economic development in partnership with the private sector. The inability to sustain a coherent focus for federal urban policy has not been the fault of the nation's policymakers but rather was inevitable given the inherent complexity and diversity of the federal system and the economic turmoil that characterized the past fifteen years.

Considering the resurgent role of the states, the long-term fiscal constraints that face the federal government, and the diminished political clout of the big cities, renewed efforts to establish a national urban policy that channels significant federal resources to the nation's distressed cities are likely to be futile.

"The inner cities are starved for private investment, not more government aid. "

Private Enterprise Can Improve Inner Cities

Mark Alpert

Because of deteriorating conditions in inner cities, many businesses have fled and banks are fearful of financing new enterprises. In the following viewpoint, Mark Alpert argues that businesses can improve economic conditions in inner cities by relocating there and investing in these areas. Alpert maintains that large retail stores could succeed in inner cities by moving in and profiting from the lack of competition. Such stores, Alpert contends, would create jobs and cater to inner-city residents who now are forced to shop outside their neighborhoods. Alpert is a reporter for *Fortune*, a biweekly business magazine.

As you read, consider the following questions:

1. What criticisms does Alpert make about government social programs?
2. In Alpert's opinion, why are underground economies important to inner cities?
3. How can private groups safeguard their business loans, according to the author?

Instead of viewing America's inner cities as doomed urban wastelands, think of them as undeveloped countries, like Peru or Poland or Bangladesh. With that perspective in mind, what's the best way to revitalize their economies? The advice Peruvians, Poles, and the Bangladeshis get is, "Free your markets from government control and encourage private enterprise." As more and more community leaders are beginning to realize, this is also the best strategy for America's underdeveloped neighborhoods.

The inner cities have become small pockets of socialism in the American capitalist economy. Over the past three decades, private businesses have fled from places like Harlem, Watts, and Chicago's South Side. Largely as a result, the public sector—federal, state, and city agencies—became the dominant force in the ghetto economy. For example in East Harlem, a Hispanic and black community known as "El Barrio," the city government owns 62% of the neighborhood's acreage. Almost two-thirds of the local residents live in public housing, and about 30% receive welfare or some other form of public assistance.

Such social programs at best maintain the status quo. They won't solve the problems over the long run any more than socialism did in Eastern Europe. The inner cities are starved for private investment, not more government aid. Consumers need better places to shop, and would-be entrepreneurs need financial and managerial help to launch new businesses.

Business Opportunities Abound

Incredible as it may seem, there are tremendous business opportunities in the inner cities. Just look at the Concourse Plaza Shopping Center, a $150 million project that opened in 1991 in one of the most notorious sections of the Bronx—not far from the courthouse celebrated in *The Bonfire of the Vanities*. In its first day of operation, the shopping center's anchor tenant—a 60,000-square-foot outlet of the Waldbaum's supermarket chain—sold over $250,000 of groceries to 10,000 customers. Says shopping center developer Bernard Rosenshein: "Until recently, most retailers have been too scared to go into inner-city areas. The developers chased easy deals in the suburbs. But now that the suburbs are saturated, the greatest opportunities are in the inner cities."

To see such opportunities, one must set aside several myths about the inner-city economy. Not everyone belongs to the so-called urban underclass, the catch-all term used to describe the chronically unemployed and socially dysfunctional. The residents of East Harlem, for example, include middle-class families, a substantial number of working poor, and a growing stream of gung-ho immigrants from Mexico and South America. Their median household income is about $14,500, according to a 1989 study done by Urban Decision Systems, a market research firm in Los Angeles. That's half the national median, but it still adds up to an aggregate neighborhood income of $1.35 billion a year. And that doesn't include the value of in-kind forms of public assistance, such as food stamps and Medicaid. Nor does it include the income flowing from the neighborhood's thriving underground economy—meaning not the drug trade, which leaves little real wealth behind, but everything from street peddlers to unlicensed livery services.

On their infrequent visits to the ghettos, market researchers discover that inner-city consumers are gravely underserved by the local retailers. The East Harlem study concluded that the neighborhood, despite its poverty, could support a wide variety of retail stores with total revenues of $374 million. But since most national chains have shied away, East Harlem's stores are generally small, poorly stocked, and have aggregate sales of only $192 million.

That means local residents have to make difficult treks outside the neighborhood—sometimes as far away as New Jersey or Westchester County—for about half their shopping needs. On Saturday evenings, the Metro-North train station at 125th Street, Harlem's Main Street, is packed with shoppers returning from malls 20 miles away in Westchester. Joe Holland, a Harlem resident who owns a travel agency and a restaurant on 125th Street, laments the lack of variety and quality in Harlem's stores. Says Holland: "There are some clothing shops here, but they don't have the range of options you'd find in an ordinary commercial strip. So the middle-class people tend to shop elsewhere."

One company taking advantage of this retailing vacuum is Woolworth, which operates 450 of its 1,000 variety stores in predominantly minority areas. In one year the company opened two new Woolworth Express outlets in Harlem. "If we see a need in the community, we're willing to take a risk and go in there," says Robert Lynn, head of Woolworth's variety store division. "And we don't run away from a neighborhood when bad things start happening."

A Lack of Competition

It takes extra work to succeed. Says Lynn: "Inner-city merchandising is very different from merchandising in the suburbs. The size assortments for shoes are different, the popular colors are different. We've had focus groups tell us what they want. But it's worth doing all these things." The operating profit margins of Woolworth's inner-city stores are a percentage point higher, on average, than the margins of its suburban stores. Security costs more, but rent is generally lower, so the overhead works out to be the same. One reason Woolworth does so well

210

is that the competition is so weak. Woolworth can offer lower prices and provide better customer service than most mom and pop stores.

The opportunity for supermarket chains is even greater. The large New York City chains—Sloan's and D'Agostino, to name a couple—have tended to shun low-income neighborhoods. Like other outside businesses, they underestimate the market potential and overestimate the difficulties and dangers. Many inner-city shoppers must rely instead on the bodegas, or local convenience stores, which offer less variety than the supermarkets and are more expensive. As a result, according to a report by New York City's Department of Consumer Affairs, grocery prices in the poor neighborhoods are 8.8% higher than in middle-class areas.

Enlisting Corporate Support

Most of the cities advertised as success stories of the 1980s—Indianapolis, Pittsburgh, St. Paul—are places where the local political leaders spent massive amounts of time talking to corporate executives about the notion of a metropolitan community and their responsibilities to it.

So far, the positive results of that effort have been seen mostly in downtown redevelopment. And they have not been small. Even Mike White's Cleveland, where the inner-city desperation is undeniable, made remarkable progress over the past decade, building a new skyline, cleaning up the Cuyahoga River, redeveloping an industrial part of the city into both a working port and a suburban tourist attraction. All of those changes have involved the co-opting of businesses, some of them suburban-based, into the role of committed metropolitan players.

Alan Ehrenhalt, *The Washington Times*, September 16, 1991.

Given the lack of competition, a well-run supermarket can make a mint in such neighborhoods. Example: the Tops market that opened in April 1991 in East Harlem. A Bronx-based chain that specializes in meat and poultry, Tops is an anchor tenant of La Marqueta, a decrepit mall specializing in Latino foods that is being redeveloped under the elevated Metro-North tracks. The clean, well-stocked store has been packed with customers since the day it opened. Says Philip Aarons, who is rebuilding La Marqueta with a Hispanic advocacy group: "Quality retailers will always do well here, because their competition is shoddy, overpriced merchandisers."

With greater opportunities, however, come greater risks, and merchandisers must face them squarely. One is security—protecting the store from robberies, shoplifting, and pilferage by employees. Inner-city businessmen have come up with ways to cut these losses. Consider Smart & Final, a West Coast food wholesaler with outlets in poor Los Angeles neighborhoods. Chairman Robert Emmons says his store managers go out of their way to protect customers and employees: "We don't want to open ourselves up to robberies, so we're very careful about receiving shipments late at night. We won't do it if there's just one or two people in the store." Managers deposit receipts several times a day instead of just once, to minimize the amount of cash that could be stolen.

Labor and the Underground Economy

Another challenge is finding skilled labor to man the cash registers and answer the phones. Woolworth's Lynn says it isn't hard to get people to work on the sales floor, but locating managers is a problem. Lee Dunham, who opened the first McDonald's franchise in Harlem and now owns three in the area, says half his employees are recent immigrants from Africa and the Caribbean. Says Dunham: "The immigrants will do anything to pay the rent. Because where they come from, it's either work or starve."

Stores alone can't provide all the jobs inner-city neighborhoods need. The largest private employer in Harlem is Alexander Doll Co., a 68-year-old manufacturer of collector dolls that sell for up to $500 in such stores as F.A.O. Schwarz and Neiman-Marcus. The privately held firm employs more than 600 people, most of whom live within walking distance of the company's three-story plant in West Harlem. In 1989, Alexander considered moving to a larger plant outside New York City, but it is now planning to relocate to another site in Harlem. According to CEO Ira Smith, one of the attractions of the area is its labor force. "We're the No. 1 premium doll manufacturer in America," he says, "and our work force is the reason." Many workers come from the Dominican Republic and learned their sewing skills in Caribbean factories.

But a great many inner-city people are employed in the underground economy, by businesses that can only make a profit because they pay low wages and avoid burdensome city regulations and codes—not to mention taxes. During the Seventies and Eighties, while the legitimate private sector was withering in the ghetto, the underground economies were booming. The International Ladies' Garment Workers' Union estimates that the number of illegal sweatshops in New York City, for example, has jumped from 200 to 3,000 over the past 20 years. Most of the workers in these sweatshops are immigrants from Latin

America, and their pay ranges from $20 to $100 per day.

Urban planners have mixed feelings about the underground economy. While they despise the deplorable conditions in sweatshops, they wouldn't want to see them eliminated since that would take away one of the few sources of economic vitality in these neighborhoods. Saskia Sassen, a Columbia University professor who has studied New York City's underground economy, believes that selective regulation could curb the worst abuses—such as workplaces with no fire escapes—without forcing the underground entrepreneurs out of business. "The underground economy shouldn't be criminalized," says Sassen. "But it should be regulated enough to avoid the worst forms of exploitation."

Access to Loans

Easier access to capital could help channel some of the inner city's latent entrepreneurial energy into legitimate enterprises. Some community groups are pushing local banks to make more loans to inner-city residents and businesses. Their main weapon is the Community Reinvestment Act of 1977, which obliges banks to meet the credit needs of the neighborhoods where they operate. In a typical CRA proceeding, the community group will accuse a bank of "redlining" their district—that is, surreptitiously making the area ineligible for loans. (To gain leverage, the group will try to lodge its complaint as the bank is applying to the Federal Reserve Board for approval of an expansion or merger.) Typically the bank will agree to earmark a certain amount of mortgage loans to the community to settle the complaint.

The CRA process amounts to government-sponsored coercion, but it does force bankers to find profitable ways to invest in the inner cities. As a result of CRA proceedings, dozens of banks across the U.S. have agreed to provide $7.5 billion of new credit for low- and moderate-income areas, and most money-center banks have established community development divisions. Chase Manhattan's community development corporation, established to meet the bank's CRA requirements, has committed over $100 million of loans in low-income areas of New York. President Mark Willis vows that Chase will profit from these loans. Says Willis: "Our portfolio looks better than the traditional real estate portfolio. You can do this kind of thing prudently."

But the right kind of banker, like the right kind of retailer, needs no coercion to inject capital into the inner cities. In 1973 three Chicago idealists—two white, one black—bought an ailing bank in the city's South Shore neighborhood, which at the time was rapidly deteriorating into an inner-city slum. They turned South Shore Bank into the nation's first for-profit community development bank and started making single-family mortgages and small-business loans in the immediate area. By the mid-1980s, the decline of the South Shore neighborhood was reversed and other Chicago banks began to make loans. "The presence of South Shore Bank made the area more attractive to investors who otherwise wouldn't have gone in there," says Richard Taub, a University of Chicago professor who has written a book on the South Shore phenomenon.

South Shore Bank has done well by doing good; it has an above-average 98.5% repayment rate on the $173 million of loans made since 1974, and it posted a $1.5 million profit in 1990. Says bank senior vice president Joan Shapiro: "We've nurtured an extraordinary group of borrowers, a bunch of true entrepreneurs." Encouraged by its success, South Shore has now set its sights on revitalizing the neighborhood of Austin, a low-income area on Chicago's West Side.

Many inner-city businesses, too small and too risky to attract interest from bank lenders, need an alternative form of capitalization. Immigrants often make use of informal sources of credit. Korean grocers get much of their startup capital from revolving credit associations, while West Indians have a traditional group savings plan called a "sou sou"—members make periodic donations, and each gets a turn at receiving the whole pot. This access to capital gives immigrants the edge over people who have lived their whole lives in the inner cities. In East Harlem, for example, about half the store owners are Asian.

Invest in the Inner Cities

When I hear someone say they're not investing in a business or a person or an idea because it's in the inner city or because it involves a person of color, I say you're not assessing your risk the right way or in the way you do in other situations. Bankers always say it's a high-risk area, but these are the people who lent to Latin America and bought junk bonds and financed every half-empty high-rise tower in the country.

Bernard W. Kinsey, *The New York Times*, August 9, 1992.

To bring long-term inner-city residents into the marketplace, a growing number of community groups are borrowing an idea that was first applied by development agencies in the Third World—the micro-enterprise loan. In Chicago, a group called the Women's Self-Employment Project has been making loans that range from $100 to $5,000 and are designed to help low-income women set up small businesses with minimal capital requirements, such as day care or catering. The Chicago group's program employs an ingenious payback scheme that was first used in Bangladesh in the late Seventies. The borrowers must form peer groups of five. If any of the five defaults on her loan, then the line of credit is revoked for the whole group. Due to the built-in peer pressure of this system, there have been no defaults so far on the $175,000 in loans made. Financial assistance alone is not enough. Inner-city entrepreneurs also need training in basics such as balancing the books and writing a business plan. . . .

Government Must Heed the Market

What clearly does *not* work are grandiose, politically inspired development schemes charted without regard to marketplace realities. Recalling Harlem's glory days as a center for black culture, local politicians have leaned toward projects intended to spur tourism, such as the restoration of the famous Apollo Theater on 125th Street. But that proved too ambitious—the restoration went way over budget, and the theater's broadcasting studios attracted less business than expected. Facing huge losses, the Apollo's owners had to renegotiate loans owed to Manufacturers Hanover and the New York State Urban Development Corp.

The proposed Harlem International Trade Center—a $135 million, 30-story office tower to be built on 125th Street and Lenox Avenue—is another questionable project. Public agencies have kicked in $50 million, and officials plan to rent the office space to a collection of federal agencies, city agencies, and trade representatives from Third World countries. So far they've received lease commitments for only half the 400,000 square feet available. Bill Stern, a former chairman of the Urban Development Corp. and vocal critic of big government projects, predicts that this one will never get off the ground. Says Stern: "It's a complete boondoggle. There's no demand for office space in Harlem. The government can't create a viable business when the market won't support it."

Peruvian economist Hernando de Soto argues that the way to reinvigorate Third World countries is to unleash the innate entrepreneurial energies of their people. And so it is with America's inner-city neighborhoods. They won't revive until they rejoin the national economy. That means empowerment of the residents as consumers, workers, and entrepreneurs—with help from businesses that can make money as they create wealth. Look at these places not as pits of despair but as regions of opportunity.

> *"The institution by far best suited to [improving ghettos] is the federal government. "*

Government Can Improve Inner Cities

Nicholas Lemann

In the following viewpoint, Nicholas Lemann argues that the federal government should lead efforts to improve race relations and living conditions in inner cities because only it can undertake such an enormous task. Lemann contends that as the traditional leader for civil rights, the federal government can improve race relations and bring the ghetto poor into the mainstream of society. Lemann concludes that state and local governments would follow the federal government's lead and create their own social programs once ghetto improvements were shown to be effective. Lemann is a national correspondent for the monthly magazine *The Atlantic* and the author of the book *The Promised Land: The Great Black Migration and How It Changed America*, from which this viewpoint is excerpted.

As you read, consider the following questions:

1. Why does Lemann believe that local government social workers can succeed in improving ghettos?
2. In the author's opinion, how could a successful government program actually save money in the long run?
3. Why must society unite in order for government efforts to succeed, according to Lemann?

From Nicholas Lemann, *The Promised Land: The Great Black Migration and How It Changed America*. New York: Alfred A. Knopf, 1991. Reprinted with permission.

Thinking about the history of American race relations can easily give rise to bitterness and fatalism, but it is encouraging to remember how often in the past a hopeless situation, which appeared to be completely impervious to change, finally did change for the better. The framers of the Constitution, idealists though they were, couldn't imagine an American nation without slavery—but in the long run slavery was ended. In this century legal segregation looked like an unfortunate given, impossible to eliminate, until well after the end of World War II. That black America could become predominately middle class, non-Southern, and nonagrarian would have seemed inconceivable until a bare two generations ago.

Bridging the Class Gap

Today the racial problem that is regarded as insuperable is the condition of the black slums in big cities. At the level of conversation, if not of political oratory, there seems to be a conviction that we don't know what can possibly help the ghettos, that even if we did know it couldn't be done for lack of political support, and that some unbridgeable gap between blacks and whites makes the amelioration of any problem related to race unlikely. These sentiments are not, in fact, either clear-eyed or realistic; they really belong on the long list of dolorous racial attitudes that turn out to be merely resistance to change wearing the garb of pessimism. . . .

Without ending any efforts to improve the ghettos that are now under way, we should change our reigning idea about what will help most: we should be trying to bring the ghetto poor closer to the social and economic mainstream of American society, not encouraging them to develop a self-contained community apart from the mainstream.

American society in the wider sense is not now a real presence in the ghettos, except via television, which only creates a continuous cognitive dissonance between everyday slum life and overall American life. Police officers don't walk the beat, most schools don't teach, fathers don't live at home, crime goes unpunished, the ward and precinct bosses who once offered a link to the political system are disappearing, and the old-fashioned settlement-house and social-agency training functions have withered away. Outside the ghettos, especially in the black middle class, sentiment has begun to run strongly in favor of reestablishing the social linkages between poor blacks and the rest of black society, but right now there is no mechanism in place to bring that about. The number of middle-class people who voluntarily return to the ghettos to live and help—or who move there for the first time—is always going to be tiny. Given the poverty and dispiritedness in the slums, it is unlikely that their residents will suddenly mobilize around some new figure who preaches moderation and bourgeois values. Any planned undertaking that would have a chance of affecting the ghettos substantially would have to be of enormous scope. For both practical and moral reasons, the institution by far best suited to the task is the federal government. . . .

Government Programs Work Well

In the specific case of the ghettos, the idea that the government can't accomplish anything is a smokescreen obscuring the useful and encouraging results of a quarter century's worth of research on antipoverty programs—research of a kind that didn't exist when the war on poverty began. We now know that the easiest problem to solve is simple material need: the food stamps program plainly reduces hunger, for example. In the ghettos, where material need is only part of the problem, the mission is more complicated, and the kind of programs that would help are less dramatically successful. Still, programs that come under the banner of "intervention," in which the government becomes a guiding presence in the lives of the ghetto poor, do demonstrably work.

Help for the Law-Abiding Poor

Urban blacks must be given—and especially must feel—a stake in the system.

Only with a personal stake can they acquire that essential ingredient—hope. Hope that their personal plight will improve. Hope that the fate of their children will be even brighter. . . .

Individuals who "follow the rules" should be helped, much more than now. The federal government, along with state and local governments, can provide more temporary financial assistance, firm law enforcement, marketable job training programs, drug rehabilitation centers, interim medical aid—whatever it takes people who themselves act responsibly to get back on their own feet.

Ken Adelman, *The Washington Times*, May 6, 1992.

Programs offering education, counseling, and birth control devices in high school clinics can reduce teenage pregnancy rates. Programs that send nurses and social workers to the homes of expectant mothers to provide prenatal care or food reduce infant-mortality rates and the incidence of low-birth-weight babies. Head Start (which was studied most comprehensively at a preschool in Michigan for more than twenty years) leads to higher graduation and employment rates and lower rates of arrest and teenage pregnancy. James Comer, of the Yale University Child Study Center, has impressively raised the achievement scores of ghetto elementary school students through a system of unusually intense school involvement in the lives of students and their parents. Various job training programs, including the Job Corps (which is now in much better shape than it was during its early years), increase the long-term likelihood of their graduates' being employed.

All these programs are relatively expensive per participant, and their payoff is not immediate and tangible, but in the long run they can save the government money that would have gone to welfare and incarceration. The work of planning them and carrying them out could provide a locus where many thousands of blacks and whites can work together to bring something new and worthy into being; this would be a far better public dialogue about race than one consisting mainly of squabbling over the distribution of resources and arguing about whose fault it is that things are so bad. Short of the kind of major cataclysm that wholly reorders a society, such as a war, an ambitious wave of new programs of this kind is the best chance we have to make a real difference in the ghettos.

Break the Ghetto Culture

It is not at all difficult to sketch out the framework of such a wholesale government effort—an effort so comprehensive that it would stand a good chance of substantially affecting the life of everyone who lives in the ghettos. The rather casual official attitude toward street crime, for example, which has existed ever since there have been ghettos, could finally end, and police officers could be put back on the streets and criminals quickly punished. Welfare could become a temporary program leading to a job. Housing projects could begin screening tenants again, and kicking out bad ones. We could try to improve the chances that every ghetto child is born healthy, learns to read and write in elementary school, graduates from high school, gets trained for the job market as it now exists, puts off parenthood until he or she can manage a family, and has a job waiting at the end of the process. The government could provide the job itself, in the form of New Deal-style projects that produce tangible results and impart real work experience. Obviously the precise conception and the management of all the programs require painstaking, detailed work, but the overall concept is simple and direct: the government should be trying to break the hold on individuals of those aspects of the ghetto culture that work against upward mobility, by providing a constant, powerful force that encourages the people of the ghettos to consider themselves part of the social structure of the country as a whole. . . .

Racial Progress Needs Leadership and Support

For most of our history, the issue of race has been linked to the issue of nationhood. During periods of fragmentation—periods when a multiplicity of local, ethnic, and economic interests held sway—racial problems have been put on the shelf. It is during the times when there has been a strong sense of *national* community that the problems have been addressed. The Civil War was one such time, at least in the Union states, and the long stretch between the New Deal and the Vietnam War was another; these periods brought us emancipation and civil rights. It has always been the federal government, not local governments or private business, that has led the way on race relations (though often the government had to be prodded into action by a political movement); the personal involvement of the president himself has usually been necessary. Like national defense and foreign policy, the management of racial issues seems to require a capability for national action. That the idea of the federal government's ameliorating race relations seems strange today is only a symptom of a much broader problem, which is that we are insufficiently unified as a society to be able successfully to undertake ambitious, organized national projects of any kind. If we can heal the ghettos, which are the part of the country most hurt by our current fragmentation, it will be a sign that we are on the way to a restoration of our spirit of community.

Protecting Health in the Inner Cities

The health of the nation's inner-city residents is directly related to the safety and quality of their environment, the home in which they live, the educational and working opportunities available to them, their access to culturally relevant information about disease prevention and health maintenance, and their ability to obtain appropriate and timely health care services. The federal government must support the local institutions that recognize the interrelated nature of the problems facing inner-city residents and can provide streamlined, efficient services in support of inner-city families and individuals from birth to death.

Ripon Forum, December 1990.

It is essential that any attempt to address racial issues quickly wins public support, even if it doesn't have public support to begin with. Otherwise, it will suffer the fate of Reconstruction and the war on poverty—a short life followed by a period of reaction.

The most straightforward way for new federal programs to win acceptance is to show that they work, not in the sense of dramatically eliminating the underclass overnight, but in the sense of being demonstrably honest, well run, committed to mainstream values, and devoid of the punitive, ram-it-down-their-throats quality that the shortest-lived reforms have had. The forces of practicality can be made to move from opposition to support of government programs if it becomes clear that a better work force and calmer cities would be the result. State and local governments would feel a pull to create social programs of their own once they saw that ghetto conditions are susceptible to improvement. Yet another argument for the federal government's centrality in the first wave of new programs is that it is best equipped to maintain their quality and ensure consistency of purpose. A radically decentralized approach, like the community action program, is bound to produce at least some disasters among its thousands of independent agencies, and these cause the whole idea of social welfare programs to lose legitimacy.

Do Not Ignore the Ghetto Poor

The way new programs are received depends not only on how they are run, but also on the way the case is stated for them. Our lack of faith in Americans' ability to put aside selfish concerns and address the big problems has produced a conviction, even among people who want to mount a new assault on ghetto poverty, that it would have to be camouflaged in some way. So the call to action is always couched as something else: as a new family policy, or children's policy, or drug policy, or civil rights policy. New antipoverty initiatives are thought to be doomed to failure unless they are buried in the tax code or loaded up with middle-class beneficiaries to give political cover. Those aspects of ghetto life that are characterized by self-destructive behavior rather than by victimization of the innocent—drug use, out-of-wedlock childbearing, dropping out of school—are, quite often, played down for fear that Americans will leap to the conclusion that the black ghetto poor are undeserving and should be written off. The old threat has not quite died out that riots will occur unless there are new programs, because there is a feeling that only the self-preservative urge can motivate the public to support anything aimed specifically at the ghettos.

The result of all this well-intentioned fuzzing up of the true nature of the tragedy in the ghettos is a loss of moral urgency, and all causes need moral urgency if they are to be fulfilled. The ghettos, and race relations in general, are the one area in American domestic life where the whole country agrees that there is something terribly wrong, where the vocabulary of crisis and national responsibility is not in the least trumped-up.

221

The United States has an undeniable strain of racial prejudice in its character, but it also has a racial conscience, which periodically comes to the fore. What brings it out is the demonstration of conditions in black America that are intolerable and that are clearly linked to the country's history of departing from its democratic ideals in the case of blacks.

Emphasize Ghetto Conditions

The ghettos bear the accumulated weight of all the bad in our country's racial history, and they are now among the worst places to live in the world. Programs for middle-class blacks—affirmative action and minority set-asides—are never going to set the country aflame with a sense of righteous purpose. Neither will family allowances or an increase in the Earned Income Tax Credit. The conditions that now prevail in the ghettos, honestly presented and openly discussed, could. To be born into a ghetto is to be consigned to a fate that no American should have to suffer. The more clearly we can be made to see that and to understand the causes of the situation, the less likely it is that we will let it stand.

"Enterprise Zones don't bribe the rich. They give poor people a chance to get rich, or at least richer."

Enterprise Zones Would Improve Inner Cities

Jack Kemp

Jack Kemp became secretary of the U.S. Department of Housing and Urban Development (HUD) in 1989. As secretary of HUD, Kemp has promoted the creation of enterprise zones in inner cities. These zones would be areas in which businesses would be exempt from capital gains taxes on income in order for them to become profitable and succeed. Kemp believes that these tax breaks would help create many new jobs and in turn provide much-needed revenue for cities.

As you read, consider the following questions:

1. According to Kemp, why is it difficult for blacks to start businesses?
2. Why does the author believe it is more important to create new businesses rather than lure big businesses into inner cities?
3. In Kemp's opinion, how does the welfare system sustain poverty?

From Jack Kemp, from a speech delivered to the U.S. Conference of Mayors, Houston, Texas, June 22, 1992.

In June 1992, Russian President Boris Yeltsin delivered an historic address to a Joint Session of Congress. What a thrill it was for me to be there in person to hear the first democratically elected leader of Russia in a thousand years tell Members of Congress and the American people: "It is in Russia that the future of freedom in the 21st Century is being decided. We are upholding your freedom as well as ours."

President Yeltsin is right about freedom—it's indivisible. And he richly deserves our political support, our financial assistance, and our liberalized trade. But I would add, our mission here at home is no less historic than Yeltsin's and just as morally profound. How can we claim democratic capitalism, free markets, and private property will work in the cities of Russia, Eastern Europe, and the Third World if we can't make them work in our cities here at home?

Indeed, we must demonstrate to the whole world that we can rebuild our cities. For what would it profit America to gain freedom and democracy for the whole world but lose our soul here at home? And make no mistake, the soul of America is revealed by how we treat the poor, how we treat the family, and how we treat inner-city pockets of poverty. I firmly believe that in saving our cities we are saving our families, saving our children, and saving our Nation's future. . . .

There can be no urban renaissance without a revitalization of entrepreneurship in our cities. Can any one doubt that an alliance between a radical, bleeding-heart, progressive-conservative HUD Secretary and equally activist mayors from all across the political spectrum would be unbeatable? Working together, nothing can stop us from waging—and this time winning—a new war on poverty. . . .

Poverty Has Worsened

There's no question the first war on poverty was an earnest and noble attempt to reduce poverty in America. But while some were helped, many were left behind. We didn't fail for lack of trying or for lack of money. After spending more than $3.2 trillion since 1965 on antipoverty programs, conditions have gotten worse, not better. Most of the tax dollars we spent fighting poverty did not end up empowering the poor. Instead, they empowered bureaucracies, developers, and politicians.

According to one study of welfare spending in the Chicago area conducted by Northwestern University, about two-thirds of every dollar spent by federal, state, and local governments went to social service bureaucracies. Only one-third trickled down to the poor.

Since at least the late 1960s, our ever-expanding web of welfare rules has gradually cut the ties between the poor and the rest of American society, creating a separate and unequal economy in the inner cities, segregating the poor from the rest of us and shattering the link between effort and reward.

Not long before his death, Senator Robert Kennedy wisely recognized and courageously began to talk about this problem. He said pointedly, ". . . we have created for the poor a separate economy, a second-rate system of government agencies keeping the poor apart from the rest of us."

Incidentally, Robert Kennedy was one of the first to argue for the use of tax incentives to restore free enterprise in the inner cities. He was one of the intellectual Founding Fathers of the Enterprise Zone concept, along with Luis Munoz Marin of Puerto Rico. He said then, "To ignore the potential contribution of private enterprise is to fight the war on poverty with a single platoon, while great armies are left to stand aside."

Years of Enterprise Zone Success

We have more than 10 years experience with enterprise zones—experience that spells success. At the state level, the District of Columbia and 36 states—including my home state of Wisconsin—have adopted enterprise programs. In total, according to the 37 state economic development offices, enterprise zones have created more than 250,000 new jobs and attracted more than $28 billion in capital investments. This has all been achieved without the federal tax incentives, which are critical to expanding the success of enterprise zones.

Bob Kasten, *The Washington Times*, August 10, 1992.

Robert Kennedy was right. We cannot succeed in reducing poverty and creating jobs without unleashing the entrepreneurial spirit of our economy. We must discard the old bureaucratic model for fighting poverty.

As President Bush said at the Cochran Gardens public housing community in St. Louis, "If the system's not helping build a better life, then we must change the system."

Whenever possible, we must empower individuals to take control of their lives by restoring the rewards for working, saving, acquiring private property, accumulating assets, owning a home, getting an education. We must open up access to new sources of capital and credit that can transform people's ideas and dreams into businesses and turn neighborhoods into wellsprings of opportunity. We should set a national goal of at least doubling the number of minority businesses by the end of 1996, vastly increasing the number of minority homeowners, and drastically

reducing the intolerably high rate of minority unemployment.
The classic American formula for escaping poverty is home-ownership, jobs, and education. That's how our parents and grandparents made it in America. Why should it be any different for the poor today? A new war on poverty is not only a moral imperative, it is an economic and strategic imperative. The 34 million Americans living in poverty represent a vast loss of human potential to the Nation. That's why a top priority of our Administration is to get Congress to finally enact a new urban agenda based on entrepreneurship, private property, and an asset-based welfare system.

Enterprise Zones are not the sole answer, but they are central to that effort. Enterprise Zones would allow investors to "expense" up to $50,000 of stock purchased from Enterprise Zone businesses; allow for expensing of capital equipment in a new business; provide an Earned Income Tax Credit for all low-income workers living in an Enterprise Zone; eliminate the Alternative Minimum Tax in Zones; and provide for liberalized "passive loss" tax relief.

Eliminate Capital Gains Taxes

Finally, the capital gains tax would be totally eliminated for anyone who works, saves, or invests in a Zone. Many people have asked me why eliminating the capital gains tax is the cornerstone of our Enterprise Zone proposal. The reason is that the generation of capital gains goes to the very heart of the wealth creation that is central to our entrepreneurial capitalist economy. You just can't have democratic capitalism without capital. Every time a business is created or expands, a capital gain is created. Taxing those gains is a direct tax on the increase in jobs, incomes, opportunity, wealth, and the expanding tax base that new and growing businesses create.

When most people view the depressed areas of your cities they see poverty and urban blight. But when I visit these neighborhoods I see a vast supply of wealth and talent, but a drastic shortage of opportunity and incentives. There is no lack of good and capable people with a desire to improve their lives. All they need is a system that allows them to fully develop their talent, pursue their dreams, and realize their potential.

Because the capital gains tax is targeted at economic growth, it stands as the major barrier to the revival of our inner cities. In precisely the same way, our high, unindexed capital gains tax inhibits economic growth in our mainstream economy. That's why President Bush wants to dramatically reduce the capital gains tax to 15% and why I believe we must index it.

No country in the world taxes capital gains the way we do. A high capital gains tax keeps capital locked up in mature assets and out of reach of the poor, especially minorities who have most of their capital gains ahead of them.

According to surveys of black entrepreneurs by *Black Enterprise* magazine and the *Wall Street Journal*, the No. 1 obstacle to black entrepreneurship is a lack of access to start-up capital. Seventy-five percent of black entrepreneurs had to start their businesses relying entirely on their own savings, versus just 25% for all entrepreneurs.

Today's high capital gains tax favors the sure bet over the long-shot, it favors existing wealth over new wealth, and very frankly, it favors the suburbs over the inner cities.

Taxing capital gains for those who live, work, or invest in our inner cities does not raise any revenue. Let me ask you something: How much tax revenue are you gaining by taxing businesses which don't exist?

Denying poor people access to capital perpetuates poverty and despair. It prolongs the legacy of Jim Crowism and racial discrimination because minority entrepreneurs are locked out of the vast capital stock in America. That is why the capital gains tax must be eliminated in every Enterprise Zone in the country.

The capital gains tax is not a tax on the rich, it's a tax on poor people who want to get rich; it's not a tax on wealth, it's a tax on wealth creation; it's not a tax on capital, it's a tax on the formation of capital.

The Need for Start-Up Capital

Our aim is not to lure companies into poor neighborhoods. Our aim . . . is to create new businesses, new jobs and new wealth by getting start-up capital into the hands of low-income entrepreneurs and inner-city residents. Eliminating the capital gains tax for those who live, work and invest in poor neighborhoods, and allowing investors to "expense" as much as $50,000 in stock purchased from an enterprise zone business, would dramatically expand the supply of capital in the inner cities and poor rural areas.

Jack Kemp, *The New York Times*, July 21, 1992.

Eliminating the capital gains tax would dramatically increase the rewards for entrepreneurs and investors who put capital at risk to create new businesses and new jobs.

For mayors, that means transforming distressed neighborhoods from tax revenue *consumers* into tax revenue *producers*. It would broaden the tax base and reduce social welfare expenditures. Many of you have seen first-hand what happens when high taxes create a shrinking tax and jobs base. Mayor Ed

Rendell can tell you what happened when Philadelphia tried to tax its way to growth. Before he took over, Philadelphia had raised taxes 19 times in 10 years. Yet, according to a recent article in the *Washington Post*, the city collects no more revenues today—after inflation—than before. Why? Because 130,000 jobs have been destroyed by these tax increases.

Enterprise Zones Are Essential

The best way to expand the urban tax base is to expand the urban jobs base. Enterprise Zones in 36 states and the District of Columbia have saved or created 260,000 jobs and generated at least $28 billion in new investment, but they lack the powerful incentives only the federal government can provide.

Enterprise Zones would "greenline" the "redlined" inner cities by eliminating the capital gains tax for the people who live, work, and invest there. Right now, in "redlined" inner-city neighborhoods, there's not enough mortgage money to buy a home, not enough venture capital to start a business, and not enough credit to build affordable housing.

Enterprise Zones are widely misunderstood to be a mechanism for inducing existing firms to relocate to inner-city neighborhoods. Let me say once and for all: Our aim is not to play a zero-sum game shifting a fixed number of existing enterprises from one place to another but rather to help the residents of inner cities start *new* businesses, create *new* wealth, and *new* jobs for their neighbors.

Big Business doesn't care about Enterprise Zones because the incentives are not aimed at large established firms. Enterprise Zones are designed to remove barriers to the creation of new wealth, not to shelter existing income. For a tiny start-up enterprise, even a small injection of capital can make the difference between success and failure.

Other opponents of Enterprise Zones argue that they will cost too much. But their static models fail to account for the revenues generated by new businesses, additional jobs, and newly employed workers. Cynics on the Left, like Michael Kinsley of the *New Republic*, claim that Enterprise Zones resort to "bribing rich people to help poor people." But Enterprise Zones don't bribe the rich. They give poor people a chance to get rich, or at least richer. And on the Right, critics at *National Review* say that "only people with the character, energy, and persistence to work and keep a family together will benefit from the right incentives."

Both are wrong! The truth is poor people *have* the right values, it's the welfare system that doesn't! Poor people respond to rewards, but the rewards are wrong. The rules of the welfare system are upside-down. Our welfare system rewards consumption over saving; dependency over work; and families that break apart or never form over families that stay together.

Frankly, Enterprise Zone critics have no faith in the inherent talents and abilities of inner-city residents. They are wrong. Most Americans—rich and poor, black and white, young and old—share the same values, hopes, and dreams. This is the lodestar of the Declaration of Independence . . . "that all men are created equal."

I said earlier that Enterprise Zones alone are not the sole answer. As my friend [U.S. representative] Charlie Rangel of Harlem says, we need job training, Head Start, Weed and Seed, and more. Peace must also be restored to the streets of our cities. Securing the safety of people in their homes, on their streets, and in their businesses is the fundamental purpose of government. Peace is a precondition if prosperity is to take root in our communities. But it is unambiguously clear that there can be no answer without Enterprise Zones and the job opportunities they will create.

"The record and objective analysis demonstrate that the enterprise zone is an idea whose time has not come."

Enterprise Zones Would Not Improve Inner Cities

Ralph Estes

Critics of enterprise zones argue that business tax incentives alone are insufficient to improve inner cities. Ralph Estes agrees and argues in the following viewpoint that businesses give little consideration to incentives as reasons to locate in particular areas. Estes maintains that other factors, such as improved public safety and transportation, are more likely to induce business start-ups. Estes believes that enterprise zones can succeed only if government is committed to creating jobs and funding education and other vital services for inner-city residents. Estes is a resident scholar at the Institute for Policy Studies and an accounting professor at American University, both in Washington, D.C.

As you read, consider the following questions:

1. Why does Estes oppose using tax revenues to subsidize business start-ups in inner cities?
2. In Estes' opinion, why should government ensure the success of inner-city communities over that of businesses?
3. According to the author, how can government directly create jobs in inner cities?

From Ralph Estes, "Enterprise Zones: A Critical Analysis," a briefing paper for the Institute for Policy Studies and the Center for Advancement of Public Policy, July 1992.

The basic concept of enterprise zones, not always made explicit, is to provide tax incentives to induce business to expand or relocate into targeted distressed areas. An enterprise zone is a defined geographical area of a city designated to qualify for certain benefits. Zones are often, but not always, selected on the basis of level of unemployment, condition of residences and neighborhoods, and lack of business activity. The implicit assumption is that business expansion in run-down areas will create jobs and revitalize the community better than will more direct social, jobs, and training programs.

Businesses that start up, relocate, or expand within the defined area receive tax breaks and other prescribed benefits. Benefits used most frequently by the states have included sales tax credits, wage credits, employer income tax credits, easing of or exemption from regulations, tax credits for hiring disadvantaged residents of the area, capital financing, property tax credits, and investment tax credits.

The term "enterprise zone" was coined in 1978 by Geoffrey Howe, a member of the British Parliament. Prime Minister Margaret Thatcher then used the zones as part of a supply-side attempt to rebuild some of the run-down areas of Great Britain. Stuart Butler, a British economist, sold the idea to HUD [Housing and Urban Development] Secretary Kemp—then a U.S. representative—but it never became part of President Reagan's domestic strategy, so the states started legislating enterprise zones on their own in 1982. To date 37 states and the District of Columbia have created over 600 zones.

Inner Cities See Little Improvement

The evaluation of state-sponsored enterprise zones is mixed. Some zones appear to have attracted at least some new businesses. In several, perhaps most, cases, businesses have moved in, but inner-city areas have seen little or no improvement. In virtually every case, it is impossible to draw a firm conclusion that the social and economic benefits of enterprise zones to communities and to taxpayers have outweighed their tax cost.

Some of the larger state enterprise zone projects include:

Baltimore. Park Circle is the home of 60 businesses that employ 1,400 people, but the adjacent neighborhood has not improved, and teenage unemployment among blacks in the area still hovers near 40 percent. A GAO [General Accounting Office] study on Maryland's enterprise zones found "little or no program-related effect on employment."

Connecticut. Eleven cities and towns in the state have enterprise zones, but the state has no way to assess whether the programs have been cost-effective. In spite of a 50 percent credit on corporate business taxes for the first ten years, the zones have not helped the state recover from its disastrous economic slump.

Kansas. Several years' experience led to cancellation of the program in 1991. Cities gerrymandered zone boundaries to include wealthy and prosperous neighborhoods and to take in existing facilities of healthy companies such as Boeing, Beech Aircraft, even the Coors distributorship. Cities also established zones entitling businesses to ten-year tax abatements, then moved the zones to take in a new set of businesses without cancelling the previously granted abatements. They thus created a shell game with enterprise zone boundaries that benefited business but had little effect on jobs and inner-city conditions.

**"Haven't you heard? We don't live in slums anymore.
They're called 'enterprise zones.'"**

© Bruce Beattie/*Daytona Beach News Journal.* Reprinted with permission.

Los Angeles. Since 1988, the Pacoima zone has created 212 jobs, the Watts zone 159, and the Central City zone 220. Pacoima has seen a spurt of industrial activity, but city planners doubt that it has been a result of enterprise zone tax incentives. Some businesses simply moved in from other areas, leading to no net gain in jobs.

Milwaukee. State tax credits in the inner city during 1990 helped create 384 new jobs; 20 percent of the new businesses had relocated from the suburbs.

New Jersey. Job growth in enterprise zones has been larger than in communities outside the zones, but researchers have been unable to trace the growth directly to the program.

Researchers did find that only a third of the businesses in the zones say the tax breaks were a big factor in their decision to locate in the inner city.

St. Louis. Since a zone was established in the Manchester Avenue area in 1983, only four small businesses have been created. Of the 328 new jobs created by these businesses and others that expanded or relocated into the zone, only 25 have gone to area residents.

San Diego. The Barrio Logan zone is described as one of the most successful in the state, hiring over 1,600 unemployed or government job-training program graduates since 1987. But the city government has no way of knowing what these employees are being paid, whether they would have been hired without tax credits, or whether they end up on unemployment when they leave their jobs.

How well have state-authorized enterprise zones worked? The brief answer is: nobody knows. Some jurisdictions have assembled extensive data on the tax expenditure costs of enterprise zone legislation, but none has developed credible estimates of benefits to depressed areas. State and local economic development officials who were interviewed consistently voiced the view—never for public quotation—that the social benefits were unlikely to equal the tax costs.

Tax Credits Alone Are Insufficient

No consensus exists on the enterprise zone issue. Some of the questions being debated are:

• Is it more important to provide incentives for *businesses* to locate or expand in the area, or to provide jobs for *individuals* living within the zone?

• Are tax incentives alone sufficient inducement for a company to locate in a run-down or burned-out area, when the increased costs of insurance and security are taken into account? A 1988 study by the General Accounting Office found that financial inducements ranked 12th out of 13 when employers in two enterprise zones were asked to rate the importance of factors in their location decisions. *Business Week* reported that infrastructure and access to markets are more important than fiscal incentives in choosing a location.

Richard Cowden, executive director of the American Association on Enterprise Zones, argues that the most effective zones provide additional funds for improved law enforcement, social services, job training, and infrastructure, in addition to providing tax breaks. He warns that programs that consist only of tax incentives are unlikely to work.

• Will companies find skilled laborers or managers in the zone area? If a company simply brings in employees from outside the zone, then there is little or no benefit to the zone.

• Once tax credits and other benefits have been granted, will companies stay in the enterprise zones, or will they merely "take the money and run"?

• Will there be a relocation tradeoff? If a company moves from one neighborhood into another that is designated as an enterprise zone, are jobs just being moved around to take advantage of tax benefits with no net gain?

• Most importantly, are enterprise zones cost-effective? Is this the best use of limited public funds, or are more direct forms of assistance to inner-city areas and the unemployed more effective?. . .

In a simple sense the enterprise zone idea can be appealing: stimulate business expansion and new enterprise creation in depressed areas, which will provide jobs to the unemployed and be a catalyst for neighborhood renewal. But current proposals, including the compromise version worked out by the Bush administration and the House of Representatives, involve *subsidizing business and investors using the national treasury*. There is little likelihood of concomitant benefits to economically depressed areas.

These tax expenditures, totaling billions of dollars, must come from the pockets of other taxpayers or from reduced spending on other programs. Given Congress's self-imposed barrier to transferring budget funds from military programs to social programs, any such reductions would almost certainly come out of the hide of already starved social programs and most likely out of existing programs to aid cities and communities.

The policy question is straightforward: is this the best use of taxpayers' money to help cities? The answer is no. Enterprise zone legislation, whether originating with the Republicans or the Democrats, is a cosmetic response to a newly perceived crisis in the cities. It is another card in the supply-side, trickle-down economics deck. The President and the Congress ought to put enterprise zone proposals aside and turn to seriously addressing the economic, health, structural, and human problems of inner cities. A gimmicky quick-fix will not cure a generation of neglect.

Focus on Jobs and Accountability

The record and objective analysis demonstrate that the enterprise zone is an idea whose time has not come. But if the administration and Congress persist in considering enterprise zone legislation despite the evidence, it is imperative that they address the following issues:

1) The focus should be on jobs, not simply enterprise creation or expansion. Tax credits should apply only for net *new hires* of employees *who live in the zones*; this requirement was added by the House, but was not in the Bush administration's proposal

and may not be retained by the Senate. It doesn't help a depressed area if employees come from stable areas across town, supplies are bought from outside the area, goods are shipped out of the area, and the business facility is virtually a fortress surrounded by a chain-link fence, and is not a real part of or contributor to the community. As a 1989 Urban Institute study noted, "Few of the tax benefits in the leading proposals accrue directly to the disadvantaged residents."

2) The experience of the states demonstrates that the enterprise zone concept has a reasonable chance of working *only* when it is integrated with a comprehensive program that includes job training, improvement of public transportation, better law enforcement, necessary social services, education of both inner-city residents and of business, and strong support—beyond mere lip service—from the city, state, and federal administrations.

3) Proposed reductions or elimination of capital gains on enterprise zone assets should be dropped. Any such reduction will not give venture capitalists a meaningful incentive to undertake projects that will provide long-term benefits to the inner cities. This proposal appears to be simply a renewed effort to cut capital gains taxes with no demonstrable benefit to depressed urban areas. If incentives *are* going to be given to business, they must be much more closely tied to the desired outcomes.

No Jobs Without Skills

We could have the finest enterprise zone in the country [in Los Angeles] and we could have all the widget companies in America move there. But they're not going to hire the Crips and the Bloods if they don't have the skills and the education. You've got to put the two together and train these kids for the opportunities they are going to be given.

John B. Breaux, *Los Angeles Times*, June 4, 1992.

---

4) Accountability must be required. The record of the states shows that companies obtain long-term benefits, such as exemption from sales taxes, with no requirement of continued evidence of eligibility. Economic development officers report that claims for new jobs created are often nothing more than double-counting, exaggeration, and creative bookkeeping.

5) To insure that companies do not simply "take the money and run," performance bonds should be required for benefits granted in advance. These could be returned to the company at the rate of so much per year, but retained by the government if

the company does not earn the benefits already collected. Taxpayers would thus be fairly compensated for tax subsidies previously granted but not fully earned.

6) An audit mechanism should be established to insure that benefits granted to business are indeed earned, and continue to be earned. The record is too clear that we cannot simply take business's word.

7) If the problem is inner-city distress and decay, the zones should not be allocated half to rural areas as the present legislation proposes. This appears to be nothing more than pork-barrel politics designed to generate support from members of Congress who represent rural districts.

8) Finally, any serious attempt to create federal enterprise zones *must* be preceded by careful testing in a small number of sites, probably no more than five. Thorough accountability must be achieved in such tests to provide even a moderately reasonable basis for objective evaluation—a basis that is simply not available in the past experience with state enterprise zones.

Target Aid to the Unemployed

These "fixes" won't change the fact that enterprise zones are not a cost-effective use of taxpayers' dollars. The concept is flawed: bribing business to induce it to help the inner cities will always mean that the bulk of the benefits will go to business, not to the targeted communities; otherwise business would not be interested.

This nation needs to turn its attention to the needs of the inner city. Washington should take the billions of dollars it is talking about putting into enterprise zones and invest it more productively and efficiently in direct aid to communities (the U.S. Conference of Mayors has already identified 7,252 projects that would put people back to work and repair the urban infrastructure). Invest in public employment programs to hire the inner-city unemployed. Equip them with training, transportation, appropriate health support. Give them jobs repairing streets, sewers, and sidewalks, cleaning vacant lots, renovating buildings, planting trees and shrubbery, removing graffiti, building and staffing libraries, parks, and recreation centers.

In other words, invest taxpayers' dollars in people, not in corporations.

"There is no municipal government function that has not been privatized successfully in some American city."

Privatization Would Improve City Services

National Center for Privatization

Privatization involves the sale of government enterprises or the contracting out of public services to private businesses. In the following viewpoint, the National Center for Privatization (NCP) argues that businesses can provide necessary services to residents more efficiently than city governments. Businesses must compete for government contracts, and this competition would improve the quality of service and ultimately lower costs to the public. The NCP asserts that government is unsuited for providing most of its services because it has no incentive to ensure quality or to control costs. The NCP is a Wichita, Kansas, organization that promotes the privatization of government enterprises and services.

As you read, consider the following questions:

1. Why does the NCP believe that Americans are not more receptive toward the concept of privatization?
2. In the center's opinion, why are businesspeople more adept at considering the long-term future than politicians?
3. According to the NCP, what services should city governments be limited to?

"Our Town 2001." The National Center for Privatization adapted its paper "Our Town 2001: A Wichita Countdown" for inclusion in the present volume.

American cities are in a crisis. Interest groups cry for varying solutions while all demanding their piece of the money that is not there. The likely upshot—municipal bankruptcy under chapter 9; the obvious solution—privatization of many public services. Yet privatization is a word applied at the moment mostly to the desperate and late moves of the crumbling economies of Eastern Europe. In the United States, which with its capitalist tradition should best understand the advantages of privatization and the real reasons for the failure of centralized planning in the Soviet Union, it is, to many, an "unthinkable thought."

Yet provision of urban public services by competitive free enterprise is at least as old as Peter Drucker's suggestions of the early 1960s that in any legitimate need there is a profitable business, and in the basic tenet that, no matter how you hide them, all costs must be paid in full, ultimately and always by the consumer. Privatization has been successful. What did people think of the possibility of a private package service before UPS or Federal Express? Were not private hospitals once in the same category as the idea of competitive schools with parental choice is now? Is it not inertia in our ideas, the fear of change and the hold of special interest that keeps us from opening our minds to privatization more than unfeasibility in practice? Most services that are now public or are quasi-public monopolies or franchises were private during the historical periods of some of the United States' most vigorous economic growth.

Principles of Privatization

Urban privatization is based on several principles: 1) government has no business in business 2) competitive enterprise is the way to get the best service at the lowest price 3) government does not have to provide most services itself, only see that they are provided 4) good intentions are no substitute for performance 5) providing service to a market at a profit, when patronage is voluntary, is one of the most unselfish of enterprises 6) government has no incentive to control costs.

Walter Lippmann, as a young political scientist, proposed that it was time for a science of human society that would replace the "drift" of individual initiative with the "mastery" he imagined could be provided by "disinterested" experts organized into regulatory boards or ensconced in positions of elected power in government. These superior beings would be free of the corruptions of money-making and attuned, as Robespierre always claimed to be while ordering decapitations in the French Revolution, with the "will of the people." It was a dangerous illusion. By 1937 Lippmann himself wrote: "The question was not whether [a planned society] would be desirable, but whether it was possible." Out of well-intentioned vision and concern, out of a desire for rationality and order, came to our country and cities the "swarms of officers who eat out our substance," mentioned in the Declaration of Independence. So easily does fantasy become fanaticism.

Urban Transit Savings

In 1989 Denver became the first large city to contract out a full 20 percent of its transit service. A number of smaller cities are doing more than that. The Southern California Rapid Transit District, a Los Angeles County-wide transit agency, which is a nightmare of inefficiency and corruption, has been mandated by the County Board of Supervisors to go to competitive contracting for a full 20 percent of its service area. As a result, the entire San Gabriel Valley in southern California is now served by private contractors rather than by the RTD at a savings of 30 percent to 40 percent in actual operating costs. Cities like Miami, Seattle, New Orleans, Cincinnati, and Dallas are also moving to competitive contracting.

Robert Poole, from a speech given at The Heritage Foundation, March 13, 1990.

Why does government not work? First, there is the impossibility of controlling complexity. Only the market is a planning system that is constantly corrected by real human needs honestly expressed by willing buyers and sellers. Second, government planning cannot allow adequately for innovation and radical change. There is a joke that if planners in the 19th century had been asked to imagine the problems of our time, they would have predicted we would be inundated by horse manure. Centralized planning is based on past experience and past technology. In 1923 a planning report for Wichita, Kansas, stated there was no need to provide streets to carry people by car from downtown to the growing east and west suburbs. The reason given was that there was a fine streetcar system, and it was logical for people to prefer this. However, they did not. Just over ten years later there was not a streetcar left in Wichita, but the planning bureaucracy was still in place and growing. Third, government often discourages change. To limit the complexity with which it cannot deal, government bureaucracy is rule-oriented, form-driven and obsessed with standardization. It enforces equality of outcome, blunting the impact of equality of opportunity for unequal individuals. The truth is that the more people create, the more necessary it is that they be free. Fourth, politicians are less likely to consider the long-term future than private businesses, which have an equity in the years beyond the next election. Fifth, in government bureaucracies there is little incentive for outstanding performance, nor is there an incentive to solve the problem. In fact, the possibility of elimination of the bureau with the elimination of its problem may create an unconscious disincentive to solve urban problems.

Decision Making by Government

The results of dependence on government action in cities can be documented. A survey comparing various kinds of private and public municipal services found that public operation costs an average of over 40% more. There is no municipal government function that has not been privatized successfully in some American city. Yet, with over 50% of every consumer dollar going to government, spending decisions are increasingly in the hands of the few rather than with the many where they philosophically and practically belong. It is often a situation where, according to Lippmann, "the opinion of unqualified men is artificially, by the mere arbitrary intervention of the police, made to prevail over the opinion of men who are specially gifted and have labored to qualify themselves." Decisions in the political forum are defensive, and since the risk must be taken involuntarily by taxpayers, the documentation of each move must be extensive, and public access and input at each stage intensive, thus adding inevitably to costs. Public commitment complete with bonds or a mill levy also decreases flexibility in dealing with new conditions. An unsuccessful private venture can and does pass out of existence when it fails: the public project not only stays in place, but is likely to ask for increases in funding and more staff *because* it has failed. Governments are not good asset managers, and the most desirable form of urban privatization, therefore, is asset shedding and turning whole functions over entirely to the regulated market, rather than mere contracting out to perhaps politically favored bidders.

How do you privatize in cities? It is often startlingly easy: the government simply ceases providing the service and does the minimum to hamper those who take its place. During bus strikes, for instance, jitneys and other private services take up the slack almost immediately if they are not prevented from doing so. They quickly find the most efficient and cost-effective way of solving transit problems that really exist and cease addressing those "needs" that are purely political. In Wichita, where NCP is headquartered, the trash service was privatized during a labor emergency in the 1970s overnight by the city simply stepping out of it and allowing the private trash haulers to contract for the routes. People think the government must do it because self-help and family and neighborhood cooperation have been as crippled by the "Progressive" central-control dream as has the spirit of enterprise. However, given the chance

240

and the rain of economic incentive, the roots which remain will regenerate the plant which once flourished.

The mission for cities of the future should be to limit government to its legitimate roles of protecting life, liberty and property and to encourage (or at least allow) private substitutes for the functions it has usurped. The keys are individual action, entrepreneurship and voluntary association, and the privatization of public services is the single biggest business opportunity of the 21st century. When individuals take responsibility for themselves and can see that their actions make a difference without being overrruled by a capacious central power, formal government is automatically limited. It is there to prevent coercion, not to be the agent of it. We predict the result will be tax-paying rather than tax-eating entities providing service more efficiently, at lower cost and at a profit to themselves. The economic as well as the social benefit will be enormous.

The Efficiency of Private Industry

We have found that private industry can more efficiently perform some services traditionally provided by [Chicago] at less cost to the taxpayers. For example, two years ago, we privatized the towing of abandoned vehicles. Since its inception, the abandoned vehicle towing program has resulted in the removal of over 100,000 vehicles from our streets and more than $2 million paid to the city.

Richard J. Daley Jr., *The World & I*, June 1991.

Government has centralized power through its monopoly on taxation. It has become unresponsive to the citizens of our cities and it has usurped the prerogatives of the local citizen and his/her family. It has effectively brainwashed three generations of citizens through monopoly of education. It will do no good to put "better people" into government, as it is not the people, but the system that is the problem. "The most entrepreneurial, innovative people," Peter Drucker writes, "behave like the worst time-serving bureaucrats or power hungry politicians six months after they have taken over the management of the public service institution, particularly if it is a government agency. The forces that impede innovation in a public service institution are inherent in it and inseparable from it." It has a great deal to do with spending other people's money, which there is absolute power to extract for any purpose deemed to be for the "public good." G.K. Chesterton observed that "the sin and sorrow of despotism is not that it does not love men, but that it loves them too much and trusts them too little. . . . When a man begins to think that the grass will not grow at night unless he lies awake to watch it he generally ends up in an asylum or on the throne of an emperor."

Shakespeare put the question well: "On what meat hath this Caesar fed, that he has grown so fat?" Don't we all know the answer to that one? It is from the resource of individual, responsibly self-interested human energy that America's cities will create in the next century local satisfactions no less spectacular for being unpredictable. Because so many people think they are dependent upon government for income and are doubtful of their capability without it, and because we often think of short-term advantage for interest groups rather than the long-term good of everyone, individuals hope the octopus will eat them last, and fear to change. Ted Gaebler, who was mayor in 1986 of America's most privatized city, Visalia, California, delighted in his town's fiscal strength compared with the bankruptcy of similar-size cities elsewhere. His secret: "I am trying to get people to think like owners, not bureaucrats." There is a difference, and in that difference lies the best cities have to offer.

"Contracting out often results in higher costs, poorer quality of service, . . . [and] corruption. "

Privatization Would Impair City Services

American Federation of State, County, and Municipal Employees

In the following viewpoint, the American Federation of State, County, and Municipal Employees (AFSCME) argues that contracting out city services such as trash collection to businesses would be harmful because the practice is fraught with shoddy service and higher prices. The AFSCME asserts that companies that win city contracts are not held accountable for their quality of service and that corruption is often involved when contracts are awarded. The AFSCME contends that city governments and their employees can successfully work together to improve city services without relying on the private sector. The federation is a national labor union located in Washington, D.C.

As you read, consider the following questions:

1. Why does the AFSCME believe that contracting out would disproportionately harm the incomes of minority and female city employees?
2. How do private businesses inflate the prices of some services, in the federation's opinion?
3. According to AFSCME, how could companies use political influence to win city contracts?

From "Government for Sale," a pamphlet of the American Federation of State, County, and Municipal Employees, 1991. Reprinted with permission.

The idea of contracting out exploded in the 1980s. Prodded by the Reagan Administration's anti-public sector rhetoric and favorable tax policies, companies launched a major marketing effort in the public sector extolling the virtues of private provision of public services. In addition to the companies' promises of cost-savings, jurisdictions also receive the added boon of threatening the clout of public employee unions.

However, as the 1980s concluded, the benefits of contracting out proved to be more elusive than its proponents claimed. As AFSCME has been saying for years, contracting out often results in higher costs, poorer quality of service, loss of government flexibility and accountability, corruption and social costs. Competition for contracts is more often the exception rather than the rule. Where bidding ostensibly occurs, there is often collusion, and as the number of political scandals on all levels of government indicates, the safeguards do not work very well.

The Public Pays Dearly

The public eventually pays dearly for contracting out, both in economic terms such as price increases and unemployment, and in social terms. Contracting out disproportionately hurts women and minorities because they, more so than white male workers, rely on public employment as a means of economic and social advancement. Additionally, contracting out results in a lower economic standard of living for the individual worker and the community as relatively good jobs with benefits become low wage, no benefit jobs.

Responsible government needs to improve the quality of public management and services, not sever the contract between government and its citizens. Governmental agencies can achieve the goal of effective provision of services without adding the problems of contracting out.

A History of Privatization

Early in this century, cities and towns around the country turned to private companies to run local streetcar systems, to collect garbage, to provide fire protection, and to perform other basic public services, often because their communities lacked the necessary public resources. However, serious problems arose. Contractors frequently overcharged municipalities; under-the-table payoffs by contractors were common; contractor-provided services were often poor. Big city political machines like Tammany Hall in New York and later bosses like James Curley in Boston used municipal contracts as a way to reward political cronies.

Because of gross abuses, a reform movement swept the country in the 1920s and made the delivery of public services part of the municipal government. Now contracting out has again become big business, and again is often used for political patronage. Big corporations, such as Waste Management and ServiceMaster, and a host of smaller firms have moved vigorously into the public sector in recent years.

A growing circle of widely respected experts and academics have been voicing their concerns from a variety of perspectives: legal, economic, social, and ethical. . . .

Problems in Boston and Los Angeles

In late 1988, state inspectors randomly inspected 53 of the Boston public school district's school buses and found that 30 failed routine inspections. Inspectors found broken headlights, worn tires, damaged tailpipes, and faulty parking brakes. The School District had contracted with National School Bus Service, Inc. to provide school bus transportation; the company was responsible for maintenance.

As a result of the failed inspections, the buses were immediately removed from service and could not be used to bus students after school. As a result, hundreds of students from 27 schools were forced to find alternate means of transportation.

A representative from the state Department of Motor Vehicles noted that National School Bus Service, Inc. was lax in their maintenance regimen and that these buses should have been pre-inspected before the State inspected them. He added that an average of 10-15% of vehicles usually fail routine inspections—a percentage far lower than the 57% failure rate of the buses serving the Boston public schools. Several months prior to the inspections, the Boston public school district received an audit report critical of the preventive maintenance and other upkeep services provided by National School Bus Services, Inc.

In October 1988, the Los Angeles County Board of Supervisors hired a private firm, Holmes & Narver, Inc., to manage and maintain most county vehicles. The County signed a 5-year contract for $12 million per year. Supporters of the deal stated that the County would save $2 million dollars annually.

Before the contract was even six months old, massive backlogs, shoddy services, and delays in providing information dismayed county officials. In February 1989, county officials realized that the contract was drafted incorrectly so that it was unclear who (the City or the company) bore the costs of repairs. By March 1, 1989, the County had assessed Holmes and Narver $80,000 in penalties.

In August 1989, Holmes and Narver requested an additional $3.2 million for the first contract year, which raised its price well above the $14 million per year the County had spent on its own maintenance program. In December, the County agreed to pay

Holmes and Narver $1.2 million to settle this contract dispute. Problems with Holmes and Narver persisted throughout 1990. The county auditor released a report documenting the greater-than-expected costs of the contract. The auditor noted a high rate of repair order errors; numerous billing irregularities; widespread dissatisfaction with the quality of fleet maintenance services; failure to meet annual state vehicle registration and smog certification requirements; and the failure to establish an effective vehicle and equipment maintenance program that the contract required. As a result, the County Board of Supervisors voted unanimously to cancel the contract with Holmes and Narver.

Holding Philadelphia Captive

In 1988, Lomax Health Services, now Correctional Healthcare Solutions (CHS), won a contract from the City to provide all medical services to Philadelphia inmates. Right from the beginning, inmates complained that medical charts were missing and medical personnel were unprofessional and slow to respond. Even wardens complained about the quality of service. Still, the problems persisted. In 1990, reports showed repeated staffing problems—nurses were not on duty and patients often had to wait months for appointments. An inmate gave birth in her housing unit before CHS personnel arrived to provide assistance even though they had been called 2½ hours earlier. In November 1990, CHS admitted that the prison health system did not have enough dentists: two dentists cared for 5,000 inmates. CHS did not improve in 1991. Nurses failed to lock appropriate doors or secure medication before leaving to answer emergencies. Nurses overmedicated patients and distributed medicine on the advice of inmates.

Leaving Cities in the Lurch

Private companies will provide services only so long as they are profitable. But once the profit has gone, the company has no legal obligation to continue the service, perhaps leaving the city and its residents in the lurch. Just as important, deregulation of private service providers may well result in differential fee structures for different neighborhoods: Those that generate the most demand will pay higher subscription rates than those with lower demand.

Lawrence J.R. Herson and John M. Bolland, *The Urban Web*, 1990.

CHS's problems were not limited to patient service. In the beginning of 1990, the City found that CHS personnel improperly dumped infectious medical waste. Furthermore, CHS thwarted the City's efforts to investigate the dumping procedures.

While all these problems were festering, the City was also paying more to CHS. The City originally agreed to pay CHS $62,832 per month—approximately $754,000 per year. Yet, by 1990, the City contracted with CHS at a cost of $534,780 per *month* which equals $6.4 million per year. It is also worth noting that Dr. Walter Lomax, the company's president, is a well-known Philadelphia physician who made significant contributions to then Mayor Wilson Goode's campaign.

Sleaze in the Garbage Industry

Illegal price-fixing and bid rigging plague the solid waste industry. Waste Management Inc. (WMI) and Browning-Ferris Industries (BFI) together account for roughly one-half of the nation's waste disposal business and have been in trouble with the law for many years.

In 1987, WMI and BFI pled guilty to antitrust charges for price-fixing and customer allocation in the Toledo, OH area. They were each fined $1 million.

In 1988, WMI's Fort Lauderdale, FL division paid a fine of $1 million after pleading no contest to federal price-fixing charges. WMI, in collusion with other haulers, allocated territories and charged artificially high rates to customers in Dade and Broward counties.

In 1989, Waste Management of California was fined $1 million for price-fixing and conspiracy, following a three-year investigation of the solid waste disposal industry in Los Angeles. WMI pled no contest to charges that it, along with several other companies, had conspired to eliminate competition and charge inflated prices.

In 1990, the federal government charged BFI and WMI with conspiring on a nationwide basis to fix prices, allocate customers, and rig bids for contracts to remove trash and other waste. Prosecuting attorneys declared that WMI and BFI indiscriminately violated laws across the country and reaped immense profits from their illegal activities. The companies denied any wrongdoing but WMI paid $19.5 million and BFI paid $30.5 million to those who complained. . . .

Water Meter Problems

Vanguard Meter Systems, a small company based in Kentucky, was awarded over $50 million in contracts from New York City between 1988 and 1991, in spite of serious financial difficulties. Vanguard hired two politically well-connected attorneys—one who was a friend of Mayor David Dinkins and one who was the brother of Senator Alfonse D'Amato. After hiring these consultants, the company won approximately ⅔ of the City's 10-year, $290 million program to install 630,000 water meters in New York City buildings. The owner of the company conceded that his financial difficulties eased when these consultants helped speed up payment checks from the City.

Limited Access to Services

Some of the worst drawbacks of privatization are distributional—that is, the methods used to finance them may put a disproportionate burden on lower-income consumers. For instance, the recreation services provided by Fort Lauderdale [Florida] are financed by user fees, with instructors collecting their fees directly from the student consumers. This limits access by lower-income consumers, a population that, in Fort Lauderdale, is predominantly minority.

Robert E. Suggs, *Minorities and Privatization*, 1989.

By March 1991, Vanguard was the subject of four government investigations focussing on labor law violations and other improprieties. New York City cited Vanguard for falling behind schedule, for hiring rude and incompetent employees, and for providing shoddy service. Also, Vanguard was investigated for paying employees for piece work rather than at the hourly wage required by state law. . . .

Contracting Out Is No Cure-All

Many jurisdictions have found that contracting out is not the cure-all that they were sold, and that they can achieve real cost savings and improve services by enhancing their own systems.

New York City reassumed the responsibility of parking meter collections after the contractor was caught stealing; the Department of Transportation Commissioner stated that "with public employees, we get better service and save money."

After years of touting the approach of public-private competition to maximize efficiency, the City of Phoenix now has public employees providing all sanitation services. Time after time, the City has shown that its public employees can do the job more efficiently than the private sector. Phoenix could have saved millions by first working with their employees to improve the service, without adding the cost of setting up bidding and monitoring systems for partly contracting out the work.

The City of Saratoga Springs, New York, decided to keep the funds for city improvement within the geographic area. By incorporating suggestions from Department of Public Works employees and union officials, the city workers began to repair sidewalks, work that was previously contracted out. Then, they moved on to doing historic restoration work which is a source of pride for the employees and their management.

Government Can Improve Its Services

AFSCME believes that, at minimum, public management should first explore alternatives to contracting out. If there is dissatisfaction with the performance of a public service, administrators should not automatically assume that contracting out is the answer to their problems. Much can be done to improve the cost and quality of the delivery of public services without selling off government. Labor and management can work together to improve efficiency and effectiveness before contracting out enters the picture.

In Madison, WI, labor and management worked together across departmental lines to save valuable time and money by reducing vehicle turnaround at the City's Motor Equipment Division from approximately 9 days to 2.5 days. In Philadelphia, PA, sanitation services improved dramatically when AFSCME worked with the City to redesign routes and modify work rules. In Phoenix, AZ, the City purchased state-of-the-art equipment and streamlined routes so that the City now provides sanitation services at a lower cost than any private company who tries to capture the City's business.

Public officials all too often have used contracting out to prop up weak management. Whenever the quality and efficiency of a public service deteriorates and the cost increases, whenever public officials lose control over services provided to the community, whenever a jurisdiction is tainted by a corruption scandal, the public endures the consequences and the public pays the bills.

Recognizing Statements That Are Provable

We are constantly confronted with statements and generalizations about social and moral problems. In order to think clearly about these problems, it is useful if one can make a basic distinction between statements for which evidence can be found and other statements which cannot be verified or proved because evidence is not available, or the issue is so controversial that it cannot be definitely proved.

Readers should be aware that magazines, newspapers, and other sources often contain statements of a controversial nature. The following activity is designed to allow experimentation with statements that are provable and those that are not.

The following statements are taken from the viewpoints in this chapter. Consider each statement carefully. *Mark P for any statement you believe is provable. Mark U for any statement you feel is unprovable because of the lack of evidence. Mark C for any statement you think is too controversial to be proved to everyone's satisfaction.*

If you are doing this activity as a member of a class or group, compare your answers with those of other class or group members. Be able to defend your answers. You may discover that others will come to different conclusions than you do. Listening to the reasons others present for their answers may give you valuable insights in recognizing statements that are provable.

P = provable
U = unprovable
C = too controversial

1. The federal government's anti-urban attitude is obvious in its reduced aid to cities and its granting of tax loopholes to individuals and businesses.

2. Privatization of city services would lower operating costs and reduce taxes.

3. As the leader in civil rights progress, the federal government is best suited to mending racial and class differences.

4. Contracting out city services to the private sector usually results in corruption and waste.

5. Eliminating the capital gains tax would incite entrepreneurs to start new businesses.

6. Underground economies in inner cities are comprised of businesses that disregard city regulations and do not pay taxes.

7. Welfare regulations segregate the poor from mainstream society by discouraging hard work.

8. Most Americans support spending more money to improve cities.

9. Most businesspeople regret moving out of the inner cities and are eager to return and earn profits.

10. Individual states rather than the federal government now bear the burden of aid to cities.

11. Prospective inner-city businesses weigh the danger of crime against the benefits of tax incentives.

12. Conditions in cities actually worsened as federal urban aid increased.

13. The only legitimate role of local governments is to protect life, liberty, and property.

14. Many women and minority city employees would lose their jobs if their departments were privatized.

15. Most of America's personal income is generated in metropolitan areas because more people live there.

Periodical Bibliography

The following articles have been selected to supplement the diverse views presented in this chapter.

Business Week	"The Economic Crisis of Urban America," May 18, 1992.
Tristram Coffin	"The Urban Crisis and Some Answers," *The Washington Spectator*, August 15, 1992. Available from The Public Concern Foundation, PO Box 20065, New York, NY 10011.
David N. Dinkins	"Will Washington Heed the Marchers?" *The New York Times*, May 5, 1992.
Peter Dreier	"Bush to Cities: Drop Dead," *The Progressive*, July 1992.
Ralph Estes	"Enterprise Zones: Urban Hope or Trickle-Down Hokum?" *In These Times*, September 16-29, 1992.
M. Stanton Evans	"How Federal Programs Create Our Urban Problems," *Human Events*, May 23, 1992. Available from 422 First St. SE, Washington, DC 20003.
Stephen Goldsmith	"Bureaucracy Shackles the Urban Poor," *The Wall Street Journal*, June 10, 1992.
Albert Holzinger	"Entrepreneurs to the Rescue," *Nation's Business*, August 1992.
Alan Keyes	"Restoring Community," *National Review*, June 8, 1992.
Richard I. Kirkland Jr.	"What We Can Do Now," *Fortune*, June 1, 1992.
Peter Kwong	"The First Multicultural Riots," *Village Voice*, June 9, 1992. Available from 842 Broadway, New York, NY 10003.
Salim Muwakkil	"L.A. Lessons Go Unlearned as Despair Deepens in Nation's Ghettos," *In These Times*, May 27-June 9, 1992.
Michael Allan Wolf	"How to Do Enterprise Zones Right," *The Wall Street Journal*, June 1, 1992.
Martin Morse Wooster	"Alms After the Storm," *Reason*, October 1992.

Organizations to Contact

The editors have compiled the following list of organizations that are concerned with the issues debated in this book. All have publications or information available for interested readers. For best results, allow as much time as possible for the organizations to respond. The descriptions below are derived from materials provided by the organizations. The list was compiled upon the date of publication. Names, addresses, and phone numbers of organizations are subject to change.

American Alliance for Rights and Responsibilities (AARR)
1725 K St. NW, Suite 112
Washington, DC 20006
(202) 785-7844

AARR supports community interests and rights and provides legal assistance when such interests and rights are jeopardized. It advocates community activism to rid neighborhoods of drug-related crime. AARR publishes the quarterly newsletter *Re: Rights and Responsibilities* and the book *The Winnable War: A Community Guide to Eradicating Street-Drug Markets*.

American Federation of State, County, and Municipal Employees (AFSCME)
1625 L St. NW
Washington, DC 20036
(202) 452-4800

AFSCME is a labor union representing government employees. It believes that city administrations and employees must work together to improve the quality of public services and considers the privatization of such services a detriment to the public. Publications include the *AFSCME Leader* weekly newsletter.

Enterprise Foundation
505 American City Bldg.
Columbia, MD 21044
(301) 964-1230

The foundation seeks to reduce poverty and works for affordable housing of all poor people by assisting nonprofit housing organizations. It advocates low-income housing tax credits and increased funding for federal community block grants. Publications include the report *A Decent Place to Live: Revisited* and the monthly newsletter *Network News*.

National Center for Privatization (NCP)
300 W. Douglas, Suite 1000
Wichita, KS 67202
(316) 261-5315

NCP is an organization that advocates the privatization of government services and enterprises. It believes that competition among businesses to provide city services benefits residents by reducing costs. NCP publishes the bimonthly newsletter *Private Solutions*.

National Coalition for the Homeless (NCH)
1621 Connecticut Ave. NW
Washington, DC 20009
(202) 265-2371

NCH serves as a clearinghouse of information concerning the homeless. It advocates emergency shelters and food assistance as first steps to help the homeless, followed by education, employment, and housing programs as long-term benefits. Publications include the monthly newsletter *Safety Network*.

National Council for Urban Economic Development
1730 K St. NW, Suite 915
Washington, DC 20006
(202) 223-4735

The council is comprised of business and economic development professionals and corporations interested in city development. It advocates federal aid to cities and supports enterprise zones as a means to stimulate inner-city economies. Publications include the quarterly *Commentary* and the semimonthly newsletter *Economic Developments*.

National Housing Institute (NHI)
439 Main St.
Orange, NJ 07050
(201) 678-3110

NHI is an information clearinghouse and technical advisor dealing with issues such as rent control and tenant rights. It advocates the creation and preservation of affordable housing. NHI publishes the bimonthly magazine *Shelterforce*.

National League of Cities (NLC)
1301 Pennsylvania Ave. NW
Washington, DC 20004
(202) 626-3000

NLC is a federation of cities that has developed a national municipal policy with the goal of helping cities solve common problems. It offers training and assistance to municipal officials and represents cities before Congress and federal agencies. Publications include the annual *National Municipal Policy*, the monthly *Urban Affairs Abstracts*, and the *Nation's Cities Weekly* newspaper.

National Urban League
500 E. 62d St.
New York, NY 10021

(212) 310-9000

The league is comprised of professionals and religious leaders who aim to eliminate racism and provide services to minorities in employment, housing, and community and business development. It proposes a ten-year, $50 billion annual public/private investment plan for America and its cities. Publications include the quarterly *Urban League News*.

The United States Conference of Mayors
1620 I St. NW
Washington, DC 20006
(202) 293-7330

The conference promotes improved municipal government through co-operation between cities and the federal government and advocates in-creased federal aid to cities. Publications include the annual *Resolutions Adopted* and *The Federal Budget and the Cities* and the semimonthly *The Mayor*.

The Urban Institute
2100 M St. NW
Washington, DC 20037
(202) 833-7200

The institute is a policy and research organization that investigates so-cial and economic problems confronting the nation. To reduce social tensions and the lack of opportunities in cities, it advocates the use of housing vouchers to enable poor families to move from central-city public housing projects into more integrated neighborhoods. Publications include the triannual *Policy and Research Report*, the report *Confronting the Nation's Urban Crisis* (1992), and various books and re-search papers.

Urban Policy Research Institute (UPRI)
PO Box 3647
Dayton, OH 45401
(513) 848-7199

UPRI is a research group that studies urban issues. It believes that much of urban decline is caused by the criminalization of drugs and calls for the repeal of drug laws to reduce urban crime. It also believes that no government aid will help cities unless government changes its "war on drugs" policy. UPRI believes that small businesses should lead urban redevelopment efforts because they are more beneficial to com-munities than larger businesses. It advocates enterprise zone plans that remove most business regulations. UPRI publishes the quarterly *UPRI Update*.

Bibliography of Books

Elijah Anderson — *Streetwise: Race, Class, and Change in an Urban Community*. Chicago: The University of Chicago Press, 1990.

Gregg Barak — *Gimme Shelter: A Social History of Homelessness in Contemporary America*. New York: Praeger, 1991.

Larry Bennett — *Fragments of Cities: The New American Downtowns and Neighborhoods*. Columbus: Ohio State University Press, 1990.

Martha R. Burt — *Over the Edge: The Growth of Homelessness in the 1980s*. Washington, DC: The Urban Institute Press, 1992.

Stella M. Čapek and John I. Gilderbloom — *Community Versus Commodity: Tenants and the American City*. Albany: State University of New York Press, 1992.

Allan Carpenter — *Facts About the Cities*. New York: H.W. Wilson, 1991.

Roger L. Conner and Patrick C. Burns — *The Winnable War: A Community Guide to Eradicating Street Drug Markets*. Washington, DC: American Alliance for Rights and Responsibilities, 1991.

Mike Davis — *City of Quartz: Excavating the Future in Los Angeles*. New York: Verso, 1990.

Janet Foster — *Villains: Crime and Community in the Inner City*. New York: Routledge, 1990.

Ester R. Fuchs — *Mayors and Money: Fiscal Policy in New York and Chicago*. Chicago: The University of Chicago Press, 1992.

George C. Galster and Edward W. Hill, eds. — *The Metropolis in Black and White: Place, Power, and Polarization*. New Brunswick, NJ: Transaction Publishers, 1992.

Joel Garreau — *Edge City: Life on the New Frontier*. New York: Doubleday, 1991.

William W. Goldsmith and Edward J. Blakely — *Separate Societies: Poverty and Inequality in U.S. Cities*. Philadelphia: Temple University Press, 1992.

M. Gottdiener and Chris G. Pickvance — *Urban Life in Transition*. Newbury Park, CA: Sage Publications, 1991.

William J. Grinker and Anne Sommers — *Drugs and Poverty in Urban America: Helping Communities to Help Themselves*. Washington, DC: The Twentieth Century Fund, 1992.

Adele V. Harrell and George E. Peterson — *Drugs, Crime, and Social Isolation: Barriers to Urban Opportunity*. Washington, DC: The Urban Institute Press, 1992.

Edward C. Hayes, ed. *The Hidden Wealth of Cities: Policy and Productivity Methods for American Local Governments*. Greenwich, CT: JAI Press, 1989.

Don Hazen, ed. *Inside the L.A. Riots*. Washington, DC: Institute for Alternative Journalism, 1992.

Joe Homeless *My Life on the Street*. Far Hills, NJ: New Horizon Press, 1992.

John A. Jakle and David Wilson *Derelict Landscapes: The Wasting of America's Built Environment*. Savage, MD: Rowman & Littlefield, 1992.

Christopher Jencks and Paul E. Peterson, eds. *The Urban Underclass*. Washington, DC: The Brookings Institution, 1991.

Marshall Kaplan and Franklin James, eds. *The Future of National Urban Policy*. Durham, NC: Duke University Press, 1990.

Helen F. Ladd and John Yinger *America's Ailing Cities: Fiscal Health and the Design of Urban Policy*. Baltimore: The Johns Hopkins University Press, 1991.

Philip Langdon *Urban Excellence*. New York: Van Nostrand Reinhold, 1990.

Wilhelmina A. Leigh and James B. Stewart, eds. *The Housing Status of Black Americans*. New Brunswick, NJ: Transaction Publishers, 1991.

Clarence Lusane *Pipe Dream Blues: Racism and the War on Drugs*. Boston: South End Press, 1991.

Laurence E. Lynn Jr. and Michael G. H. McGeary, eds. *Inner-City Poverty in the United States*. Washington, DC: National Academy Press, 1990.

National Crime Prevention Council *Preventing Crime in Urban Communities*. Washington, DC: National Crime Prevention Council, 1986.

William J. Pammer Jr. *Managing Fiscal Strain in Major American Cities*. Westport, CT: Greenwood Publishing, 1990.

Russell K. Schutt and Gerald R. Garrett, eds. *Responding to the Homeless: Policy and Practice*. New York: Plenum Press, 1992.

David C. Schwartz, Daniel N. Hoffman, and Richard C. Ferlauto *Employer Assisted Housing: A Benefit for the 1990s*. Washington, DC: Bureau of National Affairs Inc., 1992.

Wesley G. Skogan *Disorder and Decline: Crime and the Spiral of Decay in American Neighborhoods*. New York: The Free Press, 1990.

Herbert H. Smith *Planning America's Cities: Paradise Found? Paradise Lost?* Chicago: The University of Chicago Press, 1991.

Sam Staley *Drug Policy and the Decline of the American City*. New Brunswick, NJ: Transaction Publishers, 1992.

Thomas M. Stanback Jr.	*The New Suburbanization: Challenge to the Central City*. Boulder, CO: Westview Press, 1991.
Michael A. Stegman	*More Housing, More Fairly*. Washington, DC: The Twentieth Century Fund, 1991.
Mercer L. Sullivan	*"Getting Paid": Youth Crime and Work in the Inner City*. Ithaca, NY: Cornell University Press, 1989.
Studs Terkel	*Race: How Blacks and Whites Think and Feel About the American Obsession*. New York: The New Press, 1992.
Michael Tonry and James Q. Wilson, eds.	*Drugs and Crime*. Chicago: The University of Chicago Press, 1990.
William Tucker	*The Excluded Americans: Homelessness and Housing Policies*. Washington, DC: Regnery Gateway, 1990.
William Tucker	*Rent Control and the Housing Crisis*. Washington, DC: Cato Institute, 1991.
Margery A. Turner	*Housing Market Impacts of Rent Control: The Washington, D.C. Experience*. Washington, DC: The Urban Institute Press, 1990.
Twentieth Century Fund Task Force	*In the National Interest: Report on the Mayors' Urban Summit 1990*. Washington, DC: The Twentieth Century Fund, 1991.
The Urban Institute	*Confronting the Nation's Urban Crisis: From Watts (1965) to South Central Los Angeles (1992)*. Washington, DC: The Urban Institute Press, 1992.
U.S. Conference of Mayors	*A Status Report on Hunger and Homelessness in America's Cities*. Washington, DC: U.S. Conference of Mayors, 1992.
Steven VanderStaay	*Street Lives: An Oral History of Homeless Americans*. Philadelphia: New Society Publishers, 1992.
Richard W. White Jr.	*Rude Awakenings: What the Homeless Crisis Tells Us*. San Francisco: ICS Press, 1992.
William H. Whyte	*City: Rediscovering the Center*. New York: Doubleday, 1988.
William J. Wilson	*The Truly Disadvantaged: The Inner City, the Underclass, and Public Policy*. Chicago: The University of Chicago Press, 1987.
Arlene Zarembka	*The Urban Housing Crisis: Social, Economic, and Legal Issues*. Westport, CT: Greenwood Publishing, 1990.
Morris Zeitlin	*American Cities: A Working Class View*. New York: International Publishers, 1990.

Index